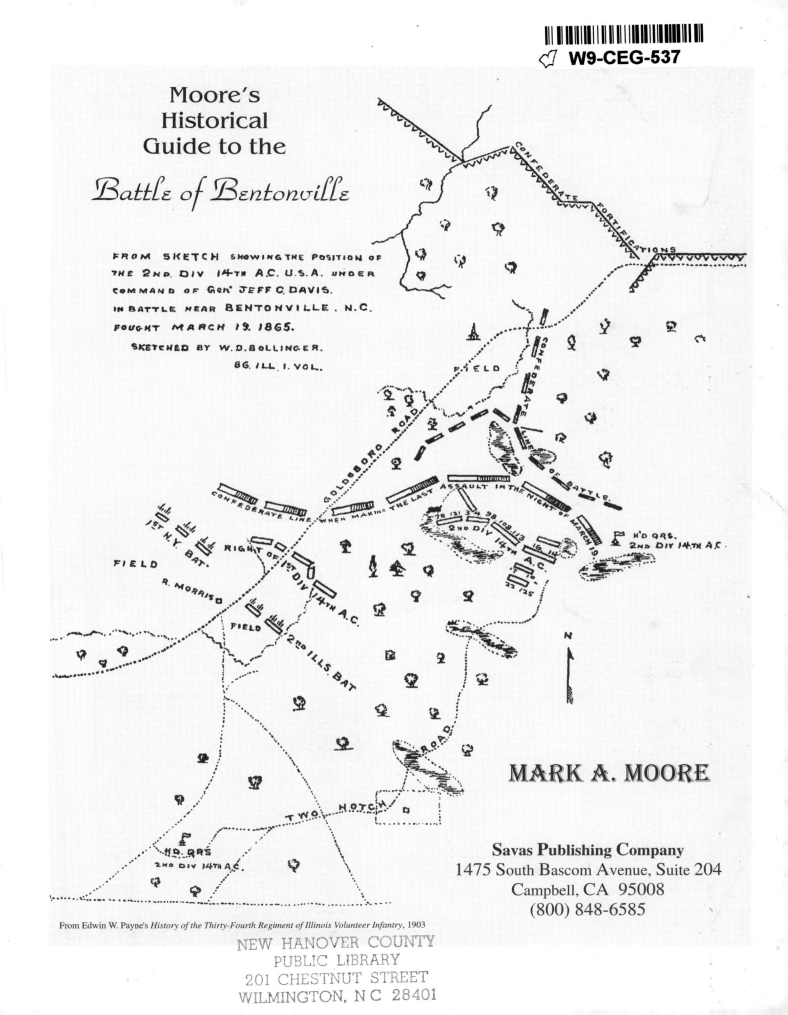

Moore's Historical Guide to the

Battle of Bentonville

FROM SKETCH SHOWING THE POSITION OF
THE 2ND. DIV 14TH A.C. U.S.A. UNDER
COMMAND OF Gen JEFF C. DAVIS.
IN BATTLE NEAR BENTONVILLE, N.C.
FOUGHT MARCH 19. 1865.
SKETCHED BY W.D. BOLLINGER.
86. ILL. I. VOL.

MARK A. MOORE

Savas Publishing Company
1475 South Bascom Avenue, Suite 204
Campbell, CA 95008
(800) 848-6585

From Edwin W. Payne's *History of the Thirty-Fourth Regiment of Illinois Volunteer Infantry*, 1903

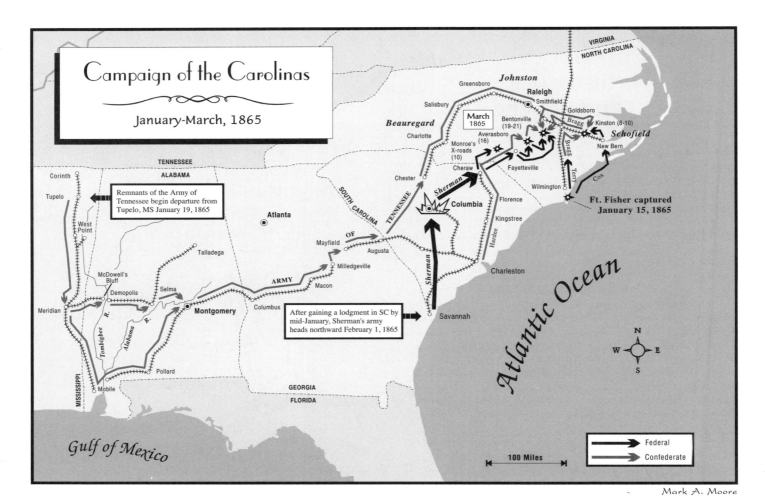

Campaign of the Carolinas

January-March, 1865

Remnants of the Army of Tennessee begin departure from Tupelo, MS January 19, 1865

After gaining a lodgment in SC by mid-January, Sherman's army heads northward February 1, 1865

Ft. Fisher captured January 15, 1865

100 Miles

Federal
Confederate

Mark A. Moore

Moore's Historical Guide to the Battle of Bentonville

Copyright © 1997 by Mark A. Moore

Includes bibliographical references, index, and appendices.

SAVAS PUBLISHING COMPANY
1475 South Bascom Avenue, Suite 204
Campbell, California 95008

Printing Number
10 9 8 7 6 5 4 3 2 (Second Edition)

ISBN 1-882810-15-5

This book is printed on 50-lb. acid-free stock.
The paper in this book meets or exceeds the guidelines for performance and durability of the Committee on Reproduction Guidelines for Book Longevity of the Council on Library Resources.

Modern photographs and book design by the author.
Cover design by Theodore P. Savas. Cover map design by the author.

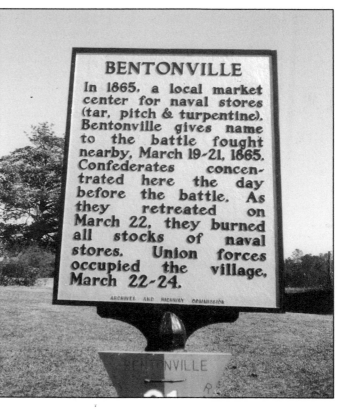

BENTONVILLE

In 1865, a local market center for naval stores (tar, pitch & turpentine). Bentonville gives name to the battle fought nearby, March 19-21, 1865. Confederates concentrated here the day before the battle. As they retreated on March 22, they burned all stocks of naval stores. Union forces occupied the village, March 22-24.

ARCHIVES AND HIGHWAY COMMISSION

Table of Contents

Foreword

I first met Mark Moore in November 1992. I received a phone call from John Goode, the site manager at Bentonville Battleground State Historic Site, that someone had just left a series of hand-drawn maps detailing the March 19 battle at Bentonville. John told me, "I think you'd better see these maps." I could tell from his tone of voice that he was impressed.

When I first saw Mark's maps I, too, was impressed. What first struck me about his maps was their comprehensibility—though detailed to an exacting degree, they were also easy to follow. Until that day, I had found certain parts of the first day's battle downright impossible to delineate. But I had only to look at Mark's maps and those confusing troop movements became as plain as day, in all their glorious exactitude. I knew then and there that my book would be incomplete without these maps.

Soon afterward, I met Mark and we agreed to form a partnership in which I would write the text and he would design the maps. I soon learned that Mark is a perfectionist. This perfectionism was as evident in his first hand-drawn maps as in his later, computer-designed versions. During the first months of our collaboration, Mark and I spent countless hours walking the Bentonville battlefield to determine the exact location of certain regiments and discussing the official reports and other documents which formed the basis of our research material. I should point out that up to this time Mark had intended to write his own book on the Battle of Bentonville, and with a methodical approach so typical of him, had drafted his maps to plot the troop movements in order to gain an understanding of the battle. Mark's maps set a high standard that I strove to match when I began writing *Last Stand* several months after our first meeting.

As the book progressed, Mark read the manuscript chapter by chapter, offering suggestions and tailoring his maps to *our* conception of the battle. I emphasize *our* because this was very much a collaborative effort. The result is evident to anyone who has seen the maps in *Last Stand*: Mark Moore has set a new standard for Civil War cartography. I believe that historian Ed Bearss' sobriquet for Mark Moore says it all—he is truly "the Jed Hotchkiss of North Carolina."

This volume, *Moore's Historical Guide to the Battle of Bentonville*, is the first in what I hope will be a long series of cartographic studies for Civil War battlefields, featuring the writing, drafting and research skills of today's preeminent graphic historian.

Mark L. Bradley
Raleigh, December 8, 1996

Preservation at Bentonville Battleground

In March 1865, the armies of Joseph E. Johnston and William T. Sherman collided near the village of Bentonville, North Carolina, in what was to become one of the last major battles of the American Civil War. Occurring only three weeks prior to Lee's surrender at Appomattox Court House, the Battle of Bentonville involved nearly 80,000 combatants who contested approximately 6,000 acres of land. The three-day engagement was the only significant attempt to arrest the march of Sherman's army after the fall of Atlanta, Georgia, in September, 1864.

After the battle, relative quiet returned to the torn fields of Bentonville, and all 6,000 acres remained in private ownership for nearly a century. The first effort to commemorate the battle came in 1893, when a local veterans organization erected a monument to mark the common grave of 360 fallen Confederates near the home of John and Amy Harper. The United Daughters of the Confederacy placed a second monument on the field in 1927, marking the point at which the main Confederate line crossed the Goldsboro Road on the first day of battle.

During the next decade, various groups and individuals campaigned for preservation of the battlefield with little success. Only the approach of the Civil War centennial, and the combined efforts of Mr. Herschel Rose and the Harper House-Bentonville Chapter of the United Daughters of the

Confederacy (UDC), revived interest in preserving the battlefield. In 1957, the North Carolina General Assembly appropriated $25,000 for the purchase and initial development of fifty-one acres on the battlefield. This property included the original Harper House, employed as a field hospital by Sherman's Fourteenth Army Corps during the battle, and a portion of the Union lines occupied by the Twentieth Army Corps.

In August 1957, a group of interested citizens formed the Bentonville Battleground Association to assist in fundraising and promotion of the site. The Association quickly raised $15,000 for the purpose of restoring the Harper House, and preparing the site for public access. The Bentonville Battleground Association was superseded in 1961, when the North Carolina Division of Archives and History established the Bentonville Battleground Advisory Committee. The primary function of the committee was to seek funding for the construction of a visitor center on property acquired by the state.

In 1961, the General Assembly earmarked $26,000 for the Bentonville visitor center. This amount fell short of the $40,000 estimated cost of the project. The Bentonville Battleground Advisory Committee was able to secure private and foundation gifts to bring total available funding to the $40,000 mark, and construction of a visitor center began in January, 1964. Completed in June of that year, the new visitor center was dedicated during the centennial anniversary of the battle on March 21, 1965.

In the early 1980s, new personnel at the State Historic Site implemented Bentonville's first interpretive programs. The resulting increase in visitation prompted the General Assembly to appropriate funding for the purchase of additional land in 1986, and thirty-six acres were added to the state-operated site. This land included a section of earthworks constructed by the Confederate Army of Tennessee in which the remains of original headlogs may still be seen.

Expanding interpretive programs and a successful commemoration of the battle's 125th Anniversary in 1990 brought increased national attention to the site and its preservation needs. In June 1990, the Association for the Preservation of Civil War Sites (APCWS) purchased 7.24 acres of threatened land adjacent to the site visitor center and the Twentieth Corps position. Assisting APCWS in this purchase was the Bentonville Battleground Historical Association (BBHA), which was formed in 1986.

In addition to APCWS, the Conservation Fund's Civil War Battlefield Campaign also came to Bentonville's assistance. Bentonville was featured in the Conservation Fund's Civil War Battlefield Guide, published in 1990. In addition, the Conservation Fund helped to secure the donation of a one-acre tract to the battlefield from Mr. Ross Lampe of Smithfield, North Carolina. This one-acre tract provides critical access to property purchased in 1986.

Participation in the American Battlefield Protection Program's Civil War Battlefield Survey in 1991-1992 brought Bentonville to the attention of the National Park Service (NPS). Under the guidance of the NPS Southeastern Regional Office's National Register Program, Bentonville's staff prepared a nomination application for National Historic Landmark designation, submitted in 1994. On June 19, 1996, Secretary of the Interior Bruce Babbitt designated the site a National Historic Landmark. This important new status will enable Bentonville Battleground State Historic Site to apply for Federal grants available for purchasing property and easements to protect historically significant land.

In 1993, the Civil War Sites Advisory Commission, established by the U. S. Congress, produced its report on the status of America's Civil War battlefields, along with its recommendations for ways in which private and public entities can work together to preserve these national treasures for future generations. The Commission placed Bentonville in the top class of battlefields that deserve the highest priority for coordinated, nationwide preservation action by the year 2000.

Proceeds from the successful 130th Anniversary event in 1995 enabled BBHA to purchase 3.59 acres in an area of the battlefield where significant fighting occurred on the second and third days of the battle. A $17,600 grant from the North Carolina National Heritage Trust enabled the state to purchase this property from BBHA for the purpose of incorporating it into Bentonville Battleground State Historic Site. In 1996, BBHA began working with private landowners and local, state and federal government agencies to develop a comprehensive battlefield preservation plan that can be put into effect by the year 2000.

John C. Goode
Site Manager, Bentonville Battleground State Historic Site

Introduction

This work is intended as a companion to *Last Stand in the Carolinas, The Battle of Bentonville*, by Mark L. Bradley. The maps herein are those I researched and prepared in collaboration with Mark. I have extracted them from *Last Stand*, with significant modifications, to help orient battlefield visitors to the 29 highway historical markers located in the battle area, and to offer students of Civil War military tactics a compendium of troop positions and maneuvers for Bentonville. The latter function will benefit those who may never set foot on the battlefield itself.

Until now Bentonville, the culminating event of the Carolinas Campaign of 1865, has been a difficult battle to comprehend. Most of the battlefield's 6,000 acres remain in the hands of private citizens. Consequently, battlefield walks and interpretive tours are not available to the general public. With a few notable exceptions, the state-owned areas of Bentonville Battleground State Historic Site are not battle specific. The informative highway markers, with origins in the 1960s, have long offered the beginnings of a tour of the battlefield. They are well placed, but it is difficult to view and understand them within the overall tactical context of the battle. With the aid of this volume, it will be easier for visitors to follow the battle action from the vantage point of these roadside information plaques.

Bentonville is slowly coming into its own as a nationally significant historic site. In 1993 the Congressionally-mandated Civil War Sites Advisory Commission, assigned the task of evaluating the preservation needs of the nation's Civil War sites, visited Bentonville and was favorably impressed with the site and its miles of extant earthworks. The Commission's *Report on the Nation's Civil War Battlefields* (1993) classified Bentonville in:

Priority 1: Battlefields With Critical Need for Coordinated Nationwide Action by the Year 2000. 1.1 Class A, good integrity, moderate threats, less than 20% of core area protected. (Class A is defined as "having a decisive influence on a campaign and a direct impact on the course of the war.")

Another major step forward was Bentonville's designation as a National Historic Landmark, approved in June 1996 by the U. S. Department of the Interior.

The future looks bright for Bentonville. The Bentonville Battleground Historical Association, in conjunction with state officials, has made significant strides in acquiring additional parcels of land critical to a proper interpretation of the battle. The Association recently bought an additional 10 acres of property which saw major action on March 19, 1865. For more information on the BBHA, its projects, and how you can participate in preserving the battlefield, write to:

Bentonville Battleground Historical Association
5466 Harper House Road
Four Oaks, NC 27524

In addition to a tactical presentation, the maps in this study illustrate the highway marker positions, along with their titles and text. I have included a brief synopsis of the engagement (map by map), together with an outline of the campaign. There is also a section on the Battle of Averasboro. Like South Mountain and Antietam earlier in the war, Averasboro and Bentonville cannot be viewed and understood separately. One veteran of the campaign remarked years later that one followed the other "so closely that it may almost be considered the second stand of a continued engagement." Each section is highlighted by the words of soldiers who participated in the fighting. Other features of the guide include

modern and contemporary views of the battlefield, and a highway marker reference guide.

The nature of this work precludes a formal introduction for each unit commander mentioned. The *Orders of Battle* for both sides (Appendix B) will help readers keep track of proper command structures—which can be confusing, especially on the Confederate side.

North Carolina's Highway Historical Marker Program is administered by the state's Division of Archives and History, of the Department of Cultural Resources. The marker texts in this study appear as published in the *Guide to North Carolina Highway Historical Markers (Eighth Edition, 1990)*, edited by Michael Hill and published by the division. For more information on the marker program contact Archives and History at 109 East Jones Street, Raleigh, NC 27601-2807 (Tel: 919-733-7305; Fax: 919-733-8807).

Mark A. Moore
December 1996

Acknowledgments

My thanks to the following people for their friendly assistance during my work on this project: Dr. Jeffrey J. Crow, Dr. Jerry Cashion, and Michael Hill, of the North Carolina Division of Archives and History; Walt Smith, of the Averasboro Battlefield Commission; Eugene Byrd, for access to *Oak Grove*; Capt. Mark Smith, of Fort Lee, Virginia; Si Harrington and Earl Ijames, of the North Carolina State Archives. Thanks also to my good friend Mark Murosky, of New Bern, for the early experiments with electronic graphics, and to David Woodbury, of Stanford University Press.

The citizens of the Bentonville community, *the custodians of the battlefield*, deserve special recognition. Without their kind permission, Mark Bradley and I would never have been able to walk their fields and study the topography over which the battle was fought. These many excursions allowed us to better understand the natural obstacles that governed troop deployment. While the *exact* position of individual units cannot be determined in most cases, the battlefield does provide many clues to a reasonable framework for interpreting troop placement.

I am grateful to Edwin C. Bearss, of Arlington, Virginia, for reading my manuscript and offering many helpful suggestions. Ed's interest in both battle and battlefield have been an inspiration. John C. Goode has been a tremendous help over the years, as have his colleagues Lauren and Fred Burgess, and the entire staff of Bentonville Battleground State Historic Site. It was John who, in 1992, suggested that Mark Bradley and I combine text and maps for the work that became *Last Stand in the Carolinas*.

This book owes its existence to Theodore P. Savas, publisher and fellow cartographer. It has been a real pleasure working with Ted on this and many other projects.

To Mark Bradley and his wife Nancy, good friends and fellow battlefield wanderers, I owe much. Mark reviewed the entire manuscript and contributed his expertise to the finished product. Our collaboration has been an engaging and enjoyable experience, and I look forward to our next project.

Lastly, a very special thanks to Nancy Carter, my sisters Robin Yellin and Terry Sechler, and to my parents, Dorothy Anderson Moore and Robert Perry Moore, for their continued support.

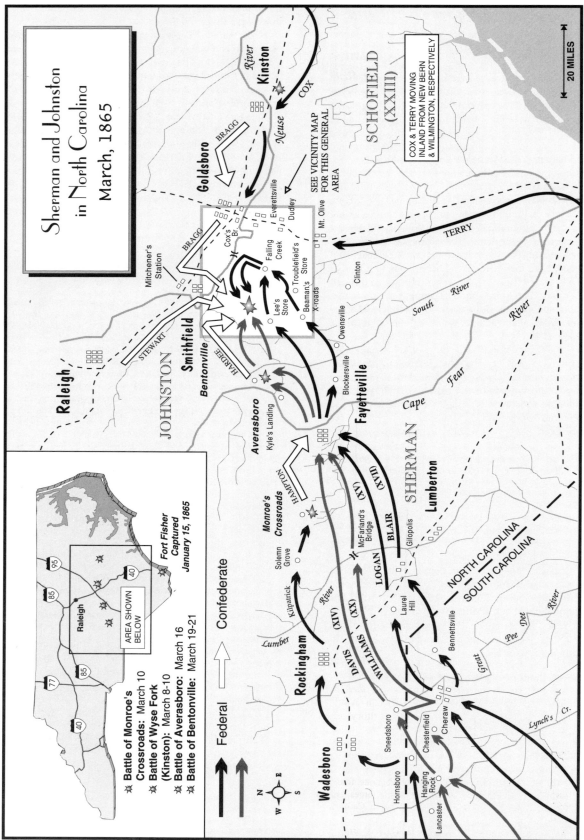

Sherman and Johnston
in North Carolina
March, 1865

Mark A. Moore

SCHOFIELD (XXIII)

COX & TERRY MOVING
INLAND FROM NEW BERN
& WILMINGTON, RESPECTIVELY

SEE VICINITY MAP
FOR THIS GENERAL
AREA

20 MILES

Fort Fisher
Captured
January 15, 1865

AREA SHOWN
BELOW

Raleigh

Federal

Confederate

☆ Battle of Monroe's
    Crossroads: March 10
☆ Battle of Wyse Fork
    (Kinston): March 8-10
☆ Battle of Averasboro: March 16
☆ Battle of Bentonville: March 19-21

N
W   E
S

Sherman Enters North Carolina

"Were I to express my measure of the relative importance of the march to the sea, and of that from Savannah northward, I would place the former at one, and the latter at ten, or the maximum."

— **Maj. Gen. William T. Sherman**

After the fall of Savannah, Georgia, in December 1864, Gen. William T. Sherman outlined his plans for a final campaign. Ulysses S. Grant, general-in-chief of all United States forces, wanted Sherman's army ferried by sea to Virginia, where it would close out the war by helping Grant defeat Gen. Robert E. Lee's Army of Northern Virginia. Sherman had other ideas for his army's route to Virginia—a march northward through the Carolinas. On Christmas Eve he wrote to Grant:

"I feel no doubt whatever as to our future plans. I have thought them over so long and well that they appear as clear as daylight. I left Augusta [Georgia] untouched on purpose, because the enemy will be in doubt as to my objective point....whether it be Augusta or Charleston [South Carolina], and will naturally divide his forces[1]....[O]n the hypothesis of ignoring Charleston and taking Wilmington, I would then favor a movement direct on Raleigh. The game is then up with Lee."

On December 27, Grant replied:

"Your confidence in being able to march up and join this army pleases me, and I believe it can be done. The effect of such a campaign will be to disorganize the South, and prevent the organization of new armies from their broken fragments....If time is given, the fragments may be collected together and many of the [Confederate] deserters reassembled. If we can, we should act to prevent this....[Y]ou may make your preparations to start on your northern expedition without delay. Break up the railroads in South and North Carolina, and join the armies operating against Richmond [Virginia] as soon as you can."

As Sherman gained a lodgment in South Carolina, Fort Fisher fell to a Federal amphibious assault on January 15, 1865. This effectively closed the port of Wilmington, North Carolina, the last major supply route to Lee's army in Virginia. Wilmington itself would fall in February to the combined forces of Gen. Alfred H. Terry's Provisional Corps, and Gen. John Schofield's XXIII Corps.[2] Schofield's orders of January 31 from Grant had specified that *"Your movements are intended as co-operative with Sherman through the States of South and North Carolina. The first point to be attained is to secure Wilmington. Goldsborough will then be your objective point."*[3] A junction there with Sherman would follow soon after. At least 425 miles of enemy territory lay between Sherman and his ultimate destination.

Columbia, South Carolina, fell to Sherman's army on February 17, 1865. Robert E. Lee, general-in-chief of all Confederate armies, questioned Pierre G. T. Beauregard's ability to oppose the Federals. He appealed to the Confederate War Department for a change in commanders, expressing that he knew of only one officer who had *"the confidence of the army & people."* Lee secured the authorization for his proposed change of commanders, and on February 22 sent the following message to Gen. Joseph E. Johnston at Lincolnton, North Carolina: [4]

"Assume command of the Army of Tennessee and all troops in Department of South Carolina, Georgia, and Florida. Assign General Beauregard to duty under you, as you may select. Concentrate all available forces and drive back Sherman."

A weary Johnston assumed command on February 23, predicting that it was *"too late to expect me to concentrate troops capable of driving back Sherman. The remnant of the Army of Tennessee is much divided. So are other troops."*

That same day Lee informed Johnston:

"If this [concentration] can be accomplished in time to strike General Sherman before he reaches the coast or unites with Schofield, I hope for favorable results. His progress can be embarrassed and retarded by removing or destroying all kinds of supplies on his route, and I hope you will spare no effort to accomplish this object....It is needless for me to call your attention to the vital importance of checking General Sherman and preserving our railroad communications as far as practicable. I rely confidently upon you to do all that the means at your disposal will permit, and hope for the most favorable issue."

The task of collecting the sundry and scattered commands at Johnston's disposal would prove formidable. When the crisis of the campaign developed in mid-March, he would effect only a partial concentration of those forces.

By March 8, 1865, Sherman's army of some 60,000 men had crossed into North Carolina. It had received little opposition thus far on the grand march. Sherman had learned of Johnston's return to command while still in South Carolina:

"I was anxious to reach Goldsboro','" he would later write, *"[but] knew that my special antagonist, Gen. Jos. Johnston, was back, with a part of his old army; that he would not be misled by feints and false reports, and would somehow compel me to exercise more caution than I had hitherto done. I then over-estimated his force at thirty-seven thousand infantry....[T]he bulk of Johnston's army was supposed to be collecting at or near Raleigh. I was determined, however, to give him as little time for organization as possible."*

Sherman's army was moving as it had in Georgia, divided into two separate wings numbering nearly 30,000 men each. *"It is plain why Sherman's army moved so rapidly always,"* wrote the Left Wing's Lt. Col. Michael H. Fitch. *"It had so many wings. It had enough wings to fly through the air, if the foraging had been as good up there as it was on the earth."*[5] Bent on occupying Goldsboro with a steadfast single-mindedness, Sherman would become less wary as the march progressed of the threat posed by his "special antagonist."

---

[1] General Pierre G. T. Beauregard, commanding the Confederate forces falling back before Sherman in South Carolina, *did* divide his forces, and Sherman's army was free to pass through the heart of South Carolina virtually unopposed.
[2] Schofield was tranferred to the east from Gen. George H. Thomas' army in Tennessee. Terry's force captured Fort Fisher.
[3] Grant realized the importance of Goldsboro as the inland junction of the Wilmington & Weldon and Atlantic & North Carolina railroads.

[4] Johnston had retired to Lincolnton after being removed from command of the Army of Tennessee by Confederate president Jefferson Davis. Johnston was sacked in mid-July 1864, during the Atlanta Campaign.
[5] Fitch himself was the commander of a three-regiment "wing" of Hobart's brigade (Carlin's division).

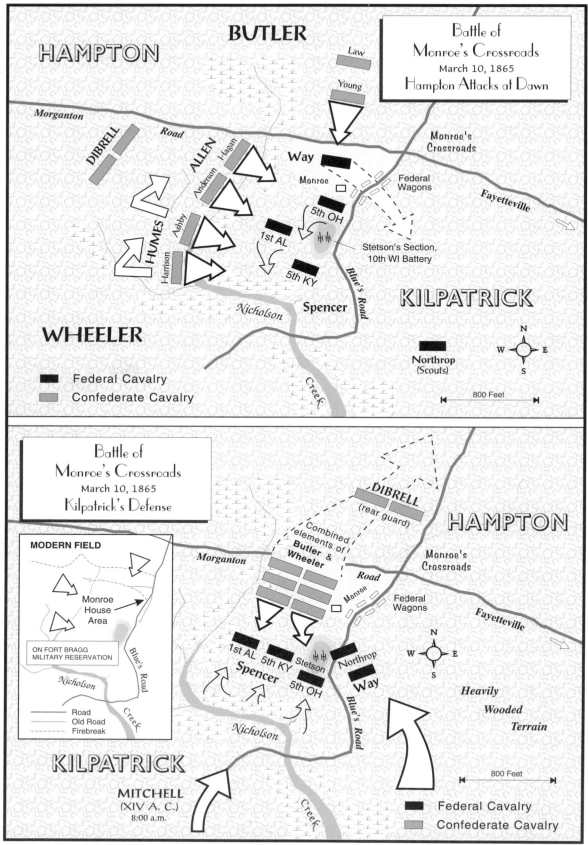

NOTE: This battlefield is not accessible to the general public

Mark A. Moore

Monroe's Crossroads and Fayetteville

"The surprise was just at daybreak, and would have been more effective but for the difficulty of crossing a swamp peculiar to the low pine-lands near the coast. The fight was desperate, but we succeeded in capturing a number of prisoners and General Kilpatrick's headquarters. The general made his escape in his night-clothes, it was said. We captured his uniform, saber, pistols, and two fine horses....In this affair Gen. Humes, Col. Harrison, of Texas, and Col. Henry M. Ashby....were wounded."

— **Lt. Col. James H. Lewis**, 1st Tennessee Cavalry[1]

♦ As Sherman's army advanced toward Fayetteville, the cavalry command of Gen. Judson Kilpatrick screened the left flank of H. W. Slocum's Left Wing column (the column closest to the enemy). At dawn on March 10, with his command divided and upon separate roads, Kilpatrick was attacked by a Confederate cavalry force under Lt. Gen. Wade Hampton.[2] This was the first organized assault on a portion of Sherman's army since its arrival in North Carolina. It was a short, confused affair fought over a small area, but it served to warn the careless Kilpatrick that Hampton's cavalry could not be trifled with.

♦ Hampton attacked the isolated brigades of Cols. George Spencer and William Way, which were bivouacked at a small crossroads near the home of Charles Monroe. Wheeler's Corps attacked from the west and Butler's Division from the north. Though driven a short distance into a swamp, the Federals quickly rallied and were able to fend off the Confederate attackers. With Dibrell's Division acting as a rear guard, Hampton's command retreated toward Fayetteville. A brigade from the XIV Corps came up in support of Kilpatrick around 8:00 a.m., but the fight had already ended.

FORCES ENGAGED:

FEDERAL:

Command	Engaged (approx.)
Spencer's brigade	800
Way's brigade	600
Northrop's scouts	50
Stetson's artillery[3]	50
Aggregate =	**1,500**

CONFEDERATE:

Command	Engaged (approx.)
Butler's Division	1,000
Wheeler's Corps	3,000[4]
Aggregate =	**4,000**

Casualty figures for this small engagement are sketchy and difficult to assess. Wide discrepancies exist between the reports and writings from each side, and some reports are missing altogether. A reasonable estimate would be few hundred casualties on both sides. Sherman was satisfied with Kilpatrick's report on the affair. *"I feared it was worse,"* he wrote, *"as the enemy claims from 200 to 400 prisoners."*

After evacuating Charleston and falling back before Sherman in South Carolina, Lt. Gen. William J. Hardee reached Fayetteville with his command on March 9, 1865. General Joseph E. Johnston was also at Fayetteville, but would leave for Raleigh that night to oversee the concentration of the Army of Tennessee troops then moving east by rail from Charlotte. As Sherman neared Fayetteville Hardee evacuated the town on March 10. Johnston ordered Hardee to monitor the advance of the Federal army: *"In general, it is important that you should be as near the enemy's line of march as possible, which will enable us to unite [our] other troops with yours."* Hardee fell back to the north and east on the Raleigh Plank Road, bivouacking at the small community of Smithville, five miles south of Averasboro.

Meanwhile, Sherman occupied Fayetteville on March 11, after a brief skirmish with elements of Hampton's cavalry. Hampton's troopers burned the bridge over the Cape Fear River as they fell back from the town. On March 12 the old U. S. arsenal was destroyed to prevent its further use by the Confederates. Sherman wrote to Gen. Alfred H. Terry at Wilmington: *"We must not lose time for Joe Johnston to concentrate at Goldsborough. We cannot prevent his concentrating at Raleigh, but he shall have no rest. I want general Schofield to go on with his railroad from New Berne as far as he can, and you should do the same from Wilmington. If we get the roads to and secure Goldsborough by April 10, it will be soon enough, but every day now is worth a million of dollars. I can whip Joe Johnston provided he don't catch one of my corps in flank, and I will see that my army marches hence to Goldsborough in compact form."*

While at Fayetteville Sherman rid his army of the thousands of refugees collected along his line of march. They were sent to Wilmington, some by river and others by land. By March 14, Sherman's forces were on the move once again. *"I am now across Cape Fear River with nearly all my army,"* he informed Gen. U. S. Grant in Virginia. *"I shall....begin my maneuvers for the possession of Goldsborough, which is all important to our future purposes....The enemy is superior to me in cavalry, but I can beat his infantry man for man, and I don't think he can bring 40,000 men to battle. I will force [Johnston] to guard Raleigh till I have interposed between it and Goldsborough. Weather is now good, but threatens rain. We are all well. Keep all parts busy and I will give the enemy no rest."*

---

[1] Lewis assumed command of Ashby's Brigade.
[2] Hampton, with M. C. Butler's Division, had transferred from Lee's army in Virginia to help defend his home state of South Carolina. He arrived in early February. By reason of rank Hampton was now in charge of Butler's Division *and* Wheeler's Corps of the Army of Tennessee.
[3] One section of the 10th Wisconsin Battery.

[4] Due to the swampy terrain his command had to cross, Wheeler later reported that only about 1,200 of his men participated in the attack.

Maj. Gen. William T. Sherman

On the grand march through North Carolina, Sherman (left) was intent on occupying Goldsboro above all else. He was banking on the notion that Joe Johnston would concentrate his Confederate forces to protect Raleigh, and thereby concede Goldsboro to the Federals without a fight. On March 18, 1865, Gen. Judson Kilpatrick told Sherman what he wanted to hear: "[Kilpatrick] reports Hardee retreating on Smithfield," a hopeful Sherman wrote to Gen. Oliver O. Howard, "and Joe Johnston collecting his old Georgia army this side of Raleigh. I know that [Johnston] will call in all minor posts, which [includes] Goldsborough. You may, therefore, move straight for Goldsborough, leaving Slocum the river road, and, if possible, the one from Lee's Store to Falling [Creek]. Make a break into Goldsborough from the south, and let your scouts strike out for [General] Schofield at Kinston."

Contrary to Sherman's expectations, there would be no easy entry into Goldsboro for the Federal army. Sherman's correspondence for the Battle of Bentonville illustrates his reluctance to concede the threat posed by Confederate forces, and his irritation at having to revise his timetable for occupying Goldsboro because of Johnston's unwillingness to retreat.

After doing all he could to avoid a general battle at Bentonville, which included allowing Johnston's army to escape to Smithfield, Sherman informed Gen. U. S. Grant on March 22: "Schofield entered Goldsborough....Terry got Cox's Bridge....and we whipped Joe Johnston, all on the same day....[I] am satisfied that Johnston was so roughly handled yesterday that we could march right on to Raleigh, but we have been out six weeks, living precariously on the collections of our foragers, our men 'dirty, ragged, and saucy,' and we must rest and fix up a little."—*OR*, Vol. 47, pt. 2.

Gen. Joseph E. Johnston

In February 1865, Confederate president Jefferson Davis reluctantly allowed Robert E. Lee to call Johnston (right) out of retirement to resist Sherman's march: "I am much obliged to Your Excellency," wrote Lee, "for ordering Genl Johnston to report to me....I know of no one who had so much the confidence of the troops & people as Genl Johnston, & believe he has capacity for the command." Davis no doubt feared Johnston would retreat in front of Sherman all the way to Richmond, Virginia. The general had behaved in similar fashion during the Atlanta Campaign of the previous summer, and as a result he incurred the wrath of the Confederate president. Reluctant as Davis, but heartened at the prospect of serving under his old friend Lee, Johnston accepted the post.

He was faced with a daunting task. Though he felt the effort to stop Sherman had come too late, Johnston methodically set out to collect the few scattered Confederate forces at his disposal. The troop concentration he effected in North Carolina on short notice, and the resulting battle at Bentonville, were probably the most decisive actions undertaken by Johnston during the war.

When the U. S. Government rejected the terms of peace agreed upon by Johnston and Sherman on April 18, 1865, President Davis urged Johnston to disband his army, that it might reassemble at some point further west. Johnston knew that such an act would bring the united forces of Grant and Sherman in pursuit across an already devastated Confederacy, and felt it would be the "greatest of human crimes for us to attempt to continue the war." Thus Johnston disobeyed the Confederate Government for the last time and chose to surrender in North Carolina.—Clifford Dowdey and Louis H. Manarin, eds. *The Wartime Papers of R. E. Lee*. New York: Bramall House, 1961. / Johnston, *Narrative*.

Johnston's *Narrative* (1874) sheds little light on the engagement at Bentonville, illustrating a seemingly cursory understanding of the particulars. While preparing to write the book, Johnston queried Gen. Robert F. Hoke for information about the battle: "I did not mean to ask you to give me minute information," he wrote in 1871. "I am compelled to write with great brevity being unable to obtain full information from the genl officers of whom I have asked it. What your own memory will furnish is all I want for the most general account....If you will write ten or fifteen lines....you can explain the part played by your division. I am particularly anxious to get this brief Material from you in regard to the affair of March 19th, at Bentonville. Because I believe that Genl Bragg's nervousness when you were first attacked....was very injurious—by producing urgent applications for help—which not only made delay, but put a large division out of position. In the afternoon too, I thought that he did not execute my instructions for the attack—nor subsequent ones. It was a great weakness on my part not to send him to Raleigh on the 18th [of March, 1865]." Hoke never supplied the information Johnston requested.—J. E. Johnston to My dear General, January 27, 1871. Robert F. Hoke Papers, North Carolina Division of Archives and History, Raleigh, North Carolina.

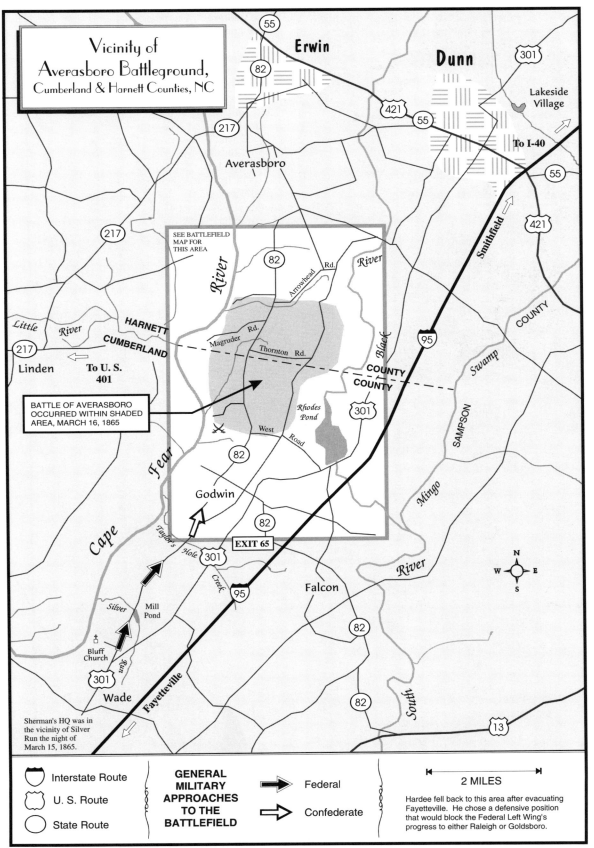

Vicinity of
Averasboro Battleground,
Cumberland & Harnett Counties, NC

Erwin

Dunn

Lakeside
Village

To I-40

Averasboro

Smithfield

SEE BATTLEFIELD
MAP FOR
THIS AREA

River

River

Arrowhead Rd.

HARNETT

Little River

CUMBERLAND

Magruder Rd.

Thornton Rd.

Black

COUNTY

COUNTY

Linden

To U.S.
401

BATTLE OF AVERASBORO
OCCURRED WITHIN SHADED
AREA, MARCH 16, 1865

Rhodes
Pond

West Road

Cape

Fear

Godwin

Taylor's Hole

EXIT 65

River

Silver

Mill
Pond

Creek

Falcon

Fayetteville

Bluff
Church

Wade

Sherman's HQ was in
the vicinity of Silver
Run the night of
March 15, 1865.

COUNTY

Swamp

SAMPSON

Mingo

South

N
W   E
S

Interstate Route

U. S. Route

State Route

GENERAL
MILITARY
APPROACHES
TO THE
BATTLEFIELD

Federal

Confederate

2 MILES

Hardee fell back to this area after evacuating
Fayetteville. He chose a defensive position
that would block the Federal Left Wing's
progress to either Raleigh or Goldsboro.

Mark A. Moore

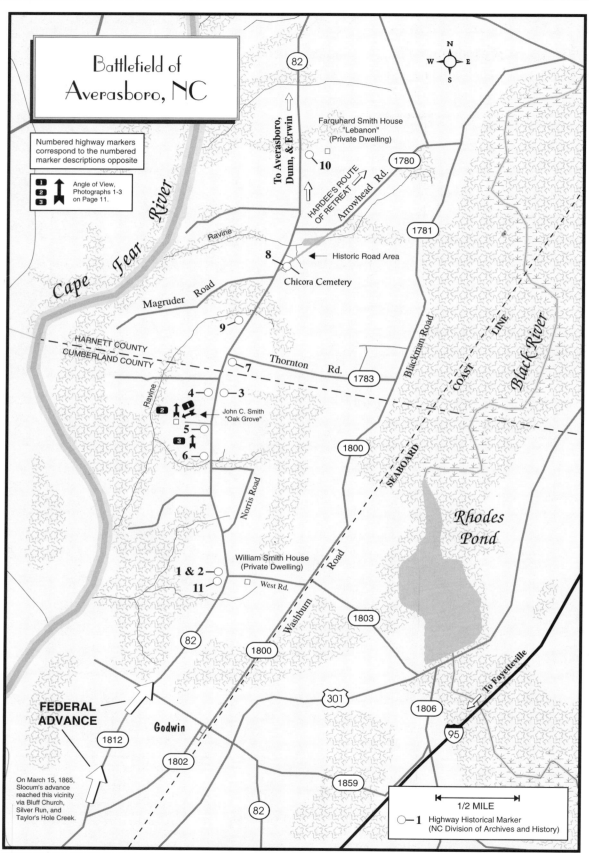

Battlefield of Averasboro, NC

Numbered highway markers correspond to the numbered marker descriptions opposite

Angle of View, Photographs 1-3 on Page 11.

Cape Fear River

Ravine

To Averasboro, Dunn, & Erwin

Farquhard Smith House "Lebanon" (Private Dwelling)

10

HARDEE'S ROUTE OF RETREAT

Arrowhead Rd.

1780

1781

8 — Historic Road Area

Chicora Cemetery

Magruder Road

9

HARNETT COUNTY
CUMBERLAND COUNTY

Thornton Rd.

1783

Blackman Road

SEABOARD COAST LINE

Black River

Ravine

7

4 — 3

2

John C. Smith "Oak Grove"

5

3

6

1800

Norris Road

William Smith House (Private Dwelling)

1 & 2

11 — West Rd.

Washburn Road

Rhodes Pond

1803

82

1800

301

1806

To Fayetteville

95

FEDERAL ADVANCE

Godwin

1812

1802

1859

82

On March 15, 1865, Slocum's advance reached this vicinity via Bluff Church, Silver Run, and Taylor's Hole Creek.

1/2 MILE

1 — Highway Historical Marker (NC Division of Archives and History)

NOTE: This battlefield remains in private ownership. No trespassing.

Mark A. Moore

Highway Historical Markers — Battle of Averasboro

1. Prelude to Averasboro

Late in 1864, two large Union armies, one in Virginia and the other in Georgia, were beginning to squeeze the Confederacy to defeat. Grant held Lee's Army of Northern Virginia immobile at Petersburg, while Sherman, with 60,000 men, captured Atlanta and began the famous March to the Sea. Savannah fell by Christmas, 1864, and in mid-January, 1865, Sherman's invasion of the Carolinas was begun. Columbia was captured on February 17th and Fayetteville on March 11th.

After leaving Fayetteville, Sherman sought to confuse General Joseph E. Johnston's Confederate forces by making a pretended advance against Raleigh with the left wing of his army. This wing, commanded by General H. W. Slocum, began its march from Fayetteville along Old Stage Road (present U. S. 401) which connected with Raleigh. Some 25 miles above Fayetteville the road branched near the village of Averasboro: one branch continued north to Raleigh, the other ran to the east toward Smithfield and Goldsboro. While Sherman's left wing moved in the direction of Averasboro, his right wing advanced toward Goldsboro on a parallel road about 20 miles to the east.[1]

The Confederates faced a difficult military situation in North Carolina by mid-March, 1865. General Johnston, ordered to stop Sherman, found his small army scattered over a wide area. It would take time to organize the various units into an effective fighting force. The only corps in position to hinder the Union advance was the 6,500 man force under General W. J. Hardee. This corps was ordered to resist Slocum's advance, thus began the Battle of Averasboro.[2]

Roadside pulloff, NC 82 North of Godwin, Cumberland County

2. Battle of Averasboro — Phase One

You are standing near the center of the first phase of fighting in the Battle of Averasboro, March 15-16, 1865.

On March 15th the left wing of General Sherman's Union army, commanded by General H. W. Slocum, was advancing along this road from Fayetteville to Averasboro. General H. J. Kilpatrick's cavalry division was in the lead, skirmishing with General Joseph Wheeler's Confederate cavalry which contested the Union advance.

At 3:00 P.M. the Union forces struck a heavy Confederate skirmish line. General Smith Atkins' 9th Michigan Cavalry drove the skirmishers back into the first of three lines of breastworks erected across the road. The Union cavalry then constructed heavy barricades in front of the Confederate works.

At 6:00 P.M. Confederate General W. B. Taliaferro, whose division was holding position [on the John Smith Farm], ordered an attack along his line. The Union forces, though hard-pressed, were able to hold their position due to the arrival of reinforcements from the 14th Corps.[3] Nightfall found the two armies in nearly the same

---

[1] The Federal Right Wing, commanded by Gen. Oliver O. Howard, was crossing South River in the early hours of March 16, 1865.
[2] Hardee chose a defensive position at Smithville, a small community about five miles south of Averasboro. Here the Cape Fear and Black Rivers were only a few miles apart. Hardee's line spanned the distance between the rivers, blocking the Federal advance on the Raleigh Plank Road.
[3] The reinforcements were actually from the XX Corps: William Hawley's brigade reached Kilpatrick's line at 12:30 a.m. on March 16.

---

positions they had held throughout the afternoon. General W. T. Sherman, Union commander, arrived on the field during the night.

At 6:00 A.M. on March 16, the Union forces attacked Taliaferro's line, driving the Confederates before them. Then the Southerners launched a desperate counter-attack. A disaster for the Union forces was averted when portions of the 20th Corps arrived upon the field. Three batteries of artillery were placed in position near the John Smith house. These began firing upon the Confederates, driving them back into their breastworks.

At 11:00 A.M. two newly-arrived Union brigades engaged the Confederates in front, while the brigade of Colonel Henry Case assaulted the Confederate right flank. This attack forced the Confederates to withdraw into their second line of works.

NOTE: For the remainder of the battle, drive two miles north on this road and read the map-marker on phase two of the battle.
Roadside pulloff, NC 82 north of Godwin, Cumberland County

3. Confederate First Line

Gen. W. B. Taliaferro's division occupied trenches crossing the road at this point, March 15-16, 1865.
NC 82 north of Godwin, Cumberland County

4. Rhett's Brigade

The brigade of Col. A. M. Rhett was repulsed 300 yds. W. on March 16, 1865, by Union troops under Col. Henry Case.
NC 82 north of Godwin, Cumberland County

5. "Oak Grove"

Plantation home of John Smith, used as a Confederate hospital during the Battle of Averasboro, March 16, 1865.
NC 82 north of Godwin, Cumberland County

6. Federal Artillery

From a point 50 yards west three batteries of artillery under Major J. A. Reynolds shelled the Confederate first line of earthworks.
NC 82 north of Godwin, Cumberland County

7. Confederate Second Line

On the morning of March 16, 1865, Taliaferro's division fell back to earthworks which crossed the road here.
NC 82 south of Erwin, Harnett County

8. Battle of Averasboro — Phase Two

You are standing at the center of the second phase of fighting in the Battle of Averasboro, March 15, 16, 1865.

On the morning of March 16th, after the fight of the preceding afternoon around John Smith's house 2 miles south on this road, Union General H. J. Kilpatrick's cavalry found a back road and circled to the rear of the Confederate position. The Union cavalry attempted to use this road to flank the Confederates, but was stopped by Colonel G. P. Harrison's brigade of McLaws' division after moving only a short distance.[4]

General W. B. Taliaferro decided to abandon the Confederate second position after finding his men in danger of being flanked. At 1:00 P.M. he withdrew to the third and final line of earthworks, where he was assisted by McLaws' division on his left and Wheeler's dismounted cavalry on his right. Rhett's disorganized

---

[4] The Confederate units that stopped Kilpatrick's men were the 32nd Georgia of Harrison's Brigade, and the 1st Georgia Regulars of Fiser's Brigade.

brigade was held in general reserve behind the junction of this road and the Smithfield road.

The Union forces soon advanced and established a strong line immediately in front of the Confederate third line. From this new position they pressed the Confederates all afternoon and part of the evening, but were unable to break the line. At 8:00 P.M. General W. J. Hardee, commanding the Confederate forces at Averasboro, having accomplished his objectives, began withdrawing his corps along the Smithfield road. Wheeler's cavalry was left behind to cover the retreat. By 4:00 A.M. on March 17th, all Confederate units had been withdrawn, leaving the Union forces in control.

General Hardee wished to accomplish two things by contesting the Union advance at Averasboro. The first objective was to determine for General Joseph E. Johnston, commander of all Confederate forces in the Carolinas, whether Sherman's army was advancing on Raleigh or Goldsboro. The Confederates learned it was moving on Goldsboro.[5] The second objective was to stretch out the distance between Sherman's left and right wings (which were moving on parallel roads) in order to give General Johnston a chance to concentrate his smaller army and destroy the Union left wing before the right wing could come to its assistance.[6] Both of these objectives were fully accomplished. The stage was now set for the greater Battle of Bentonville, fought 25 miles east on March 19-21, 1865.

NOTE: In order to better understand the battle it is best to read the large map-marker "Phase One" which is located two miles south on this road.

NC 82 south of Erwin at Chicora Cemetery, Harnett County

9. **Union Headquarters**
Gen. H. W. Slocum, commanding the Union forces, located his headquarters in this field, March 16, 1865.
NC 82 south of Erwin, Harnett County

10. **"Lebanon"**
Farquhard Smith's home was used as a Confederate hospital during the battle of Averasboro, March 15-16, 1865.
NC 82 south of Erwin, Harnett County

11. **Federal Hospital**
The 1865 home of Wm. Smith, 100 yds. E., was used as a hospital for Union troops in the Battle of Averasboro, March 15-16, 1865.
NC 82 north of Godwin, Cumberland County

NOTE: Due to vandalism in recent years most of the highway markers for this battle have been destroyed. The maps in this section show them in their proper places. Original map references in the text of marker numbers **2** and **8** have been omitted.

---

[5] Hardee's position blocked the roads to Raleigh and Goldsboro. Sherman's destination remained unclear until the Confederate retreat.
[6] The Federal Right Wing, under Gen. Oliver O. Howard, marched only six miles on March 17, as Howard awaited news of the Left Wing's battle near Averasboro. Faulty maps of North Carolina, a problem for both sides, would cause Joseph E. Johnston to exaggerate the distance between Sherman's columns. Hardee's delaying action at Averasboro gave the untried soldiers of Taliaferro's Division a chance to gain some combat experience. It also stalled the Left Wing's advance for one day, thereby gaining that much more time for Johnston to concentrate his scattered forces at Smithfield.

For more information about Averasboro Battleground contact:

Averasboro Battlefield Commission, Inc.

P.O. Box 1811
Dunn, North Carolina 28334

Civil War Sites Advisory Commission Report Status,
Battlefield of Averasboro:

Priority III.3: *Battlefields Needing Some Additional Protection*, Class C, good integrity, low threats. (Class C is defined as "having observable influence on the outcome of a campaign.")

Bluff Church: After departing Fayetteville, the Federal Left Wing advanced northeastward along the east bank of the Cape Fear River. As the lead elements of the XX Corps neared the vicinity of Averasboro, Hawley's brigade encamped at this church during the evening of March 15, 1865: "After an eleven-mile march, partly on an old plank road," remembered adjutant Edwin Bryant of the 3rd Wisconsin, "the regiment camped in the graveyard of Bluff church [above]. At 7:30 P.M., just as the supper had been disposed of and the men were preparing their places for bivouac between the grave mounds, or lying on the broad, flat stones, on which were chiseled the names and virtues of the long-since departed, an orderly dashed in. A minute later the order to 'Fall in,' caused an uprising in that cemetery....In less than two minutes the brigade was on the road. The night was the blackness of darkness, and the road, a by-road evidently, was soon bottomless....Men had their shoes sucked off by that mud embracing the feet so fondly."

Hawley's men slogged along in a thunderstorm to relieve Gen. Judson Kilpatrick's troopers, five miles distant, who were skirmishing with Taliaferro's Confederates at Smithville. Here Lt. Gen. William J. Hardee stood ready with two divisions to contest the Federal advance on the Raleigh Plank Road. Hawley's men relieved Smith D. Atkins' brigade of cavalry around 12:30 a.m. on March 16. "Encased in an armor of mud," continued Bryant, "[we] started anew the old occupation of skirmishing."—Edwin E. Bryant. *History of the Third Regiment of Wisconsin Veteran Volunteer Infantry, 1861-1865.* Cleveland: The Arthur H. Clark Company, 1891.

1. "Oak Grove": After the Battle of Averasboro, a news correspondent from Raleigh visited the John Smith house (left). After the evacuation of Confederate casualties from Averasboro, he noted, "much the larger number of wounded were left at Mr. John C. Smith's....[T]hanks to his energy, and the generous kindness of the neighbors, these men have scarcely wanted for anything. Mr. Smith gave up to the wounded six rooms of his dwelling, reserving but one for his family; and the three Smith families, and in fact, the whole community, have devoted themselves to the comfort of these brave men. We found them all lying on good beds, with male and female nurses by day and by night, while from far and near supplies of food were brought for their sustenance. Nor were they in want of Medical attendance, for Drs. McSwain, Robinson, and McDuffy relieved each other at intervals in the duty of caring for them....We found the number of wounded men at Mr. Smith's, reduced by death and removal, to twenty-seven, most of whom were from South Carolina."—*Daily Confederate*, Raleigh, North Carolina, April 6, 1865. **This house is private property and not accessible to the general public.** (See map on page 12)

2. View From "Oak Grove": This view from a second story window of the John Smith house looks northward toward the position of the first Confederate line. Alfred Rhett's South Carolinians stretched across the modern cotton field in the background. The expanse of trees on the left conceals the ravine that Case's Federal brigade crossed in attacking the right of Rhett's position. As Col. Daniel Dustin's brigade advanced to attack the Confederates in front on March 16, 1865, the right of the line was entirely exposed to enemy fire. For a short distance, the left half of Dustin's line was partially concealed by woods and outbuildings around Oak Grove. As Case's brigade attacked from the Federal left, "the commotion observed in the rebel lines," reported Dustin, "caused our men to break out in enthusiastic cheers difficult to restrain. At this moment the enemy opened a severe fire upon us, and as our line advanced it obliqued to the left, being thus partially sheltered by the woods and old buildings around Smith's house. From this point the enemy's fire was briskly returned, and a rapid advance....soon brought the entire brigade into the enemy's works."—*Official Records*, Vol. 47, pt. 1.

3. Battle of Averasboro: This contemporary view shows the Federal XX Corps artillery engaging Rhett's Confederate line on March 16, 1865. Dustin's brigade was initially posted behind these guns, but it passed through them in attacking the Confederate position. Oak Grove is rendered here as a modest, single story structure, quite unlike the plantation dwelling that it was. In truth, the house is enormous and faces almost due north. After the battle, while hospital operations were in full swing, Gen. William T. Sherman paid a visit: "In person I visited this house while the surgeons were at work," he wrote, "with arms and legs lying around loose, in the yard and on the porch."

Sherman considered his casualties at Averasboro "a serious loss," as the wounded further encumbered the Union wagon trains, toiling over muddy and difficult roads. Today Oak Grove, though in a state of disrepair, still bears visible evidence of its position between opposing battle lines. The facade is dotted with bullet holes, and there is structural damage where a few artillery rounds from Rhett's position crashed through the attic. Aside from an attached shelter and the removal of an original chimney, the house stands as it did in the 1860s.—*Harper's Weekly*, April 15, 1865 / Sherman, *Memoirs*.

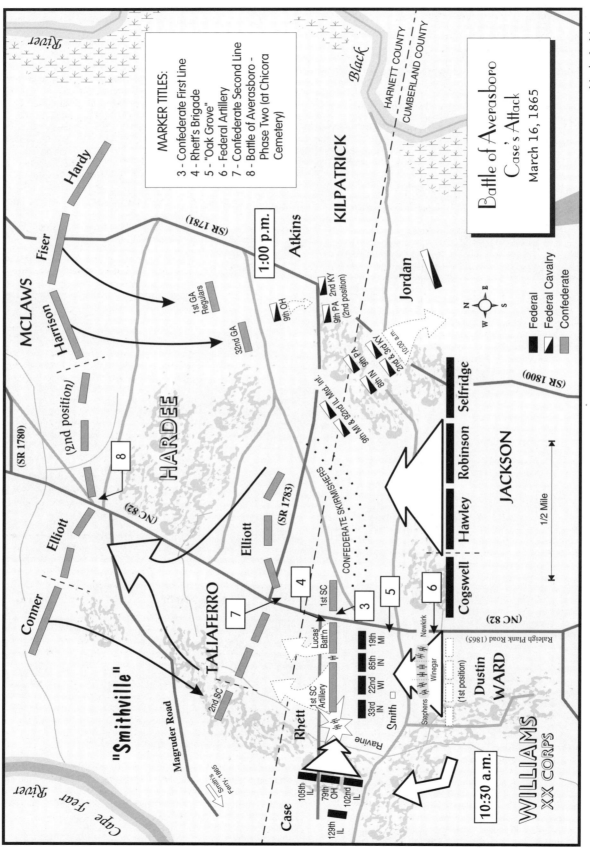

Mark A. Moore

MARKER TITLES:

3 - Confederate First Line
4 - Rhett's Brigade
5 - "Oak Grove"
6 - Federal Artillery
7 - Confederate Second Line
8 - Battle of Averasboro –
    Phase Two (at Chicora
    Cemetery)

Battle of Averasboro
Case's Attack
March 16, 1865

"About 11 o'clock [the enemy] massed and extended to our right, finally lapping and turning it....Our light artillery [three guns] was well served and operated with good results upon the enemy's infantry and opposing battery. The ground was so soft....it was found impossible to withdraw two of the guns, as every horse in Stuart's but one, and nine of LeGardeur's, were killed, and nearly all the cannoneers of both guns either killed or wounded."

— **Brig. Gen. William B. Taliaferro**, commanding division, Hardee's Corps

♦ General William J. Hardee formed his corps in three lines on March 15: Rhett's Brigade occupied the first line {3}, a short distance north of the John Smith house ("Oak Grove") {5}. Elliott's Brigade held the second line several hundred yards further north {7}. These first two lines constituted Taliaferro's Division. McLaws' Division held the third and strongest line, 600 yards in rear of Elliott {8}. Hardee's plan was for the inexperienced garrison troops of Taliaferro's command to commence the battle with the advancing Federals, and then fall back to the stronger position occupied by McLaws' veterans.

♦ Taliaferro's skirmishers were sent forward to meet the Left Wing's advance, and Gen. Joseph Wheeler's rear guard fell back through the skirmish line of Rhett's Brigade. About 3:00 p.m. Rhett's men made contact with the 9th Michigan Cavalry of Gen. Smith D. Atkins' brigade. While the 9th Michigan drove the Confederates back, the rest of Atkins' men began constructing rail works astride the Raleigh Plank Road. The 9th fell back to Atkins' main line while the sharp skirmishing continued. As night fell, a heavy rain set in. Colonel Alfred M. Rhett was captured in the afternoon by a party of Federal scouts under Capt. Theo Northrop, and command of Rhett's Brigade fell upon Col. William Butler. Infantry reinforcements arrived during the night from the Federal XX Corps: William Hawley's brigade reached Atkins' position at 12:30 a.m. on March 16.

♦ At 2:00 a.m. Sherman sent a note to Gen. A. H. Terry, whose command would soon leave Wilmington for Goldsboro: *"Thank you....for the certain knowledge that General Schofield is in possession of Kinston.[1] That is of great importance, for thence to Goldsborough there are no bridges. I will, in consequence, move straight on Goldsborough....Hardee is ahead of me and shows fight. I will go at him in the morning with four divisions and push him as far as Averasborough before turning toward Bentonville and Cox's Bridge."* To the south Gen. Oliver O. Howard's Right Wing was crossing South River, with Butler's Division of Confederate cavalry closely monitoring his advance. Sherman warned Howard: *"[A]ll is working well around us and we must not scatter, but aim to converge about Bentonville, and then Goldsborough. The rain is as bad for our opponents as for us, and I doubt if they have as good supplies or transportation as we."*

♦ On the morning of March 16 Kilpatrick's cavalry opened the battle by engaging a heavy line of Confederate skirmishers. General William T. Ward's XX Corps division arrived about 9:00 a.m. and deployed to the left of Hawley's brigade. The remaining two brigades of Jackson's division joined on the right of Hawley. Around 10:00 a.m. Atkins' troopers came up in support of Jordan's brigade. Soon the entire Federal battle line advanced to within 500 yards of Rhett's position. The XX Corps artillery unlimbered in front of Dustin's brigade {6} and began shelling the Confederate line.

♦ At 10:30 a.m. Left Wing commander Gen. Henry W. Slocum was ordered to send a force around the right flank of the Confederate position: Col. Henry Case's brigade undertook this flanking maneuver, and after crossing a ravine, advanced squarely on the right of Rhett's position. At the same time Dustin's command attacked the enemy in front, withstanding a severe fire from the Confederates. Though Rhett's men had stood well thus far in their first taste of battle, the attack of Case's brigade sent them reeling back toward Elliott's position to the north {4}. Two of the three field pieces of Stuart's and LeGardeur's Batteries[2] fell into Federal hands, and one of the captured pieces was turned and fired at its former owners.

♦ Around 1:00 p.m. Ward's and Jackson's divisions advanced upon Elliott's Brigade defending Hardee's second line. Atkins' Federal cavalry was prevented from circling around Elliott's left flank by the 32nd Georgia (Harrison) and 1st Georgia Regulars (Fiser). McLaws sent a third regiment, the 2nd South Carolina (Conner), to the right of Elliott's line, but the approaching Federals forced Taliaferro's Division to fall back to McLaws' main defensive position.

"The men sprang forward with alacrity, with a deafening yell, and the moment they emerged from the thicket in sight of the enemy they joined in a destructive fire upon their flanks." — **Col. Henry Case**, commanding 1st Brigade, 3rd Division, XX Army Corps

"There was a Rebel battery that kept annoying us [and] we received orders to take that battery and be quick about it....I suppose we were about forty rods from it....We were told that Brigadier General Dustin, our old colonel, who had been promoted and given another command, was about to charge this same battery from the right. So we wanted to get there first....As we charged up to it, they, of course, poured it into us lively. Just as we started, we heard cheers on our right and knew that Dustin and his men were racing for the guns. In three minutes we were over the fort works and the battery was ours. We got there a minute before Dustin did. The battery covered about as much ground as our front yard. On that small piece of ground I counted thirty-three dead Rebels and many wounded—and all done in a few minutes' time. Whether they did not have time to run or whether they would not run, I do not know." — **Pvt. Robert Hale Strong**, 105th Illinois, Case's brigade

[1] Schofield's XXIII Corps (under Gen. Jacob D. Cox) had begun repairing the railroad between New Bern and Kinston in early March. Terry's Provisional Corps left Wilmington for Goldsboro on the morning of March 16.

[2] LeGardeur's Louisiana Battery had two 12-pounder howitzers in line, while Stuart's Battery fielded one 12-pounder Napoleon.

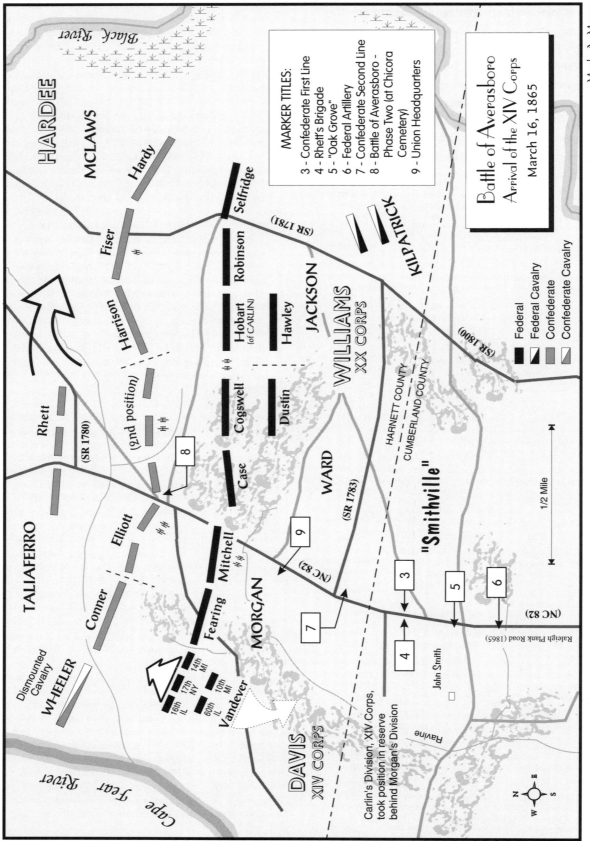

Mark A. Moore

MARKER TITLES:

3 - Confederate First Line
4 - Rhett's Brigade
5 - "Oak Grove"
6 - Federal Artillery
7 - Confederate Second Line
8 - Battle of Averasboro -
    Phase Two (at Chicora
    Cemetery)
9 - Union Headquarters

Battle of Averasboro
Arrival of the XIV Corps
March 16, 1865

Federal
Federal Cavalry
Confederate
Confederate Cavalry

1/2 Mile

Carlin's Division, XIV Corps,
took position in reserve
behind Morgan's Division

*"**B**efore the skirmishers had gained the position assigned them, the brave [Capt. William G.] Barnett fell, shot through the head, dying almost instantly....Just as his remains were carried back to our line Col. [James] Lake was struck in the right forearm, when, quietly slipping the sword knot from his wrist, he grasped the sword in his left hand, and was about giving an order 'Forward on a charge!' when he fell, severely wounded in the groin, and was carried to the rear....[W]e kept up a dull skirmishing fire until dark."*

— Sgt. **William B. Westervelt**, 17th New York Zouaves, Vandever's brigade

♦ When Taliaferro's Division fell back to Gen. William J. Hardee's third line of defense (McLaws' position) {8}, Elliott's Brigade was deployed astride the Raleigh Plank Road. Three brigades of McLaws' Division (Harrison, Fiser, and Hardy) were shifted to their left to make room for Elliott. A fourth brigade from McLaws (Conner's) formed on Elliott's right. Having received the brunt of the Federal attack, Rhett's Brigade was formed in reserve. The timely arrival of two divisions of Wheeler's cavalry (Humes' and Allen's) prolonged Hardee's line of battle to the Cape Fear River. Hardee now had roughly 8,000 men arrayed against Gen. H. W. Slocum, who would have some 20,000 men on the battlefield before the day ended.

♦ Following in pursuit of Taliaferro's Confederates, the Federal XX Corps crossed to the right of the road, and Gen. James D. Morgan's XIV Corps division soon moved into line on the left. In hopes of turning the Confederate right flank, Morgan ordered Gen. William Vandever's brigade to move out on the left and reconnoiter the enemy position. Vandever's men found that, instead of an exposed right flank, the Confederates had a well-established line all the way to the bluffs overlooking the Cape Fear. Federal skirmishers crept up to a ravine in front of Hardee's line, but were roughly handled by Wheeler's troopers on the opposite bank, and Vandever's brigade withdrew to a reserve position in the rear. At some point during the day, General Slocum established his headquarters in rear of the Federal lines {9}.

♦ The opposing forces were now in close proximity to one another, and the skirmishing remained sharp throughout the afternoon. The day's light rain gave way to a downpour in the late afternoon, worsening the muddy terrain and hampering troop deployment. As the XX Corps inched forward, Hardee sent Rhett's Brigade to the Confederate left, to guard against a flank attack from that direction. Meanwhile, Gen. William P. Carlin's Federal division reached the battlefield around dusk, and formed in reserve of the main line. Carlin's advance had been delayed by muddy roads made nearly impassable by the recent rains. General Sherman accordingly postponed any further assault on Hardee until the next morning. Scattered firing continued after dark.

♦ On the battlefield, the John Smith house ("Oak Grove") {5} was used by both sides as a field hospital. The Farquhard Smith house ("Lebanon") and William Smith house were also used as hospitals: the former by the Confederates and the latter by Slocum's Federals. (For these house locations see marker numbers 10 and 11 on the map titled *Battlefield of Averasboro, NC.*)

♦ Late in the afternoon Hardee sent word to Gen. Joseph E. Johnston that his troops had checked Slocum's advance, and that he would retire toward Smithfield after dark. At nightfall, the Confederate artillery pulled out, followed around 8:30 p.m. by the infantry. Late that night Johnston queried Hardee: *"Please give all the information you have....in regard to [the enemy's] movements, in order that we may regulate our own accordingly."* Johnston, eager to learn the direction of march of the Federal Left Wing column, was slowly gathering his scattered forces for a more substantial attempt to arrest Sherman's progress through North Carolina. Headquartered at Smithfield, roughly midway between Raleigh and Goldsboro, Johnston hoped to collect a force large enough to tackle one wing of Sherman's army while the other was beyond supporting distance. From Smithfield Johnston could move to the west to block an advance on Raleigh, or to the east to bar the way to Goldsboro. Hardee's stand at Averasboro had delayed the Left Wing's advance for one day, buying precious time for Johnston's gathering forces.

"When we started to fall back....I never paid any more attention to the men but fought my way back from tree to tree....When I jumped on top of the works, I was worse scared than I ever was in my life. I expected to find the [1st Georgia] Regulars where I left them, and therefore was in no hurry to get to the works, believing that our officers were then watching me. [I] Would have preferred being shot in front of the works than to have rushed over them like I was scared. Instead of the Regulars in the works, I found it occupied by a line of boys [of Elliott's Brigade] who would have killed me....if they had commenced firing before I entered the works....The boys where I jumped over wanted to know if the [Y]ankees were coming. I told them yes, and if they did not go to shooting like rip, the [Y]ankees would be over the works and kill the last one of them. I got them to shooting, but don't think one of them ever saw the [Y]ankees and they were not more than 40 yards away. They stuck down in the trenches and poked their guns over the works and fired....The enemy having accomplished his undertaking (feeling our lines), retreated back some 200 yards."
— Sgt. **William H. Andrews**, 1st Georgia Regulars, Fiser's Brigade.

"The lieutenant-general commanding thanks the officers and men of this command for their courage and conduct of yesterday, and congratulates them upon giving the enemy the first serious check he has received since leaving Atlanta....The lieutenant-general augurs happily of the future service and reputation of the troops who have signalized the opening of the campaign by admirable steadiness, endurance, and courage. By command of Lieutenant-General Hardee." — **Lt. Col. Thomas B. Roy**, Asst. Adjutant-General, General Orders No. 16, March 17, 1865

Johnston Gathers an Army

On March 15, 1865, Gen. Robert E. Lee again expressed to Joe Johnston the critical military situation facing both commanders:

"If you are forced back from Raleigh, and we be deprived of the supplies from East North Carolina, I do not know how this army [of Northern Virginia] can be supported. Yet a disaster to your army will not improve my condition, and while I would urge upon you to neglect no opportunity of delivering the enemy a successful blow, I would not recommend you to engage in a general battle without a reasonable prospect of success....[A]n opportunity may occur for you and [Gen. Braxton] Bragg to unite upon one of [the enemy] columns and crush it. I do not think I could maintain my position [at Petersburg, Virginia] were I further to reduce my force....I shall maintain my position as long as it appears advisable....Unity of purpose and harmony of action between [our] two armies, with the blessing of God, I trust will relieve us from the difficulties that now beset us."

Johnston traveled from Raleigh to Smithfield that same day, where he formed the hodgepodge Army of the South from the four separate commands at his disposal: the remnants of the Army of Tennessee; Hardee's Corps; Hoke's Division (under Department of North Carolina commander Braxton Bragg); and Lt. Gen. Wade Hampton's cavalry. Bragg's troops, after evacuating Wilmington and resisting the advance of Schofield's XXIII Corps at Kinston March 8-10, had fallen back to Goldsboro. On March 13 Johnston had ordered Bragg to Smithfield, where he arrived with Hoke's Division on the 15th. The Army of Tennessee troops were slowly trickling in from the west, having departed Tupelo, Mississippi, by rail in mid-January. Hardee's Corps was falling back toward Smithfield after his engagement with the Federal Left Wing at Averasboro, while Hampton's cavalry force was split to monitor the advance of both wings of Sherman's army. On March 16, Lt. Gen. Alexander P. Stewart was officially appointed commander of the Army of Tennessee remnant then at Smithfield. As his scattered units converged, an anxious Johnston awaited news from Hardee and Hampton regarding the true destination of Sherman's divided army.

On the morning of March 17, Kilpatrick's cavalry and Gen. William T. Ward's XX Corps division followed the retreating Hardee as far as Averasboro. Sherman hoped to mislead the Confederates into thinking the Federals were marching on Raleigh. Meanwhile, the main body of the Left Wing turned east toward Goldsboro. As the Left Wing advanced, Hampton fell back with Col. George G. Dibrell's Division to Willis Cole's house on the Goldsboro Road, about two miles south of Bentonville. That evening he informed Hardee: *"I think that the enemy is moving on Goldsborough....I will keep [in] between him and Smithfield and Goldsborough, until the very last moment."*

Reports from the field were slow in reaching Johnston at Smithfield, and he began to worry that events were unfolding too slowly. At 7:00 p.m. he warned Hardee: *"Something must be done to-morrow morning, and yet I have no satisfactory information as to the enemy's movements. Can you give me any certain information of the position of the force you engaged yesterday [at Averasboro]? Send it immediately by a trusted and well mounted courier, to come all the way rapidly."* Likewise Johnston queried Hampton at Cole's house: *"Please send me....all the information you have of the movement and position of the enemy, the number of their columns, their location and distance apart, and distance from Goldsborough, and give me your opinion whether it is practicable to reach them from Smithfield on the south side of the [Neuse]*

river before they reach Goldsborough." Bragg and Stewart were given orders to be ready to move out at dawn the next morning.

Hampton's reply to Johnston was encouraging. He reported that his present position at the Cole plantation would be an excellent site at which to block the advance of Sherman's Left Wing. The Federals were still a day's march away from Cole's, and were widely separated from the Right Wing. Smithfield lay some twenty miles north of Hampton's position, and he assured Johnston that his cavalry would hold Sherman's advance in check while Johnston's forces gathered at the chosen site. With this news the Confederate commander hastily prepared to unite his forces with Hampton's below Smithfield. At 6:45 on the morning of March 18, Johnston's adjutant penned a dispatch to Hardee, whose corps was encamped at Elevation, midway between Averasboro and Smithfield: *"[P]ut your command in motion for Bentonville by the shortest route....The sheriff of this county represents that there is a road leading from a point two miles this side of Elevation and striking the Averasborough and Goldsborough road a little to the west of Bentonville."* Johnston's maps of the region would prove sorely inaccurate, placing Hardee closer to Bentonville than he actually was, while exaggerating the distance between Sherman's separated columns. These discrepancies would delay Hardee significantly. At 7:40 a.m. Johnston himself notified Hampton: *"We will go to the place at which your dispatch was written [Cole's plantation]. The scheme mentioned in my note, which you pronounce practicable, will be attempted. Send all the information you can bearing upon it."*

Until now Sherman had remained wary of the intentions of his adversary: *"I think it probable that Joe Johnston will try to prevent our getting Goldsborough,"* he wrote to Right Wing commander Oliver O. Howard on March 18. *"Our map is evidently faulty....I fear Slocum [commanding the Left Wing] will be jammed with all his trains in a narrow space; but at the same time I don't want to push you off too far till this flank is better covered by the Neuse."* But soon Gen. Judson Kilpatrick reported that the enemy was retiring on Smithfield, and word came in that Joseph Wheeler's Confederates had burned the bridge over Mill Creek on the Smithfield-Clinton Road [present-day U. S. 701]. Sherman's map incorrectly indicated this road as the only approach route available to Johnston from Smithfield. (The map omitted Johnston's actual approach route, which met the Goldsboro Road two miles south of Bentonville near Cole's plantation.) It suddenly looked as though Johnston was going to defend Raleigh, instead of Goldsboro. Sherman was now confident that the Left Wing would easily reach Cox's Bridge on the Neuse River by the next afternoon. From there it would be a 12-mile march to Goldsboro.

On March 18 the Left Wing, traveling on the Goldsboro Road, advanced as far as the intersection of the Smithfield-Clinton roads. The Right Wing's XV Corps was some two miles to the south at Blackman Lee's Store, while the XVII Corps was six miles further south and east at Troublefield's Store. Sherman's army was within 25 miles of Goldsboro.

Hampton deployed Dibrell's troopers and William Earle's South Carolina Battery in a defensive line at the Reddick Morris farm, just west of Cole's plantation. At 2:30 p.m. Hampton sent word to Johnston: *"I can hold [Slocum] here for several hours more, and I do not think his advance will get beyond this point to-night."* At dusk the Confederate cavalry force was pressed hard by a 90-man party of mounted foragers from Morgan's XIV Corps division, but the thin line of Southern troopers held. Hampton had successfully defended the ground chosen for the coming fight. As Hampton clung to his position, Johnston's infantry was hard on the march from Smithfield, and Bragg and Stewart would reach the village of Bentonville during the evening of March 18.

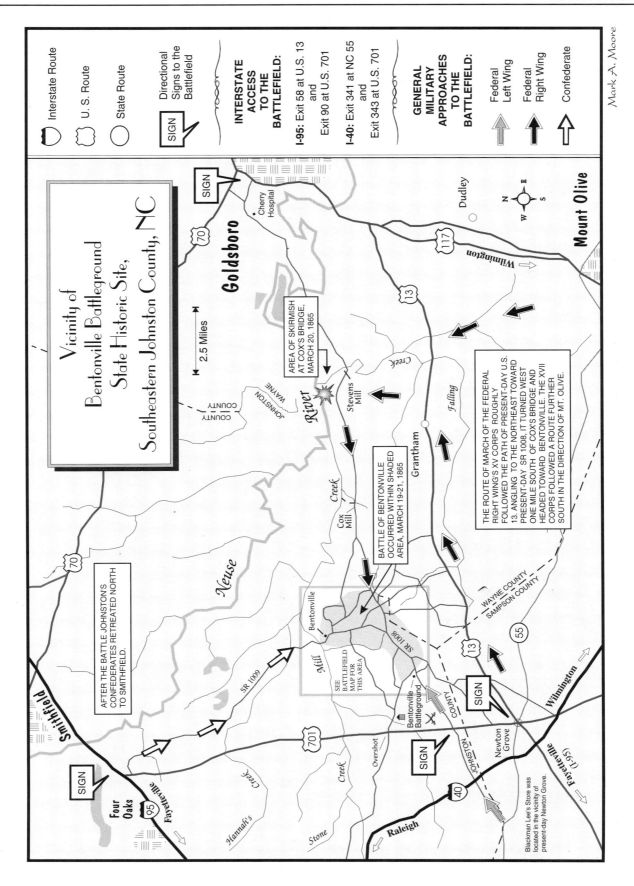

Vicinity of
Bentonville Battleground
State Historic Site,
Southeastern Johnston County, NC

Mark A. Moore

Interstate Route
U. S. Route
State Route

SIGN Directional Signs to the Battlefield

INTERSTATE ACCESS TO THE BATTLEFIELD:

I-95: Exit 58 at U.S. 13 and Exit 90 at U.S. 701

I-40: Exit 341 at NC 55 and Exit 343 at U.S. 701

GENERAL MILITARY APPROACHES TO THE BATTLEFIELD:

Federal Left Wing
Federal Right Wing
Confederate

2.5 Miles

AFTER THE BATTLE JOHNSTON'S CONFEDERATES RETREATED NORTH TO SMITHFIELD.

AREA OF SKIRMISH AT COX'S BRIDGE, MARCH 20, 1865

BATTLE OF BENTONVILLE OCCURRED WITHIN SHADED AREA, MARCH 19-21, 1865

THE ROUTE OF MARCH OF THE FEDERAL RIGHT WING'S XV CORPS ROUGHLY FOLLOWED THE PATH OF PRESENT-DAY U.S. 13. ANGLING TO THE NORTHEAST TOWARD PRESENT-DAY SR 1008, IT TURNED WEST ONE MILE SOUTH OF COX'S BRIDGE AND HEADED TOWARD BENTONVILLE. THE XVII CORPS FOLLOWED A ROUTE FURTHER SOUTH IN THE DIRECTION OF MT. OLIVE.

SEE BATTLEFIELD MAP FOR THIS AREA

Blackman Lee's Store was located in the vicinity of present-day Newton Grove.

Goldsboro
Cherry Hospital
Dudley
Mount Olive
Smithfield
Four Oaks
Raleigh
Bentonville
Grantham
Newton Grove
Wilmington
Fayetteville

Stevens Mill
Cox Mill
Bentonville Battleground

Neuse River
Falling Creek
Cox Creek
Mill Creek
Hannah's Creek
Stone Creek
Overshot Creek

JOHNSTON COUNTY
WAYNE COUNTY
WAYNE COUNTY
SAMPSON COUNTY
JOHNSTON COUNTY

SR 1009
SR 1008

70
70
117
13
13
55
701
40
95
Fayetteville (I-95)

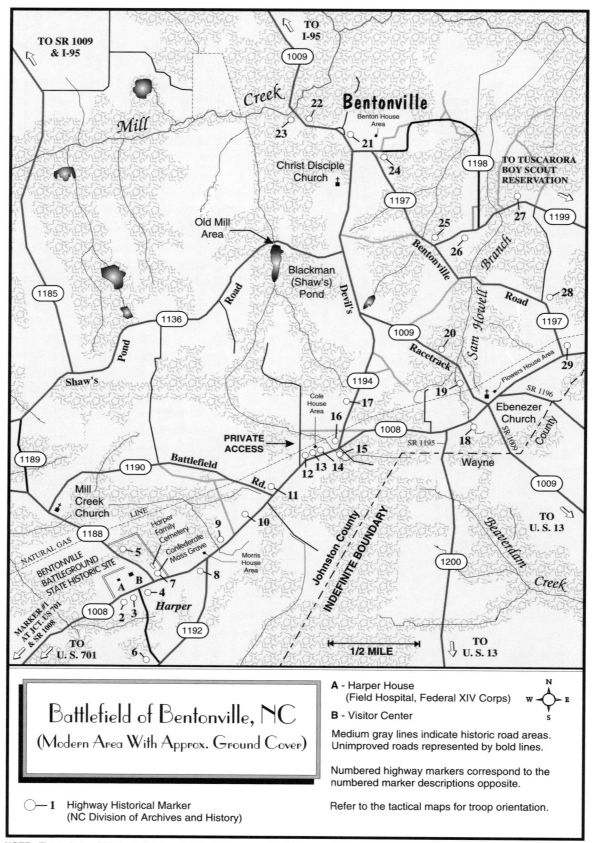

Battlefield of Bentonville, NC
(Modern Area With Approx. Ground Cover)

○—1 Highway Historical Marker
(NC Division of Archives and History)

A - Harper House
(Field Hospital, Federal XIV Corps)

B - Visitor Center

Medium gray lines indicate historic road areas.
Unimproved roads represented by bold lines.

Numbered highway markers correspond to the
numbered marker descriptions opposite.

Refer to the tactical maps for troop orientation.

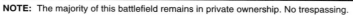

NOTE: The majority of this battlefield remains in private ownership. No trespassing.

Mark A. Moore

Highway Historical Markers —
Battle of Bentonville

1. **Sherman**

Gen. Wm. T. Sherman camped in the area with his Left Wing on the night of March 18, 1865. The following morning the Left Wing continued along this road, meeting Gen. Jos. E. Johnston's Confederates in the Battle of Bentonville, 2 miles east. Meanwhile, Sherman joined his Right Wing, marching toward Goldsboro on another road, and thus missed the first day of the battle.

Jct. SR 1008 (Harper House Road) & U. S. 701

2. **Union Hospital**

The Harper House was used as a hospital by the XIV Corps, March 19-21, 1865. About 500 Union wounded were treated here.

SR 1008 (Harper House Road)

3. **Confederate Hospital**

Following the battle, 45 Confederate wounded were hospitalized in the Harper House. Nineteen of these men died here. Surgeons moved the others to regular Confederate hospitals.

SR 1008 (Harper House Road)

4. **Union Headquarters**

Maj. Gen. A. S. Williams, commanding the XX Corps, established his headquarters here on March 19. In the woods to the north, the XX Corps erected breastworks which remain.

SR 1008 (Harper House Road)

5. **Federal Earthworks**

Constructed by First Michigan Engineers and others, March 19, 1865. Occupied by Federals throughout the battle. Works begin 75 yards behind this marker.

SR 1188 (Mill Creek Church Road)

6. **Union Hospital**

Field Hospital of the XX Corps during the Battle of Bentonville was located here. Four hundred Union soldiers, wounded in the Battle of Averasboro (16 miles west) on March 16, were brought here for treatment.[1]

SR 1008 (Harper House Road)

7. **Confederate Cemetery**

The remains of 360 Confederates who fell in the Battle of Bentonville lie here. They were moved to this plot from other parts of the battlefield in 1893. The monument was erected at that time.

Jct. SR 1008 (Harper House Road) & SR 1188

8. **Union Headquarters**

Maj. Gen. H. W. Slocum, commanding Sherman's Left Wing, had headquarters in this field, March 19-21, 1865.[2]

SR 1008 (Harper House Road)

9. **Federal Artillery**

Union batteries (26 guns)[3] formed a line here, March 19, giving cover to retreating Federals during the Confederate charges and finally halting the advance of the Confederate Right Wing.

SR 1008 (Harper House Road)

10. **Confederate Attacks**

Across the fields behind this marker the Confederate Right Wing made five attacks on Union positions to the left, March 19, 1865. They were thrown back by the XX Federal Corps.[4]

SR 1008 (Harper House Road)

11. **Confederate Main Charge**

After overrunning two Union lines above this road, the Confederates crossed here in the main assault of March 19, 1865. Union reinforcements halted their advance in the woods below the road.

At jct. SR 1008 & SR 1190 (Battlefield Road)

12. **Cole Farmhouse**

Stood in this field. Scene of heavy fighting, March 19. Destroyed on March 20 by Confederate artillery to prevent sniping.[5]

SR 1008 (Harper House Road)

13. **Fighting Below the Road**

One-half mile south of this point, across the road, Brig. Gen. J. D. Morgan's Union Division halted the main Confederate charge, March 19, 1865, in one of the fiercest engagements of the battle.

SR 1008 (Harper House Road)

14. **First Union Attack**

Brig. Gen. W. P. Carlin's Division attacked the Confederate line above the road here on March 19. Repulsed, they threw up works but were driven out by the Confederate charge.

SR 1008 (Harper House Road)

15. **Main Confederate Line**

The Left Confederate Wing, part of a long hook-shaped line designed to trap the Union forces, extended across the road here on March 19. This sector, occupied by Maj. Gen. R. F. Hoke's Division, was evacuated on March 20. A new line parallel to the road was established 500 yards north.

Jct. SR 1008 & SR 1194 (Bass Road)

16. **N. C. Junior Reserves**

Held the line along this road and repulsed the assault of Hobart's Union Brigade, March 19, 1865. This line was evacuated March 20.

SR 1194 (Bass Road)

---

[1] XX Corps wounded from Bentonville were also treated here.
[2] Evidence suggests Slocum's headquarters were several hundred yards north of the Goldsboro Road (SR 1008), behind the XX Corps line.

---

[3] The artillery line contained only 21 guns on March 19—16 north of the road, and five south of the road. The five guns below the road were located slightly west of this marker. See battle maps for clarification. Stephens' Battery C, 1st Ohio, reached this spot first. The remaining batteries were deployed during the Confederate attacks at Morris' Farm in the late afternoon of March 19.
[4] Participants in this portion of the fight (Morris' Farm) give conflicting reports, placing the number of attacks at anywhere from two to seven.
[5] The Cole House and surrounding buildings were burned to the ground by Confederate skirmishers of the Army of Tennessee on the morning of March 21, 1865.

17. **Main Confederate Line**

On March 19 the line extended 3/4 mile to the rear of this marker and one mile to the left, forming a strong hook-shaped position with a right angle turn here. On March 20 the Left Wing was pulled back to this point and the new Confederate line crossed the road here. Earthworks remain.

SR 1194 (Bass Road)

18. **Federal Junction**

Sherman's Left and Right Wings joined forces here during the afternoon of March 20, 1865. They constructed works across the road and skirmished with the Confederates.

SR 1008 (Harper House Road)

19. **Main Union Line**

Advanced to this point during the afternoon of March 21. The XV Corps established a line of works across the road here. Earthworks remain.

SR 1009 (Devil's Racetrack)

20. **Main Confederate Line**

Crossed the road at this point, March 20-21. Gen. R. F. Hoke's Division occupied this sector. Scene of much skirmishing but no heavy fighting. Earthworks remain.

SR 1009 (Devil's Racetrack)

21. **Bentonville**

In 1865, a local market center for naval stores (tar, pitch, & turpentine). Bentonville gives name to the battle fought nearby, March 19-21, 1865. Confederates concentrated here the day of the battle. As they retreated on March 22, they burned all stocks of naval stores. Union forces occupied the village March 22-24.

SR 1009 (Devil's Racetrack)

22. **Confederate Works**

Remains of breastworks on this hill mark a line of works built by the Confederates to protect Mill Creek Bridge.

SR 1009 (Devil's Racetrack)

23. **Mill Creek**

The flooded state of this creek upstream prevented an attack by Wheeler's Confederate cavalry on the rear of Sherman's Army, March 19, 1865. A bridge here was the Confederates' sole line of retreat after the battle.

SR 1009 (Devil's Racetrack)

24. **Johnston's Headquarters**

Established here on the night of March 18, 1865 and remained during the battle. Mower's Division came within 200 yards of this point in the Union assault of March 21.[6]

SR 1197 (Bentonville Road)

25. **Hardee's Charge**

Near this point Gen. William J. Hardee led the charge of the 8th Texas Cavalry and other Confederates, repulsing the advance of Mower's Division, March 21, 1865.[7]

Jct. SR 1197 & SR 1199 (Scout Road)

26. **Mower's Attack**

Advancing toward Mill Creek Bridge, Johnston's only line of retreat, Maj. Gen. J. A. Mower's Union Division broke the Confederate line near this point, March 21. Mower's Division reached a point 200 yards from Johnston's headquarters before it was driven back by Confederate infantry and cavalry.[8]

SR 1199 (Scout Road)

27. **Union Line — March 21**

After withdrawing from the advance against Mill Creek Bridge, Mower's Federals reformed here and threw up works. This was the extreme right of the Union line on March 21. Earthworks remain.

SR 1199 (Scout Road)

28. **Union Line — March 20**

Trenches in the woods behind this marker formed the extreme right of the Union line on March 20. This sector was occupied by the XVII Corps, commanded by Maj. Gen. F. P. Blair.

SR 1197 (Bentonville Road)

29. **Union Headquarters**

Sherman's headquarters were located in the field 400 yards to the rear of this marker, March 20-21, 1865. Headquarters of the XVII Corps, which included Mower's Division, were 250 yards to the left rear.

Jct. SR 1008 & 1197 (Bentonville Road)

BENTONVILLE AREA ROAD NAMES

Battle Area:

1008 - Harper House Road
1009 - Devil's Racetrack Road
1136 - Shaw's Pond Road
1188 - Mill Creek Church Road
1190 - Battlefield Road
1194 - Bass Road
1197 - Bentonville Road
1198 - Westbrook Lowground Road
1199 - Scout Road

Peripheral:

1185 - Joyner Bridge Road
1189 - Britt Road
1192 - Newton Grove Road
1195 - L. Flowers Road
1196 - St. Johns Church Road

NOTE: As a reference work, this guide offers a consistent repetition of marker positions from map to map. When the guide is read as a whole, a "visual" history of the battle unfolds around these static reference points, which may seem redundant. The repetition is for the benefit of those who wish to consult the guide piecemeal.

---

[6] Johnston's headquarters were probably in the yard of the John Benton House, which stood in the large field north of this marker.

[7] Hardee's counterattack began approximately one-half mile north and slightly west of this marker, moving from west to east.

[8] Mower's attack began approximately one-half mile north of this marker, moving from east to west. The 64th Illinois (Fuller's brigade) overran Johnston's headquarters, forcing the general and his staff to flee on foot.

North Carolina Division of Archives and History

Contemporary Sketches: The views at left, drawn by *Harper's* artist William Waud, are the only published battle scenes by an artist who was present during the fighting at Bentonville. The most recognizable battle image, depicting a portion of Mower's Charge on March 21, 1865, was drawn from a description of that action, rather than an eyewitness. (See *Last Stand in the Carolinas*, Appendix E, p. 463). The top view shows the Federal XX Corps artillery in action on the Morris farm on March 19, while the bottom view illustrates a part of the Federal XV Corps skirmish line on March 20, 1865. William's brother Alfred was the more famous of the two artists. —*Harper's Weekly*, April 15, 1865.

The detailed view of the XX Corps artillery below appeared in *The Story of the Great March, From the Diary of a Staff Officer*, by Maj. George Ward Nichols (Harper Brothers, 1865), and may have been commissioned by the publisher. Nichols was an aide-de-camp on the staff of Gen. William T. Sherman.

North Carolina Division of Archives and History

Maj. Gen. Henry W. Slocum: On the morning of March 19, 1865, as Left Wing commander Henry Slocum (above) began to realize that he faced serious opposition, Lt. Col. Henry G. Litchfield rode in from the front and confirmed that fact: "Well, general, I have found something more than Dibrell's [Confederate] cavalry—I find infantry intrenched along our whole front, and enough of them to give us all the amusement we shall want for the rest of the day." As a result, Slocum adopted a defensive plan which ensured the Federals a tactical draw for the first day's battle. At sundown, a strong Federal defense of the Morris farm staved off the Confederate "high tide" attacks of Taliaferro and Bate.—Slocum, "Sherman's March."

Maj. Gen. Daniel H. Hill: D. H. Hill (right) commanded the largest corps of the Army of Tennessee present at Bentonville, fielding 2,687 men on March 19. As in many previous fights, Hill was active on the battlefield, where four of his staff officers were wounded. "Our men fought with great enthusiasm in this engagement," he reported. "The only thing censurable in their conduct which I could perceive was an excited firing, at times resulting in the causeless waste of ammunition." Complaints of ill health from Hill were common throughout the war, and he felt poorly on the morning of March 19, 1865. "I was sick," he wrote of the first day's fight at Bentonville, "but the battle made me well." —*Official Records*, Vol. 47, pt. 1 / D. H. Hill to Daughter, March 23, 1865, D. H. Hill Papers, United States Army Military History Institute, Carlisle Barracks, Pennsylvania.

In his report on Bentonville, Hill refers to "A map of the ground, since made by Lieutenant Currie." This map has not surfaced, and remains one of the many mysteries surrounding the Confederate side at Bentonville. Several key battle reports are also missing. Most conspicuously absent are those for Hoke's Division, which were never made. But in his unpublished report, Gen. Henry D. Clayton specifically refers to the reports of Col. Osceola Kyle, commanding Jackson's Brigade, and Brig. Gen. Alpheus Baker—neither of which have been found. These would no doubt prove interesting: Clayton refers to Kyle's report for an account of the captured Federal artillery, and to Baker's for information on Baker's Brigade during Mower's Charge, March 21, 1865.—Henry D. Clayton Papers, University of Alabama, Tuscaloosa, Alabama.

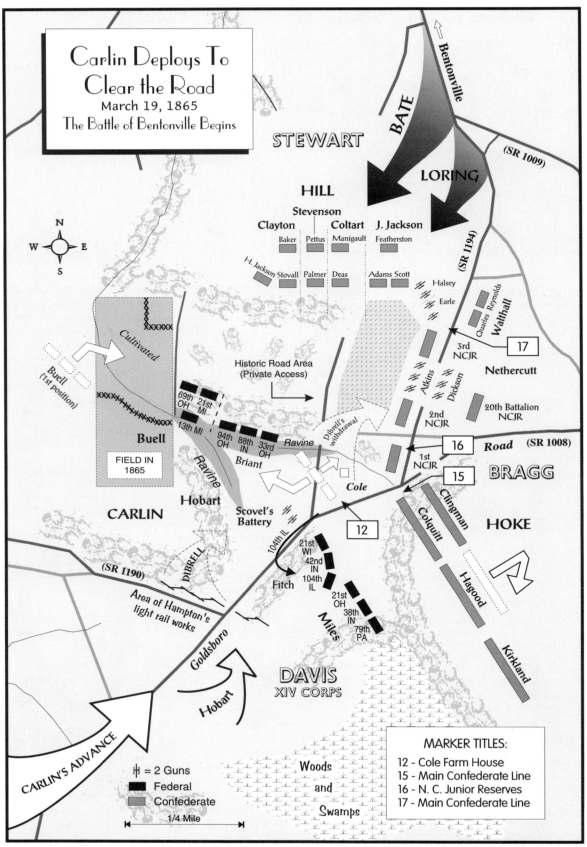

Carlin Deploys To Clear the Road
March 19, 1865
The Battle of Bentonville Begins

STEWART

BATE

Bentonville

(SR 1009)

LORING

HILL

Stevenson

Clayton   Coltart   J. Jackson

Baker   Pettus   Manigault   Featherston

(SR 1194)

H. Jackson Stovall Palmer Deas   Adams Scott

Halsey

Earle

Quarles Reynolds Walthall

17

3rd
NCJR

Nethercutt

Cultivated

Buell
(1st position)

Historic Road Area
(Private Access)

Atkins   Dickson

20th Battalion
NCJR

69th 21st
OH   MI

2nd
NCJR

13th MI

94th 88th 33rd
OH   IN   OH

Ravine

Dibrell's
withdrawal

16   Road   (SR 1008)

Buell

FIELD IN
1865

Briant

Cole

1st
NCJR

15   BRAGG

Hobart

Scovel's
Battery

12

Clingman

HOKE

CARLIN

Ravine

Colquitt

(SR 1190)

DIBRELL

104th IL

Fitch

21st
WI
42nd
IN
104th
IL

21st
OH
38th
IN
79th
PA

Hagood

Area of Hampton's
light rail works

Miles

Kirkland

Goldsboro

Hobart

DAVIS
XIV CORPS

CARLIN'S ADVANCE

⊩ = 2 Guns

Woods

Federal

and

Confederate

Swamps

1/4 Mile

MARKER TITLES:
12 - Cole Farm House
15 - Main Confederate Line
16 - N. C. Junior Reserves
17 - Main Confederate Line

Mark A. Moore

"If the foragers could not clear the way, nothing less than a brigade need try it."

— **Lt. Allan Dougall**, 88th Indiana, Hobart's brigade

◆ On the bright morning of March 19, 1865, XIV Corps commander Jefferson C. Davis and Gens. H. W. Slocum and William T. Sherman stood at the crossroads of the Smithfield and Goldsboro roads. Skirmish firing rolled up from the east as the Left Wing foragers pushed ahead on the Goldsboro Road, and Davis expressed concern over meeting *"more than the usual cavalry opposition."* Davis' adjutant overheard Sherman's reply: *"No Jeff; there is nothing there but Dibbrell's [sic] cavalry. Brush them out of the way. Good-morning. I'll meet you to-morrow morning at Cox's Bridge."* From this point forward, his earlier caution notwithstanding, Sherman's attitude concerning the threat posed by Joseph E. Johnston was marked by skepticism. As Carlin's division led the way eastward, Sherman rode off to join the Federal Right Wing as it marched on Goldsboro. Davis' adjutant, Alexander McClurg, later noted that *"three days yet lay between us and Cox's Bridge."*

◆ Hoke's Confederate Division reached Hampton's chosen ground early that morning and took position blocking the Goldsboro Road {15}. The Federals, advancing east on this road, would be forced to deploy to clear the way to Goldsboro.

◆ By 10:00 a.m. the advance of Carlin's division (Hobart's brigade) was driving elements of Dibrell's cavalry from a line of rail barricades west of Cole's plantation. As Col. Cyrus E. Briant's wing of Hobart's brigade reached the Cole house {12}, it was pinned down by fire from Atkins' Battery and the North Carolina Junior Reserves {16}. Caught in the open, Briant's men hastily attempted to improvise a breastwork.

◆ Following behind Briant was the second wing of Hobart's brigade, under Lt. Col. Michael H. Fitch. It deployed south of the Goldsboro Road, with its line refused to the right. The two wings of Hobart's brigade would remain separated for the duration of the fight. Scovel's battery (C, 1st Illinois) unlimbered to the left of Fitch's position and began shelling the Confederate line.

◆ From its exposed position north of the road, the 33rd Ohio was ordered by Hobart into *"a good position in the pines a short distance to the left and front of the [Cole] house."* The new line faced north in a deep wooded ravine, at the bottom of which flowed a sizable creek.* The 33rd began to entrench on its northern slope. About an hour later it was followed by the 88th Indiana and 94th Ohio, which fell in line on the left of the 33rd. At the time, the new position offered welcome

protection from Hoke's artillery, but the ravine would become a problem for Carlin's men later in the day.

◆ Having fanned out well to the left in developing the Confederate line, George Buell's brigade—after engaging a skirmish line from the Army of Tennessee—was directed to move to the right and into the ravine. It formed to the left of Briant's men, who remained out of sight beyond Buell's right flank.

◆ South of the Goldsboro Road David Miles' brigade filed in on the right of Fitch's three regiments. Both commands advanced a line of skirmishers through the woods in the direction of the enemy.

◆ Meanwhile, as Carlin's troops struggled with Hoke's Division, the Army of Tennessee was filing into position several hundred yards to the north. Their line was at a right angle to Hoke's, and as Hardee's Corps had not yet arrived on the field, two batteries of Hampton's horse artillery were placed at the angle {17}. Thanks to Lt. Gen. Wade Hampton, Johnston's forces had managed to find suitable ground from which to contest the Federal advance on Goldsboro. It was a timely arrival, but the Left Wing column was springing the Confederate trap just as it was being set.

◆ Up to this point the Confederate threat was dismissed by Federal commanders as merely cavalry, accompanied by a few pieces of artillery. By order of Gen. Jeff C. Davis, Carlin directed Buell to initiate a probing attack to further develop the Confederate position. Briant's three regiments and Miles' brigade would also participate, in order *"to multiply the chances of success."*

"Throwing forward skirmishers, we advanced rapidly, driving the enemy out of their skirmish line of works across the Cole farm to the woods beyond, but the enemy opened on us with shot and shell from a battery to our left oblique. We halted, hastily throwing together what rails, &c., we could find, keeping up a continuous fire at the enemy, who also were busy throwing up works in our front." — **Capt. William N. Voris**, commanding the 88th Indiana, Hobart's brigade

"We were in plain sight, in the open field, in musket range [and] we found the place a little unhealthy." — **Capt. Joseph Hinson**, commanding the 33rd Ohio, Hobart's brigade

---

"[Hoke's Division] took position on the left of a large and deserted old plantation, heavily wooded on each side, through which one main road ran, and along which the division was stationed....[Lt. Col. Joseph B.] Starr's Light Artillery, after remaining in column in the road for some time....took the right center of the line on the edge of the field....The battery was commanded by Captain George B. Atkins....This officer, finding a wooden house [Cole's] in front of a North Carolina regiment serving as a shelter for the enemy's sharpshooters, dislodged them by a few well-directed shots from two Napoleons, and they were seen hurrying out from the building, amid the cheers of the Confederates....though the never ceasing [Federal] artillery fire was causing many casualties in our ranks." — **Lt. James H. Myrover**, 13th Battalion North Carolina Light Artillery (Company B, Atkins' Battery)

---

* Curving around to the north, the stream runs from the high ground of the battlefield down to what is now Blackman (or Shaw's) Pond. From there it empties into Mill Creek. Traces of earthworks are still visible amid the undergrowth, denoting Carlin's position in the ravine. This natural obstacle was, and still is, the most prominent geographic feature on this part of the battlefield. No public access.

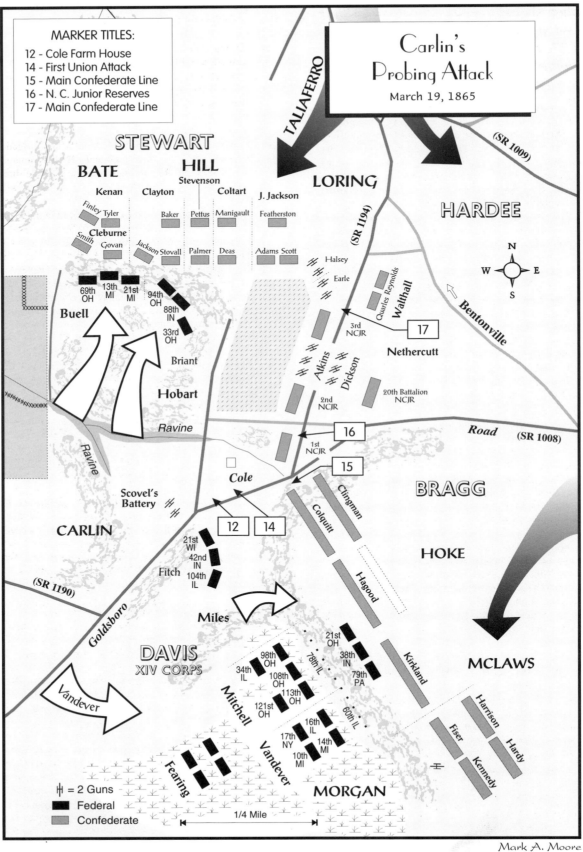

MARKER TITLES:
12 - Cole Farm House
14 - First Union Attack
15 - Main Confederate Line
16 - N. C. Junior Reserves
17 - Main Confederate Line

Carlin's
Probing Attack
March 19, 1865

Mark A. Moore

"I remember the day well. It was Sunday, a beautiful and sunshiny day, and had it not been for the terrible rattle of musketry, and the fierce roar of cannon, we would have been delighted with the warbles of the beautiful birds of the sunny south."

— **Capt. S. L. Zinser**, 86th Illinois, Fearing's brigade

♦ Around 11:00 a.m., with Miles under a severe fire on the right, Maj. Gen. Jeff C. Davis ordered Morgan's division to the front. Mitchell's brigade arrived first, and trudged into a wooded swamp to the right of Miles' brigade.* Fearing's brigade followed, taking position to the right rear of Mitchell. Morgan then deployed skirmishers to feel for Hoke's position. Accordingly, Hoke sent Kirkland's Brigade out on the left of Hagood to further extend his line in that direction.

♦ Major General Henry W. Slocum, commanding the Federal Left Wing, became anxious about the delay in clearing the road to Goldsboro: *"Fearing that the firing would be heard by General Sherman and cause the other wing of the army to delay its march, I sent Major E. W. Guindon of my staff [to tell] Sherman....that I should not need assistance, and felt confident I should be at the Neuse [River] at the appointed time."*

♦ Meanwhile, troops of the Army of Tennessee continued to move into position on the northern edge of Cole's plantation {**12**}: Bate's Corps came in on the right of Hill and Loring.

♦ Carlin's men now began their reconnaissance-in-force of the Confederate line. Miles' brigade attacked Hoke's Division just before noon, moving well to the right in front of Mitchell. The Federals, disoriented from battle smoke and the difficult terrain, were soundly repulsed by Hoke's entrenched veterans. But the uneasy Braxton Bragg, commanding Hoke's Division, began to beg for reinforcements on this part of the Confederate line {**15**}. In response, General Johnston ordered McLaws' Division down from Bentonville (where it had arrived a short time earlier), and it labored through the thickets to reach the left of Hoke's line. This turned out to be a costly tactical blunder for the Confederates, as it depleted by one-fourth the attacking force Johnston was assembling north of the Cole farm.

♦ Around noon Hobart and Buell advanced from the cover of their ravine toward Lt. Gen. A. P. Stewart's Army of Tennessee {**14**}. Forcing back Stewart's skirmishers, Carlin's Federals pushed ahead toward the waiting Confederates, whose battle line was concealed in the timber. Fire from Hampton's horse artillery partially checked the advance on the right of Briant's wing. But Briant's left and Buell's brigade advanced perilously close before receiving a concentrated fire from the Confederates. Buell and Briant suffered grievously in a stand-up fight with Pat Cleburne's and Henry Clayton's divisions. Though Buell met with some initial success in front of Cleburne, both brigades soon fell

back in disarray to the safety of the ravine from which they started their advance.

♦ During the resulting lull in the fighting, three Southern prisoners ("galvanized Yankees" formerly of the Federal army) were brought to Carlin. They warned of a large Confederate force collecting in his front. Carlin sent the men to General Slocum, reporting that *"I attacked....but failed to drive the enemy [who] is strong in men and artillery."* *"There is a very large force in your front,"* one of the prisoners told Slocum, *"all under the command of Joe Johnston."* The Left Wing commander immediately issued orders to hurry the XX Corps to the front. He also made plans to shift to a defensive position, and sent a staff officer to find General Sherman, who was several miles to the south with the Federal Right Wing. The messenger galloped off with Slocum's 1:30 p.m. dispatch to Sherman: *"I am convinced the enemy are in strong force in my front....I shall strengthen my position and feel of their lines, but I hope you will come up on their left rear in strong force."* One half-hour later Slocum accentuated the plea: *"It is reported by prisoners that Johnston and Hardee are here. I think a portion of the Right Wing should be brought forward at once."*

♦ Having been left behind with the XIV Corps trains, Vandever's brigade arrived at Morgan's position just as Hobart and Buell were being repulsed above the Goldsboro Road. Vandever moved out through the swamp to take position on Mitchell's right.

♦ The XIV Corps now had six brigades on the field confronting an unknown force of the enemy {**15-16-17**}. The line was dangerously deployed, with a large gap between the two "wings" of Hobart's brigade. Buell's left was unprotected, and Carlin's entire position was vulnerable to an enemy attack.

♦ Heading down from the direction of Bentonville, the other half of Hardee's Corps (Taliaferro's Division) pulled in behind Stewart's men, adding some needed weight to Johnston's striking force above the Cole farm. Though Slocum's advance was deployed for battle, the Left Wing column was road-bound and in danger of being attacked while on the march.

"[We] charged up the hill over a fence and into a wood under a severe front and flank fire from about twice our numbers. The [21st Michigan and 69th Ohio] went within ten rods of the [enemy] works and halted badly 'cut up' then our Reg. charged through the line and within about 5 rods of the enemy when our Major [Willard G. Eaton] was killed and our color bearer wounded." — **Pvt. John W. Daniels**, 13th Michigan, Buell's brigade

"Col. McGuire came walking leisurely by down the line and said: 'Boys, you remember the 19th and 20th of September, 1863, at Chickamauga? Well, this is the 19th of March, and you may look out for some work to-day as hot as it was there.'" — **Sgt. Thomas J. Corn**, 32nd Tennessee, Palmer's Brigade. Minutes later Palmer's troops participated in the repulse of Briant's Federals.

---

* This swampy forest appears today much as it did in 1865.

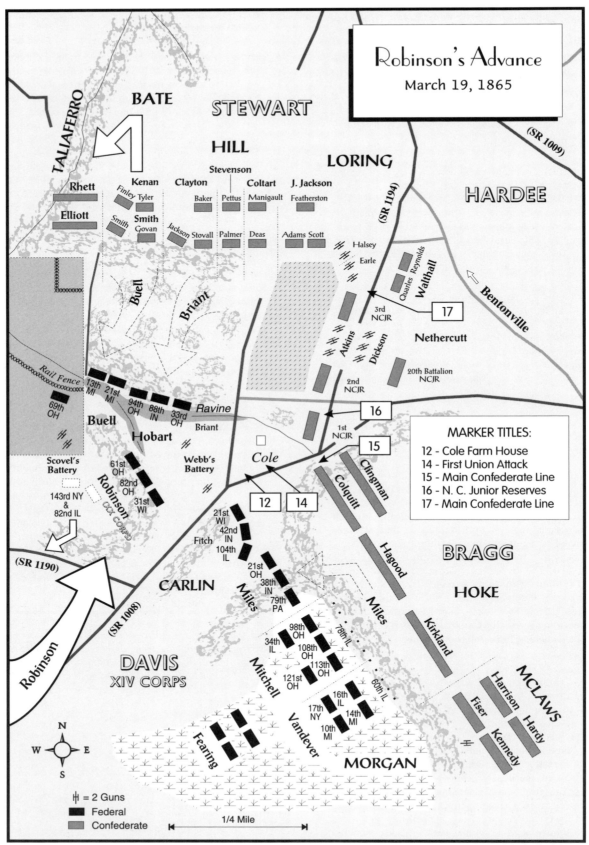

Robinson's Advance
March 19, 1865

MARKER TITLES:
12 - Cole Farm House
14 - First Union Attack
15 - Main Confederate Line
16 - N. C. Junior Reserves
17 - Main Confederate Line

= 2 Guns
Federal
Confederate

1/4 Mile

N
W E
S

Mark A. Moore

"[General A. P.] Stewart wrote just now that the enemy attacked him. Taliaferro is just going in. I think whatever we do should be done quickly. An advance of the line would break them, I think."

— **Lt. Gen. Wade Hampton**, commanding Confederate cavalry. Dispatch to Gen. Joseph E. Johnston, 12:45 p.m.

♦ Smarting from their unsuccessful foray against the Army of Tennessee {14}, Buell and Briant went to work strengthening the breastworks they had begun before the assault.

♦ Around 1:00 p.m. Webb's battery (19th Indiana) was sent to the front by Maj. Charles Houghtaling, commanding XIV Corps artillery. The 19th unlimbered on the same ground as Scovel's battery (C, 1st Illinois), which was pulled out and sent to the left. Scovel went into line behind Buell's brigade, south of the ravine which concealed the left of Carlin's position. Webb's gunners opened fire on the Confederates, receiving severe damage in the process from Atkins' and Dickson's batteries across the way.

♦ Meanwhile, the Federal XX Corps was being hurried forward. Hawley's brigade of Jackson's division had the lead, and reached the Reddick Morris farm sometime after 2:00 p.m. Robinson's brigade was next in line, followed by Selfridge's brigade.

♦ Robinson continued another mile eastward down the Goldsboro Road to the Willis Cole farm. His orders were to deploy and, if possible, fill the yawning gap between the separated "wings" of Hobart's brigade. A short distance west of the Cole house {12}, Robinson went into position behind *"a small ravine easily crossed."* Immediately afterward he was instructed to send his two reserve regiments (82nd Illinois and 143rd New York) back to the Morris farm. There the two regiments would provide support for Hawley's brigade. Robinson, to his great dissatisfaction, was left with only three regiments at the front.*

♦ All of Johnston's infantry was now on the field {15-17} and preparing to launch an attack on the enemy. From his position on the right flank of the Army of Tennessee, Maj. Gen. William B. Bate undertook a *"close and accurate"* reconnaissance of the Federal left. He found that it did not extend connectedly beyond his own right. Knowing that Taliaferro's Division lay in reserve a short distance to the rear, Bate suggested to Lt. Gen. William J. Hardee that it be deployed to extend the Confederate line to the right. Johnston had earlier placed Hardee in overall command of the Army of Tennessee and Taliaferro's Division. Hardee now informed his subordinates that the planned attack on the enemy would be delayed while Taliaferro moved into position.

♦ Several hundred yards to the south Buell's skirmishers, commanded by Capt. George M. Rowe, were strung out well to the left along the creek and ravine. Rowe sent back a report warning Buell that a large enemy column was massing to the north, beyond his left flank. Accordingly, Buell sent the 69th Ohio out to extend his line to the west. The 69th fell in behind a rail fence, slightly south of the main line.

♦ As the Confederates prepared to make their advance Lt. William Ludlow, Slocum's chief of engineers, was examining the Federal defensive position near the Cole house. In assessing the nature of Carlin's deployment, Ludlow suggested to the general that he fall back and construct a new line on the left of Robinson's brigade. This change of position would interpose the creek and ravine *between* the Federals and the enemy. Carlin chose to ignore the warning: *"[B]eing confident of my ability to hold my position until the troops in rear should come up, I decided not to fall back, but made dispositions to fortify my left flank against movements of the enemy in that direction."*

♦ Having stopped at the small ravine west of Cole's house, Robinson's brigade was just shy of the gap in Hobart's line: an area well defended by Hoke's artillery and the North Carolina Junior Reserves {16}. Lieutenant Webb moved a two-gun section of the 19th Indiana Battery to the north to help cover the open ground there. Robinson worried over the precarious alignment of Carlin's division, noting that his own troops made no connection with Carlin on either flank. Thus deployed, disaster awaited the unsuspecting Federals.

"I had not troops enough to fill the vacancy....Carlin's line on my left, instead of being refused was thrown forward, which seems to me was a most dangerous and unfortunate arrangement, as it rendered it much more easy to be flanked than it ought to have been....Having no intrenching tools, my men were compelled to build their breast-works by means of their hatchets. They had, nevertheless, succeeded in erecting a respectable shelter from the fire of the enemy's sharpshooters, when it was reliably reported....that the enemy was advancing his skirmish line, apparently with the intention of obtaining possession of the buildings in the field [around Cole's house]." — **Brig. Gen. James S. Robinson**, commanding 3rd Brigade, 1st Division, XX Army Corps.

"[A]s we marched hurriedly along the road in the direction of the firing we passed a number of wounded men coming to the rear; and then several operating tables on both sides of the road, some with wounded men stretched out on them with the surgeons at work, and all of them with several bloody amputated legs and arms thrown alongside on the grass. The sight was temporarily depressing, as it foreshadowed what we had to expect....[S]oon [we] were called to 'attention,' and received orders to create it, by an attack upon the enemy from our extreme right. At this moment Maj. A. [Burnet] Rhett, of the artillery, rode along the line and called out that news had been received that France had recognized the Confederacy and would send warships to open our ports immediately. The men cheered, few of us realizing that the end was so near. We were blinded by our patriotism....As we stood in line ready to advance my next comrade remarked, 'Well, boys, one out of every three of us will drop to-day. I wonder who it will be?'" — **Cpl. Arthur P. Ford**, Elliott's Brigade

---

* The sixth regiment of Robinson's brigade (101st Illinois) would not reach the battlefield until later that afternoon—too late to participate in the fighting.

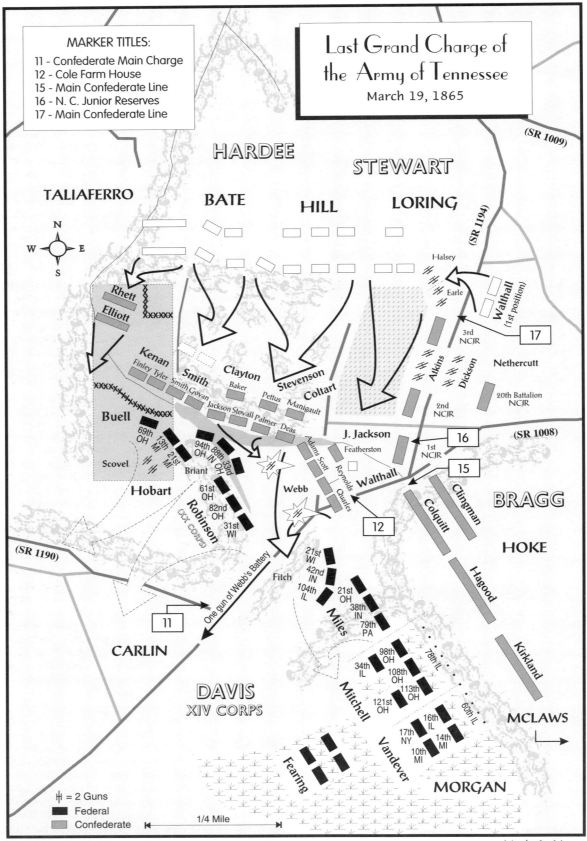

MARKER TITLES:
11 - Confederate Main Charge
12 - Cole Farm House
15 - Main Confederate Line
16 - N. C. Junior Reserves
17 - Main Confederate Line

Last Grand Charge of
the Army of Tennessee
March 19, 1865

Mark A. Moore

"[T]he most terrible battle I ever imagined....It was the most fearful scene I ever witnessed."

— **Capt. G. B. Gardner**, courier on the staff of Lt. Gen. William J. Hardee

♦ At 2:45 p.m. Hardee ordered the Army of Tennessee and Taliaferro's Division to advance on the enemy. For the last time the long gray line stepped forward, guiding on Stevenson's Division, which occupied the center. From his position at the angle behind Hoke's right flank {17}, Walthall passed through Hampton's batteries and joined on the left of Loring's Division. The North Carolina Junior Reserves {16} watched as Loring's Corps passed at right angles to their line, and disappeared into the ravine to their left. From this point forward, the Juniors would play no further part in the battle of March 19.

♦ Walthall's command and Loring's Division (under Col. James Jackson) emerged from the ravine north of the Cole house {12}, forcing back Robinson's skirmishers.[1]

♦ To the right of Loring, Hill's Corps descended the slope of the ravine and collided with Briant's wing of Hobart's brigade. Loring's Confederates passed around Briant's right flank, and the weight of the assault became too great to withstand. The 33rd Ohio broke first, followed by the 88th Indiana and 94th Ohio. Carlin's line crumbled rapidly. The ravine, which earlier had protected the Federals from Hoke's artillery, now proved difficult to negotiate in fleeing from the screaming enemy. After crossing an *"ugly swale"* at the bottom, Carlin's ranks were shot to pieces in ascending the opposite bank.[2]

♦ On Hill's right, Cleburne's Division (under Brig. Gen. James A. Smith) slammed into Buell's brigade. The 13th and 21st Michigan regiments held firm for a short time, and were able to witness the flight of Briant's wing before joining the stampede to the rear. Buell's fugitives fell back through Scovel's battery, which limbered up and headed for the safety of the Morris farm.

♦ The Army of Tennessee paused briefly on the southern slope of the ravine, and Hardee rode out in front of the line to encourage the troops to continue the advance. The Confederates surged forward. Pouring out of the ravine, Bate's Corps encountered Buell's 69th Ohio behind a rail fence in an open field. To extend his line to the west, Bate sent out Tyler's and Finley's brigades (under Col. D. L. Kenan), which fell in on Smith's right. Trailing behind in the Confederate advance, Taliaferro's Division, on Kenan's right, brushed away Buell's skirmishers and passed unopposed beyond his left flank.

---

[1] The ravine here was, and still is, at its shallowest point. Col. Henry G. Bunn, of Walthall's Division, referred to this portion of the ravine as a "dry branch." Further west, where Carlin's troops were entrenched, the gully deepens significantly and is much more swampy at its base.

[2] The Federals were further hindered by a rail fence bordering the southern side of the ravine. The Army of Tennessee crossed a similar fence on the northern side. These are mentioned by participants, and a portion of one fence is illustrated on a manuscript map that was to accompany Buell's report. They may have served to keep farm animals out of the ravine. [See Appendix A].

♦ The position of Robinson's brigade was rendered untenable by the flight of Carlin's men and the advance of Loring's Confederates. So sudden was the attack that Lt. Samuel D. Webb's 19th Indiana Battery abandoned its guns. The left section of the battery, hastily limbering up for the retreat, was overrun and captured by Hill's men. Robinson began to fall back in good order amid the mounting confusion. One gun and team of Webb's right section was pulled out and sent to the rear by a private in the 31st Wisconsin, but the remaining piece fell into the hands of Walthall's Division. As the Federals fell back toward the Morris farm, the victorious Rebels descended upon the Goldsboro Road {11}.

♦ South of the road, Fitch's wing of Hobart's brigade began pulling away from Loring's advance. Miles' brigade was also forced to retreat, and the right half of Carlin's line caved in toward Morgan's position.

♦ Carlin's division was driven from the field in a perfect rout. But as the defeated ranks streamed backward from the Cole farm, better fortune prevailed for the Federals south of the Goldsboro Road. The troops in Hoke's sector of the main Confederate line {15} had remained stationary during the attack of the Army of Tennessee. Bragg's tardiness in advancing allowed Morgan's division to construct a formidable defensive position in the swamp. Presently, Fearing's brigade would be called upon to stem the tide of the advancing foe.

"[The] Rebs strike our Left....& drive back our forces some distance. Here our Trains come near being Captured [and] we are hurried away through [a] Swamp where many [of our wagons] stick fast. Rebs send Grape [shot] through trees over our heads, but by unloading, pushing, digging & carrying loads we finally get through and Park in open fields. Rebs almost broke up [Carlin's] Div. Our Brigade came out with 100 men commanded by Lieut. Col. McMahan....Lieut. Col. Miles being wounded in fleshy part of thigh—Many men are wounded, 50 men are left of the 79th, the clothing & accoutrements of nearly all are cut in holes by Minie Balls....Many of the missing are returning. When the Rebs charged our Flank....and took the line they were close upon our Artillery, & trying to get it did not notice Brig. Gen. Carlin retreating near them, he and a Reb. Capt. were running abreast for some time, the latter trying to get the Battery, while the former, not saying a word Kept running as fast as he could.[3] [The] Rebs had possession of 3 pieces of Artillery, but could not take [the third piece] away. [W]e have it now." — **William T. Clark**, Commissary Sergeant, 79th Pennsylvania, Miles' brigade (Diary entries, March 19-20, 1865)

"Reaching the top of the slope [of the ravine,] we came in view of the Federal line and if our eyes had been closed our ears would have given us ample evidence of the fact. The rattle of the Enfields and the hiss of the minies marked the renewal of our acquaintance with our old antagonists of the Dalton and Atlanta campaign." — **Sgt. Walter Clark**, 1st Georgia (Volunteers), Smith's Brigade

---

[3] Carlin was on Buell's right flank when the attack came. William Clark's statement, while plausible, seems to have been made in jest of his division commander. The quote is of interest, for Carlin's own 1889 account of this event is equally comical.

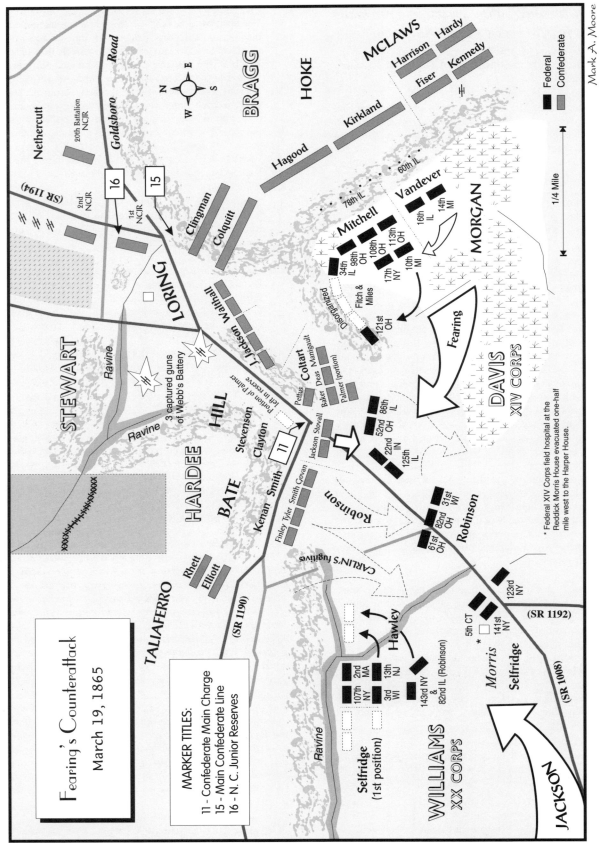

Fearing's Counterattack
March 19, 1865

MARKER TITLES:
11 - Confederate Main Charge
15 - Main Confederate Line
16 - N. C. Junior Reserves

Federal
Confederate

1/4 Mile

* Federal XIV Corps field hospital at the
Reddick Morris House evacuated one-half
mile west to the Harper House.

Mark A. Moore

"I have witnessed the conduct of many regiments in perilous situations, but I never saw a body of troops act with greater coolness or more heroic daring than the One hundred and twenty-fifth Illinois manifested on the eventful 19th instant."

— **Lt. Col. James W. Langley,** commanding the 125th Illinois, Fearing's brigade[1]

- On the Morris farm, the XX Corps brigades of Hawley and Selfridge had made good use of the delay in the attack of the Army of Tennessee. These units were strengthening their works when Carlin's division came streaming back in defeat from the Cole farm. To help provide a rallying point for Carlin, Selfridge was sent to the right, where he halted astride the Goldsboro Road. Robinson's brigade fell back and went into line a short distance in front of Selfridge. Carlin's fugitives poured pell-mell through the XX Corps line and finally halted in the rear, finished for the day as an effective fighting force.

- South of the Goldsboro Road, Gen. James D. Morgan attempted some damage control on the Federal right, as Fitch and Miles were being driven into his lines. The 34th Illinois was moved out at a sharp angle to Mitchell's front line. The 121st Ohio swung out and formed on the left of the disorganized elements of Fitch and Miles, and all efforts were made to rally the line. Vandever's second line (17th New York and 10th Michigan) was shifted to the left behind Mitchell.

- Flushed with success, the Army of Tennessee descended upon the Goldsboro Road {11}. Pettus' Brigade moved up in support of Clayton's Division, and on the Confederate left Gen. Braxton Bragg belatedly joined in the movement against the enemy: Colquitt and Clingman were deployed from the main line {15} in an effort close the gap between Hoke and Loring's troops.

- From its reserve position behind Morgan's front, Gen. Benjamin D. Fearing's brigade was ordered by Jeff Davis to deploy to the left and check the advance of the oncoming Confederates. In line of battle, Fearing's men rushed toward the Goldsboro Road.

- Shortly after reaching the road, Fearing began to feel the weight of the enemy attack. As Palmer and Baker bore down on his right flank, the 86th Illinois and 52nd Ohio pulled back to meet their advance. Meanwhile, elements of Stovall's and Jackson's brigades, under Col. Osceola Kyle, pressured the resulting angle in Fearing's line. As D. H. Hill's troops pushed further south, the right half of Fearing's line broke for the rear. The 22nd Indiana was forced to pull out as well, leaving the 125th Illinois in a position *"fast becoming untenable."* The 125th changed front to meet the enemy by deploying two companies at a time to the right. The regiment then withdrew, firing on the Confederates while retreating.

- Like Carlin's troops previously, Fearing's brigade crumbled under the weight of the Confederate attack and fell back in disorder to the right of Robinson's new position to the west. It would take the rest of the afternoon for Fearing's men to regain their composure. Though Fearing had been shoved from the field, his attack significantly delayed the Confederate advance, which bought time for the Federal XX Corps troops to prepare a defensive line at the Morris farm.

- Bragg's men (Hoke's Division) now stood poised to enter the fight on Morgan's front.

- The North Carolina Junior Reserves {16} lay idle for the remainder of March 19.

"On the morning of the 19th....[we] little dreamed that before nightfall many a brave boy would be dead on the field of strife, and many more bleeding and dying in a field hospital. The same skillful and shrewd foe who disputed our march from Chattanooga to Atlanta was again confronting us....The [C]onfederates were in their own chosen position, the country was swampy and dense with scrubby undergrowth. [They] made an attack....striking Carlin's brigades in flank and rear, knocking them back. This took time, our boys determined not to be beaten....The enemy came on step by step, our men retreating, firing volleys with terrible effect....A battery of ours was captured. At this crisis of the battle Gen. Jeff C. Davis ordered our brigade to charge upon the flank of the enemy who was following Carlin. The attack on the flank did the work. We charged them on the run and drove them at the point of the bayonet....But the battle was not over. On our right was a gap [and] the enemy made for it. [We were] in the hottest of the fight....[W]hen the rebels found the gap....the bullets came whizzing on our right flank. The 86th deployed to the right on the run....[I]t looked as though the day was going to result in defeat."
— **Capt. S. L. Zinser**, 86th Illinois, Fearing's brigade

"[W]e had been ordered to lie down. It was not necessary to repeat this order, for the stray balls were thick and very insinuating. In a few minutes a roaring in front of us—akin to a fair-sized cyclone, proved to be our own troops seeking safety in a way not taught in military tactics; they were stampeded beyond control.[2] [I]t was laughable though the occasion was a serious one....They tramped up on us, and as we would attempt to get up some fellow in his blind flight would run against us, upsetting our person and our calculations....[W]e were rushed into action without much deliberation. The Federals had become so enraged at the fleeing 'Johnny Rebs' that we killed and wounded a great many of them before we could check their mad rush....The killing and wounding was by no means unanimously in our favor, for my Captain who was right by my side about ten feet in advance of the company, fell desperately wounded in the first volley [and] we raised a yell that echoed with revenge. The regiment followed and the charge at once became general down the line." — **Pvt. Claude Lee Hadaway**, 54th Alabama, Baker's Brigade

---

[1] Langley took over command of Fearing's brigade when Fearing was wounded during the counterattack on the Army of Tennessee.

[2] These troops were probably skirmishers from Hill's and Bate's commands, which had preceded the Confederate battle line in the direction of the Goldsboro Road. These skirmishers were forced back by Fearing's advance. General Edmund W. Pettus relates a similar event in his report on the battle.

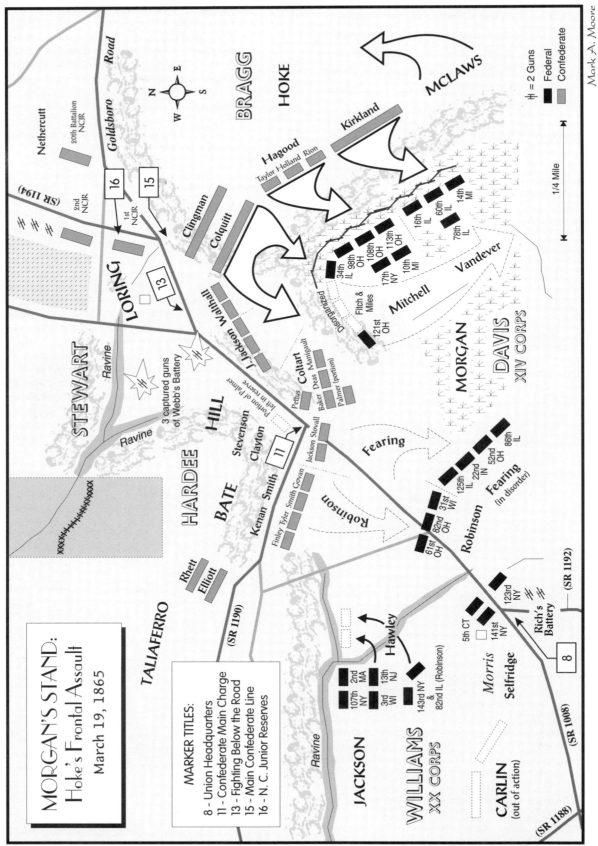

Mark A. Moore

MORGAN'S STAND:
Hoke's Frontal Assault
March 19, 1865

MARKER TITLES:

8 - Union Headquarters
11 - Confederate Main Charge
13 - Fighting Below the Road
15 - Main Confederate Line
16 - N. C. Junior Reserves

= 2 Guns

■ Federal
▨ Confederate

1/4 Mile

"[O]ur skirmishers were driven in and a strong line of battle opened fire upon both fronts of our works, making the most vigorous attack at the angle formed by the main line with the refused line. The enemy's position at this point gave them an enfilading fire down both of my lines."

— **Brig. Gen. John G. Mitchell**, commanding 2nd Brigade, Second Division, XIV Corps

♦ Having thus far carried all before it, the Army of Tennessee halted along the Goldsboro Road to reorganize itself {11}. The clash with the enemy across broken terrain had greatly disorganized the Confederate advance.

♦ South of the road, the 34th Illinois and 121st Ohio tried desperately to anchor the vulnerable northern salient of Morgan's line. The two regiments began to build breastworks on both ends of the line. Between them were the remnants of Fitch's and Miles' commands (of Carlin's division), which were trying to rally after falling back before Loring's advance. Morgan's eastern front had been busy since arriving on the battlefield, and now stood ready to meet the enemy behind a formidable redoubt of earth and logs.

♦ Since reaching Bragg's position earlier in the day, McLaws' Division had remained inactive. As Hoke prepared to assault Morgan's division, McLaws' men were pulled off the Confederate line and sent north of the Goldsboro Road. Hardee had asked Joseph E. Johnston for McLaws' return, and intended to use the division in support of the Army of Tennessee. Johnston granted the request, no doubt wishing McLaws had been with Hardee all along.

♦ Around 4:00 p.m. Hoke's Division, with a combination of seasoned veterans and untried garrison troops, finally advanced on the waiting Federals {13}. Colquitt's and Clingman's brigades had earlier left their main line {15} to close the gap between Hoke and Loring. With Clingman following in reserve, Colquitt attacked the northern front of Morgan's position. The 34th Illinois and 98th Ohio held the angle of the line, where some of the most desperate fighting occurred during Hoke's first attack. West of the angle, Carlin's disorganized remnants quickly broke for the rear under heavy pressure from Colquitt. The 121st Ohio was forced to follow, as Morgan's northern salient crumbled and fell back in disorder through the swamp to the south.

♦ Along the eastern front of Morgan's line the Federals made good use of their breastworks. Mitchell endured the attack of Hagood's Brigade, which was in turn punished severely and forced back under heavy fire. Further south, Kirkland's Brigade tangled with Vandever's troops on the right of Morgan's position. The 60th Illinois, deployed as skirmishers, was nearly overwhelmed by Kirkland's attack. They fell back to the main line, but two companies were surrounded and had to fight their way out. The 60th nearly lost its colors in the mélee.

♦ If Gen. Jeff C. Davis had remained unsure of the threat to his command, he now became convinced of what should have been an obvious fact. He sent a dispatch at 4:00 p.m.: *"Respectfully referred to Major-General Slocum for information. The enemy is beyond doubt in our front in strong force, and intends to give a general engagement."*

♦ The terrain below the Goldsboro Road could not have been less ideal for combat operations. Hoke and Morgan opposed one another in a dense swampy forest, not unlike that of the Wilderness battlefield in Virginia. For the Confederates, a well-organized advance was impossible. Morgan's men, while entrenching, found that water quickly filled any depressions that were dug in the ground. They felled trees instead, and packed the logs with the muddy soil of the swamp. Adding to a difficult battleground was the dense gunpowder smoke trapped among the trees. These conditions may go far in explaining the odd angle of attack made by a portion of Hoke's line later in the fight. (See pp. 34-35).

♦ On the Morris farm, the XX Corps troops continued to dig in. Fearing's brigade (of Morgan's division) struggled to regroup after its earlier bout with the Army of Tennessee. At some point during the afternoon Slocum set up headquarters in rear of the XX Corps {8}.

♦ Having knocked Fearing's brigade aside, the troops of D. H. Hill's command were set to exploit the resulting gap between Fearing and Mitchell. This would bring on the crisis of the engagement for Morgan's division.

♦ The North Carolina Junior Reserves {16} were held in reserve for the remainder of March 19.

"The enemy had massed a strong force on our left flank....Gen. Mitchell immediately ordered the Thirty-Fourth to change front....while a perfect mass of stragglers was crowding through to the rear....and the battle growing more furious and fearfully close every moment....The new line formed by Mitchell had ten minutes, during a lull in the battle—what an awful quietness that is—and never did men work more eagerly to place between themselves and rebel bullets a work for protection....In another instant the battle had opened. Here the rebels received their first check, but coming on again with tremendous yells, the support on the left of the Thirty-Fourth gave way, leaving that flank entirely open....and here was the crisis of the whole battle, and the most trying position in which the Thirty-Fourth or any portion of the brigade was ever in." — **Capt. W. C. Robinson**, 34th Illinois, Mitchell's brigade

"The history of this battle must always be interesting to the student of our war—showing how the Southerners fought when under the most adverse circumstances and when the Cause was almost entirely lost....Every state in the South and almost the entire North was represented on the bloody field of Bentonville. The gallant Kirkland and his surviving followers will always feel proud of the record they made there." — **Charles G. Elliott**, Kirkland's Brigade

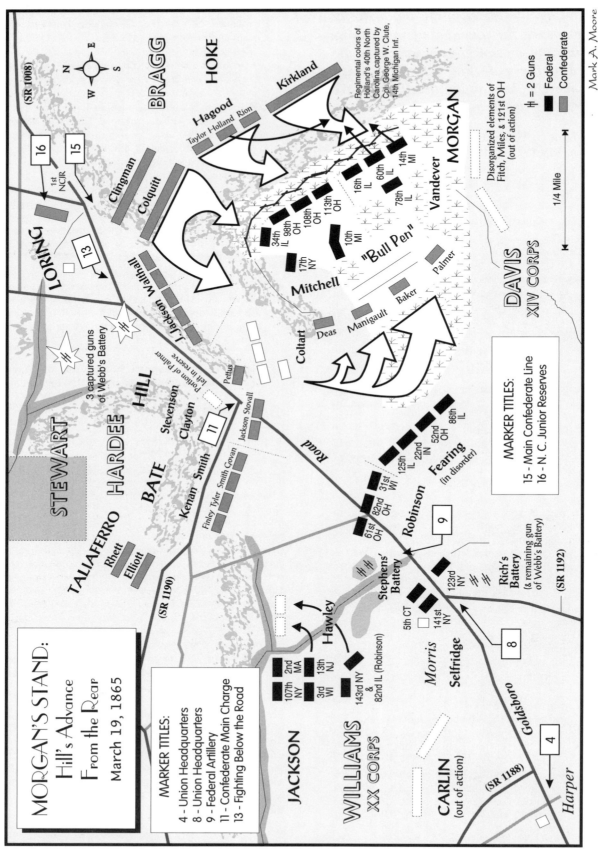

MORGAN'S STAND:
Hill's Advance
From the Rear
March 19, 1865

MARKER TITLES:
4 - Union Headquarters
8 - Union Headquarters
9 - Federal Artillery
11 - Confederate Main Charge
13 - Fighting Below the Road

MARKER TITLES:
15 - Main Confederate Line
16 - N. C. Junior Reserves

Mark A. Moore

"The charge [of Hoke's Division] was desperate and persistent, and the roar of musketry, as it rolled up from that low wood, was incessant....the smoke obscured everything in front....I rode forward toward the line to ascertain definitely how matters stood....Here the view was not a cheerful one. On the opposite side of [a clearing], at perhaps twenty-five yards' distance, was a body of unmistakably rebel troops, marching by the flank in column of fours, toward the right."

— **Lt. Col. Alexander C. McClurg**, Adjutant, staff of Gen. Jefferson C. Davis

♦ Reforming after their first assault, Hoke's Division mounted a second charge upon Morgan's entrenched Federals {13}. Maj. William A. Holland's 40th North Carolina (Hagood's Brigade) obliqued well to the left in the smoky wilderness, toward Vandever's position in the swamp. The 60th Illinois and 14th Michigan surged forward against the Confederates, and a confused hand-to-hand struggle ensued. (See pp. 32-33).

♦ After crushing the northern salient of Morgan's line, Colquitt's Brigade again bore down on Mitchell's left. From its position behind Mitchell's first line the 17th New York Zouaves (Vandever) changed front to the left and met the attacking enemy head on. The 17th was aided by the additional firepower of the 10th Michigan (also of Vandever), and the 34th Illinois and 98th Ohio continued to blaze away at their attackers from the angle in Mitchell's line. When the northern salient fell away the 34th Illinois stood firm, thereby preserving the angle (and in large measure the security of Morgan's position). Colquitt's troops were sent reeling back to the main Confederate line {15} with heavy loss.

♦ The Army of Tennessee continued to reform along the Goldsboro Road {11}. After squelching the counterattack of Fearing's brigade, the troops of Hill's Corps poured into the resulting gap and moved upon the rear of the broken Federal battle line. Disaster loomed for Morgan's division. These men were now surrounded on three sides by enemy forces. And the fourth side—an impenetrable swamp—was clogged with their disorganized comrades already routed by the Confederates.

♦ D. H. Hill's men, partially disorganized from their earlier battle with Fearing's brigade, veered to the east and struck a line of breastworks: the same works Fearing had recently vacated in rushing to check the Confederate advance. Morgan was in a perilous predicament, but at this critical juncture Hill's men began to lose their momentum below the road. Lacking formal organization, Hill's troops surged ahead in disconnected groups.

♦ On the Morris farm Lt. Judson Rich's Battery I, 2nd Illinois had gone into position south of the Goldsboro Road, behind Selfridge's brigade. The XX Corps artillery also began to arrive on the field: Stephens' Battery C, 1st Ohio, came up

first and unlimbered around 3:30 p.m. on a knoll just east of a small ravine {9}. Hawley, Selfridge, and Robinson continued to strengthen their positions.

♦ At some point during the afternoon, Slocum established headquarters in rear of the XX Corps {8}. Gen. Alpheus S. Williams, commanding the XX Corps, set up headquarters further west {4}.

♦ The North Carolina Junior Reserves {16} lay in reserve for the remainder of March 19.

♦ Morgan's division was in trouble and help would soon be on the way. But Col. McClurg observed that this unit's own actions would serve it well as the fight progressed: *"Nothing could stand that day before the veterans of the old second division."*

"In a few moments they charged again with redoubled fury, all along the right and right center of the line. In our immediate front they were again repulsed, with terrible loss, and the Fourteenth Michigan and Sixtieth Illinois, on our immediate right, charged their broken line in turn and drove them in confusion back over their own works. As serious doubts were entertained regarding the result of this charge further to the left I deemed it best to hold my regiment in their works in readiness for any emergency that might arise in that direction. The worst fears were soon realized by the enemy sweeping down in column by regiments on my immediate rear." — **Capt. Herman Lund**, commanding the 16th Illinois, Vandever's brigade

"[F]or a time it seemed as though all was lost....[A] yell of indignation resounded in our ears when every man flew to his pos. determined to shed his life's blood on that consecrated spot rather than give an inch....[A] tremendous volley cut the air and the rebellious hosts came pressing on[,] but were met by Such a terrible storm of musketry....that for a moment they were checked....Their ranks soon closed and they came so close that they could distinctly hear the clanking of our bayonets....[T]hey stood within 25 yrds of our line and fired as fast as they could load their pieces until our ammunition was [nearly] exhausted....[T]hey broke in utter confusion and left us conquerors of one of the bloodiest battle fields of the war....We examined the cartridge boxes of the dead and wounded and procured as much ammunition as possible when we returned to our posts feeling confident that it was beyond their ability to dislodge us, although they were fighting all around us, compelling us to seek shelter on first one side and then the other side of [our] works....So closely were we pressed that our Gen [Mitchell] told us to tare [sic] up our 'flag' and tramp it into the ground before Surrendering....[W]ithout any joking we came very near taking a trip to Richmond or some other rebel 'Sea port'....[We] whipped them so badly they knew not from where they came." — **William Kemp**, 98th Ohio, Mitchell's brigade

"Brig.-Gen. Alpheus Baker....one of the most renowned orators of the South, during the hard fighting on the 19th from some cause became greatly enthused, and charged with his little brigade, broke through the Federal lines [and] penetrated to the rear....Baker was very eccentric and superstitious. He said that when his brigade began to advance and was proceeding in quick time he saw a big rabbit running, and saw that it would cross his path; he stuck spurs to his horse and dashed ahead of the rabbit, and then ordered his brigade to charge, which it did, and drove everything before it, until he found that he had cut through to the Federal rear....He said he was satisfied that if he had allowed that old jack-rabbit to cross him he would have been killed and his brigade decimated....[A]fter he beat the rabbit he turned up the cuff of his left coat-sleeve—wrong side out—and felt no danger." — **Warren C. Oates**, veteran colonel of the 15th Alabama, Army of Northern Virginia, from an anecdote related by Gen. Alpheus Baker

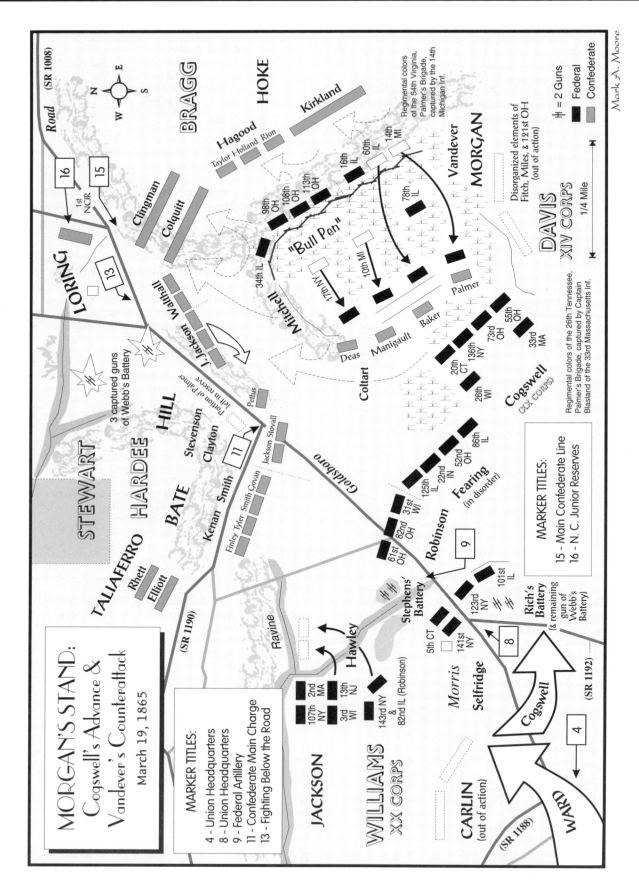

Mark A. Moore

MORGAN'S STAND:
Cogswell's Advance &
Vandever's Counterattack

March 19, 1865

MARKER TITLES:
4 - Union Headquarters
8 - Union Headquarters
9 - Federal Artillery
11 - Confederate Main Charge
13 - Fighting Below the Road

MARKER TITLES:
15 - Main Confederate Line
16 - N. C. Junior Reserves

Regimental colors of the 26th Tennessee,
Palmer's Brigade, captured by Captain
Blasland of the 33rd Massachusetts Inf.

Regimental colors of
the 54th Virginia,
Palmer's Brigade,
captured by the 14th
Michigan Inf.

Disorganized elements of
Fitch, Miles, & 121st OH
(out of action)

⊞ = 2 Guns

■ Federal
▨ Confederate

3 captured guns
of Webb's Battery

1/4 Mile

"Bull Pen"

"With some few others I made my way up in the rear of [the Federal] works. Our loss here was heavy....They gave us credit for fighting them as hard as they were ever fought....Some thought we had whiskey to incite us on. Quite a compliment."

— **Pvt. Hiram Smith Williams**, 40th Alabama, Baker's Brigade

◆ General William T. Ward's Federal division began arriving at the Morris farm around 3:00 p.m. By 4:00 p.m. Gen. Jefferson C. Davis was calling for reinforcements. He needed a brigade to fill the gap occasioned by Fearing's retreat on Morgan's left. Accordingly, Brig. Gen. William P. Cogswell's brigade (Ward's division) was called to the front to shore up the broken Federal battle line. (See pp. 30-31).

◆ Meanwhile, lack of organization and command initiative among Hill's Confederates south of the Goldsboro Road threatened their efforts to envelop Morgan's position {13}. In addition, Morgan's front line soundly repulsed Hoke's attempt to carry the Federal works, and sent that force back in defeat to the main Confederate line {15}.

◆ With enemy fire now pouring in from the rear, Morgan's men leapt to the front side of their earthworks—the side that had recently protected them from Hoke's assaults.[1] With their backs to the retreating foe, Morgan's troops prepared for a Confederate advance from the west.

◆ Cogswell passed around the right flank of Fearing's position, and plunged into the embattled swamp surrounding Morgan's division. The brigade somehow managed to move four regiments abreast through the murky forest, and fell upon the right flank and rear of Hill's troops below the road.

◆ Four regiments from Vandever's brigade chose this opportunity to strike back at the Confederates occupying Fearing's old works. Returning from their counterattack against Hoke, the 14th Michigan and 60th Illinois surged ahead toward the brigades of Palmer and Baker. The 10th Michigan and 17th New York joined in the assault as well, attacking the commands of Deas and Manigault. These counter measures helped turn the tide for Morgan's division. Any hope of Confederate success below the road was quickly extinguished. Hill's troops were forced to beat a hasty retreat toward the Goldsboro Road, but not before many were killed or captured. One party of 70 Confederates (under Col. Anderson Searcy of the 45th Tennessee) was cut off from the main body of troops, and stole away through the forest to safety—nine days later the party emerged in Raleigh, with a dozen Federal prisoners in tow.

◆ A gap was made in the Army of Tennessee's line when D. H. Hill's brigades passed to the rear of Morgan's position, and

Loring's command was shifted several hundred yards to its right in order to close the ranks. Hill's panicked Confederates now fell back in disorder through the main line of the Army of Tennessee, which was gathering along the Goldsboro Road {11}.

◆ On the Morris farm, the troops of the XX Corps continued to strengthen their position. Stephens' Battery C, 1st Ohio, having arrived around 3:00 p.m., unlimbered on a knoll north of the road and prepared for battle {9}.

◆ During the afternoon, Henry Slocum established headquarters in rear of the XX Corps {8}. Gen. Alpheus S. Williams, commanding the XX Corps, set up headquarters further west {4}.

◆ The North Carolina Junior Reserves {16} lay idle for the remainder of March 19. This was the largest brigade fielded by Johnston's army at Bentonville, numbering about 1,100 men and boys. Such a force would have been well used in swinging out behind the Army of Tennessee, adding its support to the main line when needed—especially against Cogswell's brigade. The Confederate high command may have held doubts as to the Juniors' reliability, but they would perform well enough in limited action on March 20-21, 1865.

"As the Third Division [Ward's] formed in support of the firing line....the crash of musketry and roar of artillery were deafening....[A]n officer rode rapidly to General Cogswell, commanding the Third Brigade, and explained that there was a gap [in the Federal line] which needed but one brigade to fill it, and gave an order from General Williams to advance and fill the space....The command had marched but a few rods when it discovered marching directly across its path a Rebel command which had found the gap [between Fearing and Mitchell], and was marching to flank Morgan's division. The two lines were both amazed at the encounter, and but few shots were fired. The Confederate command....at once retreated." — **Capt. Hartwell Osborn**, 55th Ohio, Cogswell's brigade

"[W]e made a left oblique move and struck the enemy's line....We did not linger there you may be sure; had nothing on our right, except a skirmish line, and that very short. This line was heavily fortified and the enemy strongly protected. In a short time we were ordered to fall back. My company fell back, leaving me there firing as I did not hear the command, and I shot at a tall man above the breastworks, our men having retreated in the meantime....I looked and saw only one man, realizing my great danger for the first time, I then fell back, and strange to say was not struck by a bullet. Notwithstanding the fact the enemy was centering their fire on me, and this other man. I then retreated back, and as some of my comrades afterwards told me fairly rolled over the breastworks, getting out of danger. We captured in this engagement twelve Yankees, taking them....on our backward journey....How we survived this fearful ordeal, I do not know."[2] — **Pvt. R. S. Cowles**, 45th Tennessee, Palmer's Brigade

---

[1] The impressive remains of a portion of these stout breastworks are visible in the pine woods below the old Goldsboro Road (SR 1008). No public access.

[2] Private Cowles was a member of the party commanded by Col. Anderson Searcy.

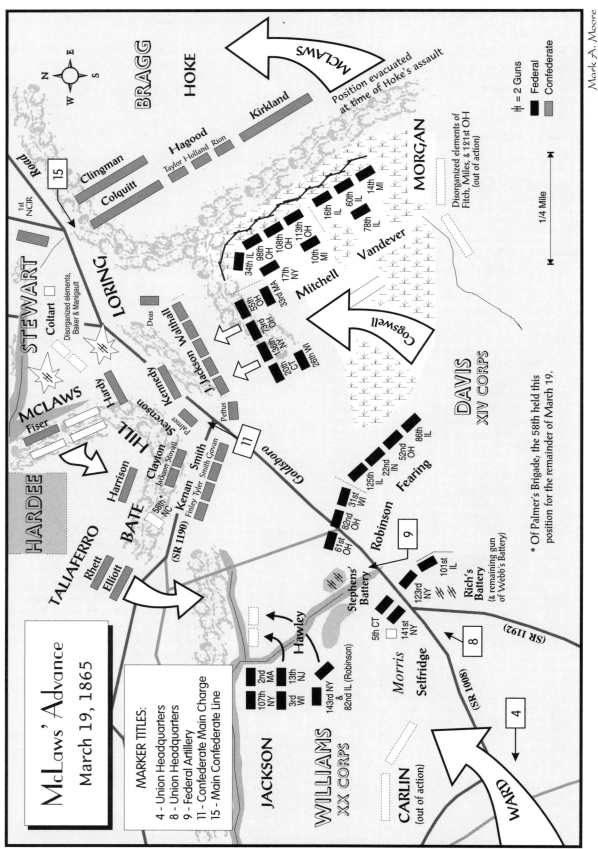

Mark A. Moore

McLaws' Advance
March 19, 1865

MARKER TITLES:
4 - Union Headquarters
8 - Union Headquarters
9 - Federal Artillery
11 - Confederate Main Charge
15 - Main Confederate Line

= 2 Guns

■ Federal
■ Confederate

1/4 Mile

* Of Palmer's Brigade, the 58th held this position for the remainder of March 19.

Position evacuated at time of Hoke's assault

Disorganized elements of Fitch, Miles, & 121st OH (out of action)

BRAGG

HOKE

Kirkland

Hagood
Taylor Holland Rion

Clingman

Colquitt

MCLAWS

1st NCJR

STEWART

Coltart

Disorganized elements, Baker & Manigault

LORING

Deas

Walthall

J. Jackson

34th IL
98th OH
108th OH
113th OH
10th MI
17th NY
33rd MA
55th OH
73rd OH
136th NY
20th CT
26th WI

16th IL
60th IL
78th IL
14th MI

Vandever

Mitchell

MORGAN

Cogswell

DAVIS
XIV CORPS

MCLAWS

Fiser

Hardy

HILL

Kennedy

Stevenson

Palmer

Pettus

Harrison

Clayton
Jackson Stovall

Smith
Finley Tyler Smith Govan

Kenan

58th NC *

(SR 1190)

Goldsboro

TALIAFERRO

Rhett

Elliott

BATE

61st OH
82nd OH
31st WI
125th IL
22nd IN
52nd OH
86th IL

Robinson

Fearing

9

HARDEE

107th NY
2nd MA
3rd WI
13th NJ
143rd NY & 82nd IL (Robinson)

Hawley

Stephens' Battery

5th CT
141st NY
123rd NY

Rich's Battery
(& remaining gun of Webb's Battery)

101st

Morris

Selfridge

(SR 1192)

8

(SR 1008)

JACKSON

WILLIAMS
XX CORPS

CARLIN
(out of action)

4

WARD

"[A]bout 5:00 p.m. the enemy in one or two lines of battle attacked and attempted to drive us from our unprotected position; but our men stood firm, not a man leaving his post except the wounded. At this point the contest was more obstinate, and the musketry more terrific than at any other time of the engagement. Having received a slight wound, I retired from the field at twilight."

— **Col. Henry G. Bunn**, 4th Arkansas, commanding Reynolds' Brigade[1], Walthall's Division

♦ As General Hardee had earlier requested, McLaws' Division was pulled from the left of Bragg's line {15} and sent to the support of the Army of Tennessee. Hardee's request had come just as Hoke was preparing to attack Morgan's division. McLaws circled around to the Cole field and formed in reserve at the abandoned earthworks built earlier in the battle by Robinson's XX Corps brigade. (See pp. 32-33).

♦ As the routed troops of Hill's command passed toward the rear, Loring's Corps and Pettus' Brigade made preparations to stop the advancing Federals {11}. While taking position they endured a long-range artillery barrage from Lt. Judson Rich's XIV Corps battery (I, 2nd Illinois), located on the Morris farm. Palmer reunited his command and formed in rear of the Confederate battle line, while the scattered commands of Baker and Manigault fled further north and remained disorganized for the rest of the day.

♦ Cogswell's XX Corps brigade rapidly followed Hill's retreating ranks in the direction of the Goldsboro Road. Advancing through the swampy woods, they struck Loring's position just south of the road—and received a devastating fire at close range. This collision brought on an extended engagement at close range between Cogswell and the left portion of the Army of Tennessee.

♦ North of the road Hardee's adjutant, Lt. Col. Thomas B. Roy, instructed McLaws to send out two brigades in the direction of the firing. Accordingly, Kennedy and Harrison were deployed toward the front, with Hardy's Brigade following in reserve. Kennedy came up behind Loring, while Harrison headed off in the direction of Gen. William B. Bate's position. As the fight with Cogswell erupted south of the road, Loring's Division (under Col. James Jackson) ran low on ammunition. At sundown Jackson pulled out to make way for Kennedy's Brigade, which then took up the fight with Cogswell. The woods caught fire below the road, and amid smoke and flames the two sides slugged it out until well after dark.

♦ Stephens' Battery C, 1st Ohio was the first XX Corps battery to take position on the Morris farm. It was followed by three

others for a total of 16 Federal guns north of the Goldsboro Road {9}.

♦ The headquarters sites of Gens. Henry W. Slocum {8} and Alpheus S. Williams {4} were established earlier in the day.

"We were Soon briskly engaged and from that time till long after dark the enemy continued to bring line after line of battle against us and pouring a perfect hail Storm of bullets at us, but they failed to drive us an inch and finally fled leaving their dead & wounded in our hands....I think I was never under such a terrible Storm of bullets in my life....It was one continued roar of musketry for about 3 hours. Our Artilly [sic] fired from our rear over our heads as rapidly as you could count sending [projectiles] into the advancing hosts of the rebels until they got tired of it and fled[2]....I with the rest of my Regt Bivouaced [sic] in line of battle on the field we had won laying down on a blanket before a fire where I slept as Soundly as I ever did in my life." — **Lt. Col. Philo B. Buckingham**, commanding the 20th Connecticut, Cogswell's brigade

"I saw Genl Johnston, Genl Bragg & Genl Stewart in an open field from which the enemy had been driven[3]....A brisk cannonade was going on just above, the shells from the enemy bursting over the field we were in....The musketry fire ceased temporarily and the opinion was that the attack was over....but immediately the musketry recommenced with great fury, and I was ordered to send two brigades toward the firing....The sun was declining rapidly, and the smoke settled heavy & dense over the country—A fog also came on, which added to the smoke made it impossible to See but a very short distance. The firing was very rapid and continuous for some time after my brigades went forward, but gradually ceased as the darkness increased." — **Maj. Gen. Lafayette McLaws**, commanding division, Hardee's Corps

"It was a hot old time, and things were lively if they were not lovely....After we had been engaged perhaps half an hour the [soldier] who had the flag was knocked down by a ball....My color-bearer companion seized the flag as it fell, and was instantly killed. I got it and was hit slightly in the face, but carried it through the fight without any further damage to my person, but I had my clothing pretty badly shot up [and] had my Sunday vest ruined....The idea of a man carrying a flag and being a target for every gun of the enemy is, to my mind, radically wrong." — **Pvt. W. A. Johnson**, 2nd South Carolina, Kennedy's (Conner's) Brigade

NOTE: Concurrent with the action on the Army of Tennessee's left (described above), another part of the battle raged further west at Morris' farm. Up to this point—*as illustrated on the maps*—the battle for Morris' farm has been "on hold." The series will now continue with events on this part of the field, digressing to the rout of Carlin's division and progressing from that point.

---

[1] Brigadier General Daniel H. Reynolds was grievously wounded early in the engagement, when an artillery round gutted his horse and mangled the general's left leg. The projectile also killed another horse standing nearby. Colonel Bunn assumed command of the brigade when Reynolds fell.

[2] Buckingham is referring to the fire from Rich's XIV Corps battery, and the surviving gun of Webb's 19th Indiana Battery, south of the Goldsboro Road.

[3] McLaws is referring to the field around Willis Cole's house, north of the Goldsboro Road.

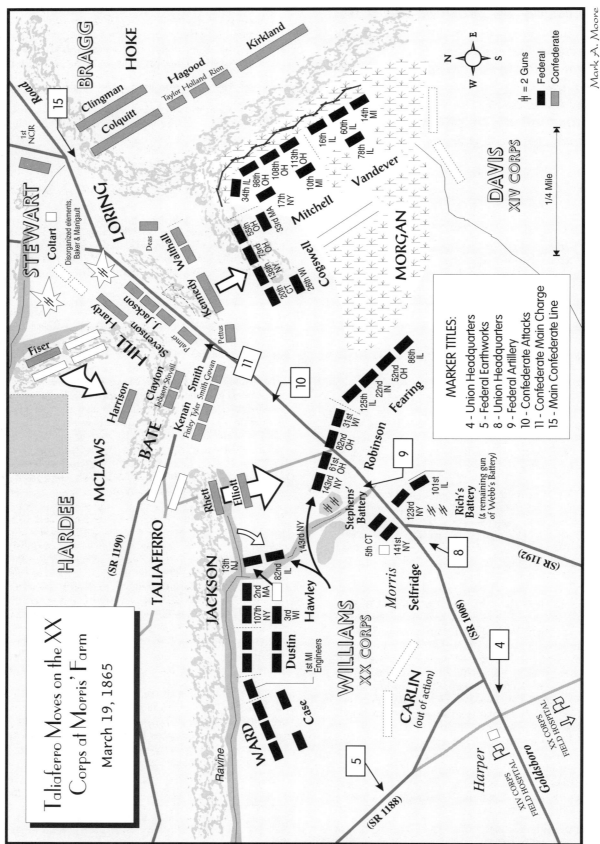

Taliaferro Moves on the XX
Corps at Morris' Farm
March 19, 1865

Mark A. Moore

MARKER TITLES:
4 - Union Headquarters
5 - Federal Earthworks
8 - Union Headquarters
9 - Federal Artillery
10 - Confederate Attacks
11 - Confederate Main Charge
15 - Main Confederate Line

▮▮ = 2 Guns
■ Federal
▯ Confederate

"If the Lord will only see me safe through this job, I'll register an oath never to vote for secession again as long as I live."

— **Unidentified Soldier** of Elliott's Brigade, prior to the Confederate attack at Morris' Farm

♦ Earlier in the afternoon, as Hawley's brigade was digging in south of a wooded ravine bordering the Morris farm, the thunder of battle rolled to the east in the direction of Carlin's position. As the noise grew louder, Colonel Hawley sent the 13th New Jersey out to his right across a small ravine. The 82nd Illinois (Robinson's brigade) was also sent to prolong the line to the right of the 13th (Refer to previous map).[1] It was hoped that as Buell's XIV Corps brigade fell back it could form in extension of this new line. (See pp. 30-31).

♦ Soon the shattered remains of Carlin's division burst into view from the east, streaming back before the advancing Confederates. The stampeding Federals poured through the large gap between Hawley and Robinson, and attempts by Hawley's men to rally their panicked comrades proved largely unsuccessful. Carlin's troops (Buell and a portion of Hobart) formed in rear of the XX Corps and were finished for the day.

♦ With the approaching enemy threatening their exposed flank, the 13th New Jersey and 82nd Illinois pulled back and dug in parallel to the small ravine they had just crossed. Their line now stood at right angles to the rest of Hawley's brigade. As Federal ordnance and commissary wagons struggled to escape the attacking enemy, the XIV Corps field hospital at the Morris house was hastily evacuated one-half mile west to the Harper farm.

♦ As General Bate's command was dressing its line west of Hill and Loring {11}, Taliaferro's Division drew up alongside to the right. Before them stretched the fields of Morris' farm, across which they could see the forming ranks of the enemy. With Elliott's Brigade leading, Taliaferro's Division moved out to attack the Federal XX Corps {10}.

♦ Stephens' Battery C, 1st Ohio promptly opened on the Rebels with spherical case shot {9}. The gunners cut their fuses short, hoping the shells would burst among the oncoming enemy.

♦ As Taliaferro approached the Federal battle line, Colonel Hawley sent the 143rd New York back to Robinson, who was preparing for the defense of his line across the Goldsboro Road. Stephens' battery ceased firing while the 143rd passed to the right in the face of the enemy, and joined on the left of Robinson's position. The brigade then unleashed a fierce fire upon the attacking Confederates.

♦ As Elliott's Brigade passed at right angles to their line, the 13th New Jersey and 82nd Illinois poured a well-directed fire squarely into its flank. Their first volley sent Elliott's inexperienced soldiers scampering for the rear. Rhett's

Brigade (under Col. William Butler) surged ahead and continued the attack.[2] Though inexperienced themselves, Rhett's Confederates drove to within 30 yards of the Federal battle line. The attack came so close that Robinson's line wavered and began to break in the center. At this crisis of the engagement, Lt. Col. Hezekiah Watkins (143rd New York) took matters into his own hands and bullied the troops back into line. Rhett's Brigade was soon compelled to retreat under a galling Federal fire of small arms and artillery.

♦ General William T Ward's division, now arriving at the front, was deployed to the left in prolongation of Hawley's position. The division was accompanied by a battalion of the 1st Michigan Engineers and Mechanics, which joined them on the front line {5}.

♦ Cogswell's brigade was formed in rear of the Federal artillery, and it was from here that it was deployed to the aid of Morgan's division. (**Note Cogswell's engagement with Loring and McLaws:** *this concurrent action is described in the previous section, pp. 38-39*).

♦ At some point during the afternoon, Slocum established headquarters in rear of the XX Corps {8}. Gen. Alpheus S. Williams, commanding the XX Corps, set up headquarters further west {4}.

♦ Having been repulsed by Morgan's division, Bragg's portion of the main Confederate line {15} made no further attempt to assault the enemy on March 19.

"[T]he Confederates came on in force, charging to within one hundred feet of our line....The boys made good use of a rail fence, making it into breastworks behind which they could lie flat and have slight protection. Evidently the Johnnies did not like the reception the boys gave them, and retreated. They soon renewed the attack with results as before. After the second charge [our] Lieutenant cautioned the boys to be ready, as there was something going on in front. In a moment a hat was tossed up, and the Lieutenant called out: 'Ho Johnny, what do you want?' and back came the reply, 'We want to come in.' The Lieutenant shouted, 'Come on,' and some twenty came running in over our rails. A guard was detailed to escort them to headquarters, when two asked to be allowed to remain and be given the use of muskets....The two recruits in gray fired as rapidly as any of us, and at each discharge would say, '[damn] you, take that; draft me, will you.' One or two more attempts were made to break through, when darkness closed the dreadful work for that day." — **Soldier** of the 143rd New York, Robinson's brigade

---

"The enemy's fire from their artillery, which had been concealed in the woods was very deadly....In approaching their battery (or batteries)....about half of our regiment on the right had come out into the open, in a field where there was nothing to conceal or protect them. Our men fell rapidly....under what seemed a tremendous concentrated firing upon us." — **Pvt. Robert W. Sanders**, 2nd South Carolina Artillery (fighting as infantry), Elliott's Brigade

---

[1] The 82nd Illinois, together with the 143rd New York, had earlier been sent to the rear from Robinson's position at the Cole farm. They were placed in reserve behind Hawley, subject to deployment as conditions warranted.

[2] Col. Alfred M. Rhett was captured March 15, 1865, below Averasboro, North Carolina.

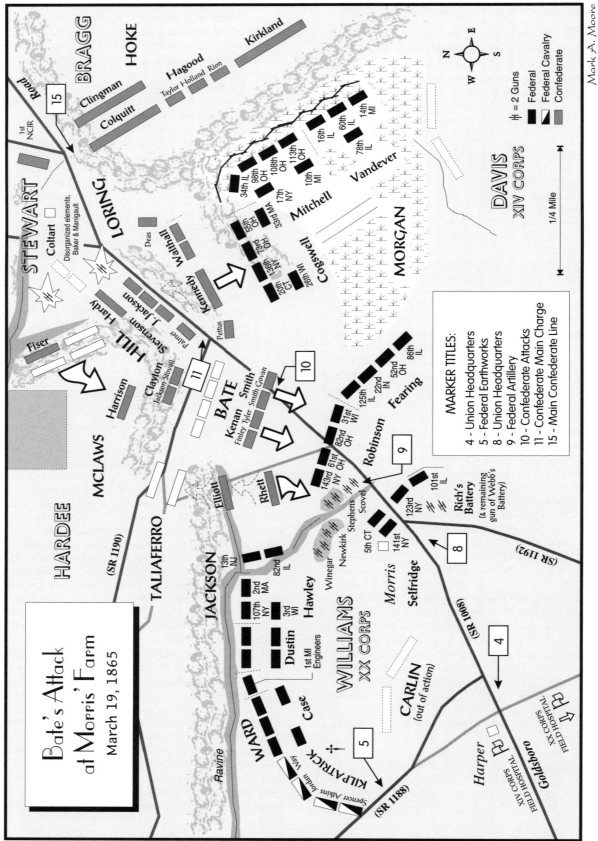

Bate's Attack
at Morris' Farm
March 19, 1865

Mark A. Moore

MARKER TITLES:
4 - Union Headquarters
5 - Federal Earthworks
8 - Union Headquarters
9 - Federal Artillery
10 - Confederate Attacks
11 - Confederate Main Charge
15 - Main Confederate Line

⊬ = 2 Guns
Federal
Federal Cavalry
Confederate

N
W E
S

1/4 Mile

"The Rebs....undertook to carry a new line I established, in the angle of which I left a marshy interval commanded at canister distance by twelve pieces of artillery.* They threw a mass into this interval and at the same time attacked in front. They were terribly punished....They left lots of dead officers and men, especially when the canister swept them on the left front. It was a worse affair for them than Kolb's Farm, [Georgia,] and somewhat reminded me of it."

— **Bvt. Maj. Gen. Alpheus S. Williams**, commanding the Federal XX Corps

♦ After Taliaferro's first assault had been repulsed, Lt. Edward P. Newkirk's Battery M, 1st New York, pulled up and unlimbered to the left of Stephens' Battery C, 1st Ohio {9}. A shallow marshy ravine separated the batteries, behind which the limber teams were held.

♦ Rhett's Brigade (Butler) moved out for a second charge against the Federal position at Morris' farm {10}. Once more advancing to within point-blank range of Robinson and the Federal batteries, the Confederates were thrown back with severe loss. Rhett's men retreated and regrouped for a third assault. At the same time Lt. Palmer F. Scovel's XIV Corps battery (C, 1st Illinois) fell in line to the right of Stephens, just north of the Goldsboro Road {9}. Scovel had fallen back from his position behind Buell's brigade during the rout of Carlin's division, and now added his strength to the powerful line of Union artillery.

♦ Amazingly, Rhett's inexperienced garrison troops advanced for a third time, in the face of 12 Federal cannon. Again they suffered in the open terrain. The 13th New Jersey and 82nd Illinois poured a flanking fire into the Rebels at every opportunity, and Robinson's men continued to punish their attackers in front. For a third time Rhett's men fell away from the devastating fusillades. As the Confederates again tried to reform their lines, Capt. Charles E. Winegar's Battery I, 1st New York, unlimbered to the left of Newkirk's position {9}. Sixteen Federal guns now completely commanded the gap between Hawley and Robinson.

♦ The final Southern attack occurred at sundown. Rhett's Brigade charged a fourth time, falling under a shower of canister rounds from Winegar's battery. To Rhett's left, after recovering from its earlier bout with Carlin's division {11}, Bate's command finally rose up to join the assault {10}. Stephens and Scovel lobbed their projectiles over the heads of Robinson's Federals, who were lying down in their front, and Bate's command was stopped short by the concentrated Federal fire. Colonel D. L. Kenan (commanding Bate's Division) and Maj. W. H. Wilkinson (commanding Tyler's Brigade) were struck down almost immediately. Bate's attack

promptly fell apart, and the beaten Confederates retired for the last time. The battle for Morris' farm, the Confederate "high tide" at Bentonville, was over.

♦ During this action Gen. Judson Kilpatrick's cavalry came up and formed on the left of the XX Corps. For the sake of simplicity, these troops are shown in compact form to the left of Ward's division {†}. They were probably spread out a little further west. Kilpatrick, however, was not actively engaged on March 19. Likewise, the XX Corps line west of Hawley's refused right flank was not attacked {5}.

♦ During the afternoon Left Wing commander H. W. Slocum established headquarters in rear of the XX Corps {8}. Gen. Alpheus S. Williams, commanding the XX Corps, set up headquarters further west {4}.

♦ (**Note Cogswell's engagement with Loring and McLaws:** *this concurrent action is described in a previous section of this study. See pp. 38-39.*)

♦ Having been repulsed by Morgan's division, Bragg's portion of the main Confederate line {15} made no further attempt to assault the enemy on March 19.

"It was a critical moment behind our line. [Gen. H. W.] Slocum stood motionless and speechless near the batteries, intently watching Robinson's thin line. Williams looked on as confident as ever in the tenacity of the red star division [Jackson's]; Jeff C. Davis, pugnacious as at Chickamauga, watched the woods, and listened for sounds from Carlin and Morgan; Kilpatrick, who was a visitor, showed all his splendid teeth in a smile of admiration at the way [the enemy] fought, and slapped his thighs ecstatically when the rebels were checked. The five batteries were opened at a distance less than seven hundred yards, throwing canister and spherical case into the wavering mass of rebels, the discharges being as rapid for a time as the ticks of a lever watch. Smoke settled down over the guns as it grew dark, and the flashes seen through it seemed like a steady, burning fire, and powder and peach blossoms perfumed the air....Captain Winegar, of the Buffalo battery, who 'drew a good bow' at Gettysburg and Chancellorsville, says he never witnessed such artillery fire. The enemy retired hastily and in confusion, and one hour later not a shot was heard along the line." — **E. D. Westfall**, war correspondent for the *New York Herald*, present with the XX Corps during the battle at Morris' farm

---

"[U]nder heavy fire we are ordered to lie down. Sam Woods and the writer seek the shelter of a large pine and while kneeling together behind it a minie passes through Sam's hand and he limps to the rear. Advancing again, we are halted just before night....A friendly log lies near....and we lie down behind it. A Federal battery open[s] on us and the color bearer of Olmstead's 1st Ga. regiment is knocked six or eight feet and disembow[e]led by a solid shot as it passes through the ranks. As the litter bearers are carrying off another wounded man....he begs piteously for his haversack, which has been left behind. They are under fire and refuse to halt. One of the Oglethorpes, in pity of the poor fellow, leaves the protection of his log and running up the line secures the haversack, takes it to him, then hastens back to his position." — **Sgt. Walter A. Clark**, 1st Georgia Volunteers, Smith's Brigade

---

* Williams seems to refer only to his three XX Corps batteries. The artillery line north of the Goldsboro Road also included a battery of the XIV Corps, for a total of 16 guns. Five more guns were in line south of the road.

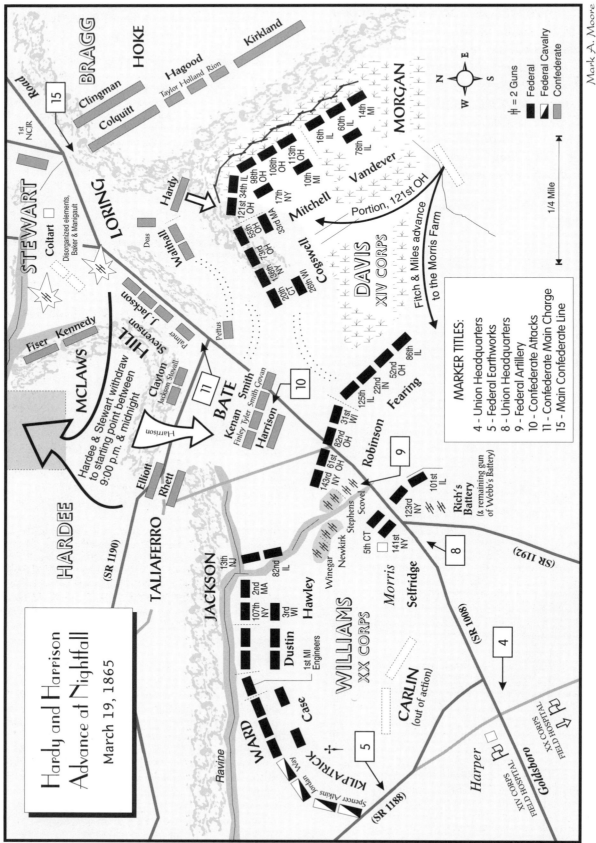

Mark A. Moore

Hardy and Harrison
Advance at Nightfall
March 19, 1865

MARKER TITLES:

4 - Union Headquarters
5 - Federal Earthworks
8 - Union Headquarters
9 - Federal Artillery
10 - Confederate Attacks
11 - Confederate Main Charge
15 - Main Confederate Line

"[Harrison's Brigade of] McLaws' division after sundown passed through my lines and halted a few paces in....front. Had these fresh troops been thrown in an hour earlier our victory would have been more complete and more fruitful of advantage. The firing continued until dark."

— **Maj. Gen. William B. Bate**, commanding Cheatham's Corps, Army of Tennessee

♦ Just after sundown Col. George Harrison's Brigade (McLaws' Division) came up in support of Bate's command, which was hugging the earth after its bout with the Federal XX Corps {10}. Harrison's men moved out a short distance in front of the main line, but were also pinned down by Federal artillery fire from the Morris farm {9}. Harrison had come up too late to be of any help to Bate's command.

♦ The XX Corps line west of Hawley's refused right flank had remained unmolested throughout the afternoon of March 19 {5}. That night Slocum pitched his tent somewhere near the Morris house {8}, while Gen. Alpheus S. Williams had headquarters further west {4}. Kilpatrick's cavalry is shown here in compact form to the left of Ward's Division {†}. They were probably spread out more to the west.

♦ On the left of the Army of Tennessee line, Kennedy's Brigade was withdrawn and replaced by a line of skirmishers. Pettus' Brigade and Walthall's Division held their ground just south of the Goldsboro Road {11}. As night fell Col. Washington Hardy's Brigade (McLaws' Division), having earlier followed Kennedy toward the firing line, chose to advance against the Federals south of the road.

♦ Hardy's advance met the 121st Ohio of Mitchell's brigade. About half of the 121st was in line between the 34th Illinois (Mitchell) and Cogswell's XX Corps brigade. The other half was en route to the Morris farm, accompanied by the remnants of Fitch and Miles (Carlin's division). These commands had remained in the swamp south of Morgan's position after being swept from the field by Confederate attacks earlier in the day.

♦ After some confusion as to whether Hardy's troops were friend or foe, Maj. Aaron B. Robinson directed the 121st Ohio to open fire. Hardy's Brigade was repulsed after a short fight of about 15 minutes. This small action marked the end of the fighting on March 19, save for an occasional shot from the XX Corps batteries at Morris' farm. Both sides busied themselves with collecting the wounded and burying the dead.

♦ At 8:00 p.m., Left Wing commander Henry W. Slocum sent a final plea for reinforcements to General Sherman, who had left Slocum that morning to accompany the Right Wing as it neared Goldsboro: *"I have positive information that General Johnston is here in person with a heavy force. I feel confident of holding my position, but I deem it of the greatest importance that the Right Wing come up during the night to my assistance....From prisoners I learn that the corps and commands of Hardee, Stewart, [S. D.] Lee, Cheatham, Hill, and Hoke are here."*

♦ Though Johnston had crushed Carlin's division and nearly enveloped Morgan's position, he lacked the numbers necessary to win the day. Slocum's strong defensive position, anchored by the massed artillery of the XX Corps, ensured that the battle of March 19 would end in a tactical draw.

♦ Between 9:00 p.m. and midnight, Johnston's Confederates began pulling back to their original starting point north of Cole's plantation. Hardee's Corps took position in rear of the Army of Tennessee. South of the Goldsboro Road, Bragg's position {15} remained unchanged during the night. At 9:00 p.m. Wade Hampton instructed Joseph Wheeler, whose cavalry command was several miles to the west, guarding the Smithfield-Clinton Road: *"[L]eave sufficient force to hold the bridge on Clinton and Smithfield road [at Stone Creek] and bring the rest of your command to Bentonville....General Johnston proposes to maintain his position to-morrow. Send out your best scouts to get information."*

"I ordered the men not to fire, but to lay close to their works and I challenged the enemy. They were plainly to be seen not thirty paces from us, picking their way through the swamp....[I] ordered the enemy to come in at once, telling them if they did not we should fire upon them. After a moment's pause I ordered the men to fire....The enemy broke and fled in great confusion, throwing away blankets, knapsacks, and guns. Thus ended the day....The affair of the evening was the first opportunity the regiment ever had of fighting behind their works. We carried in one wounded rebel and sent him to the hospital....The rebels were known to have carried off some of their wounded during the night....The deliberate aim which our men were able to take made their fire very effectual." — **Maj. Aaron B. Robinson**, commanding the 121st Ohio, Mitchell's brigade

"[T]he engagement lasted until dark, each party holding his own. The enemy seems then to have retired to his works, which were at a distance, wholly out of sight. Our pickets saw small parties of them by night, going about with torches and taking away their wounded. All their dead, we found there the next morning in large numbers." — **Lt. Col. Frederick C. Winkler**, commanding the 26th Wisconsin, Cogswell's brigade

---

*"At Bentonville....we got pretty badly mixed. We got after the Yankees and they just fired and fell back; we chased them on Sunday evening [March 19] until after dark. I think we went in twenty feet of one of their lines, when they suddenly fired a volley....If the fire had been well directed not a man of us could have escaped. The sheet of fire was blinding....I have met many of these old comrades at our annual reunions since, and some times [sic] I think we get our war stories a little mixed and rather shaky."** — **Lt. Charles S. Powell**, 10th North Carolina Battalion, Hardy's Brigade

---

* Lieutenant Powell good-naturedly hinted that his own account may be among the "mixed and rather shaky," as it was "written by request and on short notice." Indeed, Powell's statement that there was a "mighty rattling of canteens and tin cups in those woods when the enemy fell back in haste," seems to describe the actions of his own brigade that night in the swamps below Bentonville.

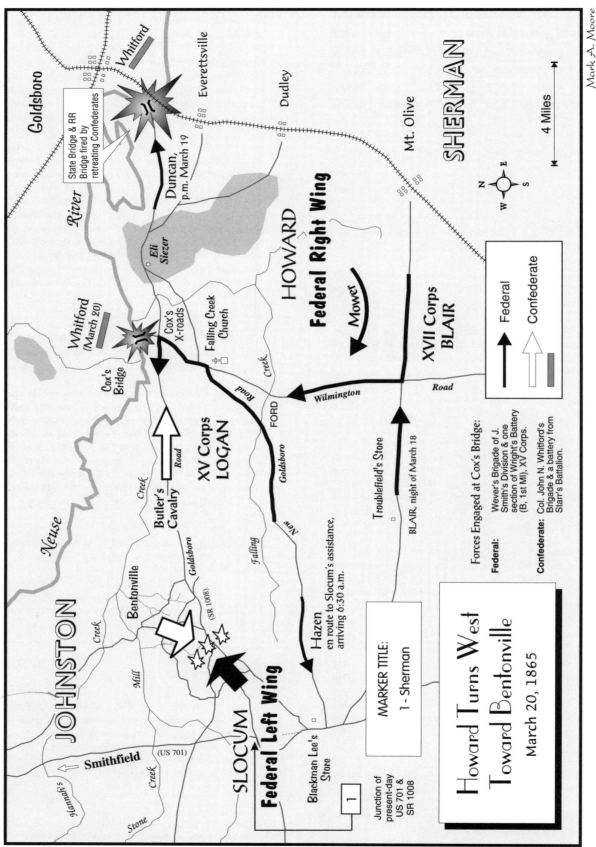

Mark A. Moore

Goldsboro

Whitford

State Bridge & RR
Bridge fired by
retreating Confederates

River

Duncan,
p.m. March 19

Everettsville

Dudley

Mt. Olive

SHERMAN

N
W E
S

4 Miles

Eli
Siezer

Whitford
(March 20)

Cox's X-roads

Cox's
Bridge

Falling Creek
Church

HOWARD

Federal Right Wing

Mower

Creek

Wilmington

Road

Federal

Confederate

JOHNSTON

Neuse

Creek

**XV Corps
LOGAN**

Butler's
Cavalry

Road

Goldsboro

FORD

Goldsboro

Road

**XVII Corps
BLAIR**

Forces Engaged at Cox's Bridge:

Federal: Wever's Brigade of J.
Smith's Division & one
section of Wright's Battery
(B, 1st MI), XV Corps.

Confederate: Col. John N. Whitford's
Brigade & a battery from
Starr's Battalion.

Bentonville

Goldsboro
(SR 1008)

Creek

Mill

Falling

New

Creek

Hazen
en route to Slocum's assistance,
arriving 6:30 a.m.

Troublefield's Store

BLAIR, night of March 18

MARKER TITLE:
1 - Sherman

SLOCUM

Federal Left Wing

Smithfield

(US 701)

Blackman Lee's
Store

Creek

Stone

Hannah's

1

Junction of
present-day
US 701 &
SR 1008

Howard Turns West
Toward Bentonville

March 20, 1865

*"**A**ll day the 19th we could distinctly hear the booming of the guns on our left, indicating that the left wing [Slocum] was being heavily engaged."*

— **Pvt. John C. Arbuckle**, 4th Iowa, Stone's brigade

♦ Early on the morning of March 19, Gen. William T. Sherman left Slocum's command to join Oliver O. Howard's Right Wing as it marched on Goldsboro {1}. Sherman felt sure that Slocum's head of column would reach Cox's Bridge that afternoon, and was anxious to communicate with Generals Schofield and Terry. Schofield's XXIII Corps was marching inland from New Bern, North Carolina. Having fought a battle with Hoke's Division below Kinston March 8-10, Schofield was now bearing down on Goldsboro. Alfred H. Terry's Provisional Corps was marching northward after having captured the port of Wilmington—which severed the last major supply line to Robert E. Lee's Army of Northern Virginia.[1] As Sherman rode off to join Howard, he was confident that the grand plan for a concentration of these forces with his own at Goldsboro was proceeding on schedule.

♦ The route of march of the Federal XV Corps lay about five miles south of the old Goldsboro Road (upon which Slocum's force was moving). It was advancing via Blackman Lee's Store on the *new* Goldsboro Road. The route of the XVII Corps lay further south, marching in the direction of Mount Olive via Troublefield's Store.

♦ By 11:30 a.m. on the 19th, the leading elements of the XV Corps reached Falling Creek Church. The column stretched all the way back to Lee's Store, and Howard called a halt to allow the ranks to close up. He also sent a party of scouts under Capt. William H. Duncan, and the 7th Illinois Mounted Infantry, to reconnoiter the approaches to Goldsboro. The party returned later that afternoon, reporting that a force of the enemy had burned the bridges south of town. During the day a mounted force under Lt. Col. William E. Strong, together with the 10th Iowa, secured the crossroads one mile south of Cox's Bridge. Here they shoved back a small force of Confederate cavalry from Gen. M. C. Butler's Brigade, which had ridden east to monitor the advance of Howard's wing. All day long the sounds of battle rumbled from the direction of Slocum's position.

♦ Late in the afternoon Lt. Joseph Foraker of Slocum's staff caught up with Sherman near Falling Creek Church. The courier bore a dispatch from Slocum, which informed Sherman of a large enemy force in front of the Left Wing. The note further requested immediate assistance from Howard. Sherman lost no time in making preparations to move the Right Wing toward Bentonville. He fired off a message to Slocum assuring him that Howard would soon be on the way, adding that *"if you find the enemy gone in the morning, follow up, as he will turn on Howard."* Sherman also ordered Maj. Gen. William B. Hazen's division to backtrack on the new

Goldsboro Road, via Lee's Store, and move up in support of Slocum. Generals John Geary and Absalom Baird were also directed to move to Slocum's assistance.[2] General Frank Blair's XVII Corps was given orders to march at 3:00 a.m. toward Falling Creek Church.

♦ Throughout the evening couriers brought news of the battle to Howard's wing. Slocum's more urgent dispatch of 8:00 p.m. reached Sherman sometime after midnight, and in the small hours of March 20 he replied to Slocum: *"We all move at 5 a.m. toward you; hold fast to your position, which I take for granted is now well fortified, but be ready to attack the enemy the moment you see signs of [his letting] go."*[3]

♦ At 5:00 a.m. on March 20, Col. Clark R. Wever's brigade advanced toward Cox's Bridge on the Neuse River. Soon it found the road blocked by Confederate troops: a small brigade commanded by Col. John N. Whitford.[4] On March 18, Joe Johnston had ordered Whitford's Brigade to move immediately from Goldsboro to Cox's Bridge. Whitford was to *"defend the bridge to the last against the approach of Sherman's forces,"* and if driven out he was to *"destroy the bridge at all hazards."* Likewise on the 18th, Col. Joseph B. Starr, commanding the 13th Battalion North Carolina Light Artillery, was directed to send a four-gun reserve battery to help defend the bridge. Keeping the Federals south of the Neuse would ensure a safe line of retreat for Johnston's army.

♦ Wever's brigade, together with Wright's Michigan battery, moved up and engaged Whitford's command. After a lively skirmish of about an hour the Confederates withdrew, torching the bridge behind them. As the remains crashed into the water, the lead division (Woods') of the XV Corps was rounding the corner at Cox's Crossroads one mile to the south. The Federal Right Wing was en route for Bentonville, and Butler's Confederate cavalry stood ready to contest its advance.

"The enemy's infantry and artillery [are] advancing rapidly from the direction of Cox's Bridge....A few regiments of infantry would check his advance, I think, very materially. Our cavalry is too weak to accomplish much."

— **Brig. Gen. Evander M. Law**, dispatch to General Johnston's adjutant on the advance of the Federal Right Wing. Law assumed command of Butler's *Division* on the morning of March 20 when Butler fell ill. (See *Order of Battle,* p. 80.)

---

[1] See map titled *Sherman & Johnston in North Carolina, March 1865, p. 2.* For a full study of the Wilmington Campaign, see Savas Publishing's *Last Rays of Departing Hope,* by Dr. Chris E. Fonvielle, Jr.

[2] These divisions had remained in the rear with the Left Wing trains during the battle of March 19.

[3] Earlier Sherman had responded to Slocum's initial pleas for assistance: *"We occupy a position dangerous to the enemy, if he thinks he is in front of the whole army....If he is there at daylight we will move straight on Cox's Bridge, and then turn toward you. I think you will find them gone in the morning....Get up your [wagon] trains between your camp and Lee's Store, and keep the enemy busy till we can get up with the four divisions of the Fifteenth Corps. If you hear firing to the front not explained by your own acts you must assault and turn the enemy, for it will not do to let him fight us separately."* Sherman remained skeptical. As late as 5:00 p.m. on the 19th he wrote to Gen. Judson Kilpatrick: *"General Slocum thinks the whole rebel army is to his front. I cannot think Johnston would fight us with the Neuse to his rear. You may remain with General Slocum until further orders."*

[4] The 67th and 68th North Carolina regiments.

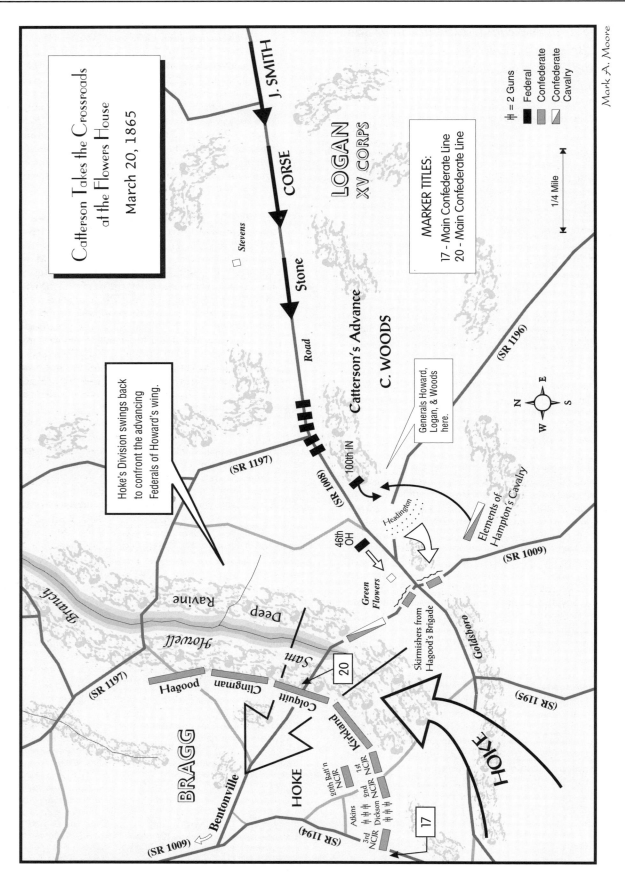

Catterson Takes the Crossroads
at the Flowers House
March 20, 1865

Mark A. Moore

MARKER TITLES:
17 - Main Confederate Line
20 - Main Confederate Line

Federal
Confederate
Confederate
Cavalry

⊞ = 2 Guns

1/4 Mile

Hoke's Division swings back
to confront the advancing
Federals of Howard's wing.

Generals Howard,
Logan, & Woods
here.

J. SMITH

CORSE

Stone

Road

(SR 1008)

Catterson's Advance

LOGAN
XV CORPS

C. WOODS

Stevens

100th IN

46th OH

Headington

Elements of
Hampton's Cavalry

(SR 1196)

(SR 1197)

(SR 1009)

Green
Flowers

Skirmishers from
Hagood's Brigade

Goldsboro

(SR 1195)

Branch

Howell

Deep

Ravine

Sam

20

Hagood

Clingman

Colquitt

Kirkland

BRAGG

HOKE

HOKE

20th Batt'n
NCJR

1st
NCJR

2nd
NCJR

Dickson

Atkins

3rd
NCJR

17

Bentonville

(SR 1009)

(SR 1194)

"The bugles sounded attention and [Catterson's] Brigade took its assigned position as the advance force on the Bentonville road.[1] Captain Orlando J. Fast....always a familiar figure at the front, spoke encouragingly to the troops as they filed into position, saying, 'Keep a stiff upper lip boys, and give them the best you have.' The enemy in considerable force was encountered only a short distance out from the camps....The battle opened at once with a crackling of small arms....The firing was brisk and the boys were hot for the sport."

— **Lt. Henry H. Wright**, 6th Iowa, Catterson's brigade, on the advance toward Bentonville.

♦ With Gen. Charles R. Woods' division in the advance, the Federal Right Wing marched in the direction of Bentonville. Colonel Robert F. Catterson's brigade led the way. About a mile out from Cox's Crossroads the brigade collided with a detachment of Confederate cavalry, which began contesting its advance on the Goldsboro Road. The enemy horsemen were from Young's Brigade (Butler's Division), commanded by Col. Gilbert J. Wright.

♦ The 97th Indiana pushed ahead to relieve the 7th Illinois Mounted Infantry[2], which had been screening the advance of the column, and a lively "running fight" ensued that would last the entire distance to Bentonville. Four companies of the 100th Indiana joined on the left of the 97th, as Catterson gamely drove the Confederates back to the west. The brigade was well-equipped for the work: it numbered seven regiments, and nearly all of its men carried repeating rifles.

♦ When the 97th ran out of ammunition, it was replaced on the skirmish line by the 6th Iowa. Elements of Gen. Joseph Wheeler's cavalry corps joined in the action with Young's Brigade, but the Confederates continued to yield ground to the Federal column. The Rebel cavalry fell back upon successive lines of rail works and began to stiffen their resistance just east of Johnston's position at Bentonville.

♦ At 10:15 a.m. Johnston received word of the approaching Right Wing from Gen. Evander Law. The Federals were advancing squarely upon the rear of General Bragg's position astride the Goldsboro Road. Accordingly, Hoke's Division was ordered to swing back to the north, *above* the Goldsboro Road, in order to keep the enemy in its front. In Hoke's new position his right ran roughly parallel with the road {**17**}, while his left bent sharply around to the north {**20**}. The line found an excellent defensive position behind the natural barrier of a deep ravine, at the bottom of which ran a creek called the Sam Howell Branch.[3]

♦ As the Federals pushed on, the 6th Iowa expended all of its ammunition and the 46th Ohio moved up to take its place. The 100th Indiana had remained in line for the entire march. The Confederate horsemen fell back to their final line of barricades: at the intersection of the Goldsboro Road and a second road that led north to Bentonville and Smithfield. As the cavalry clung to this tenuous position, Hoke's men busily completed their change of front. A squad of skirmishers from Hagood's Brigade fell in line with Hampton's troopers to help defend the barricade at the crossroads.

♦ The 46th Ohio promptly charged ahead and found the enemy *"across the road behind high and heavy rail-works."* Below the road to their left a force of Confederate cavalry burst from the woods and passed around the left flank of the 100th Indiana's skirmishers, commanded by Maj. Charles Headington. The remaining companies of the 100th moved up and stopped the advance of the Rebel troopers, who turned and fled northward. Generals Howard, Woods and John Logan (commanding the XV Corps) were nearly captured as the enemy troopers bore down on the 100th Indiana. Headington charged in conjunction with the 46th Ohio and sent the Confederates flying up the road toward the safety of Hoke's new position. Catterson now had possession of the crossroads, and the brigade began to take a position upon which the rest of the Right Wing could form.

♦ Across the way in Morgan's front (XIV Corps), as Hoke's Division pulled away, a small force of Union infantry was aggressively following in pursuit.

"[T]he Johnny Cavelry [sic] came dashing into our rear. Generals Logan, Woods, and other officers had followed our skirmish line closely. Col. [Ruel] Johnson [commanding the 100th Indiana] saw the Cavelry coming out of the woods. He faced the Regiment towards them and the men fired a volley into them that scattered them, and his quick action no doubt saved not only us but the Generals from capture." — **Sgt. Theodore Upson**, 100th Indiana, Catterson's brigade

"GENERAL: I have formed a dismounted line here very near [Green] Flower[s'] house, and can hold the enemy in check till we are flanked out of it. The line is a very short one, however. I have sent General Law back to Bentonville, with instructions to scout all roads running eastwardly from that point....Enemy are engaging us very warmly." — **Maj. Gen. Joseph Wheeler**, commanding Confederate cavalry corps, dispatch of 11:05 a.m. to Gen. Joseph E. Johnston

---

[1] The Federal Right Wing was moving west on the *Goldsboro* Road toward Bentonville.

[2] The mounted portion of the 7th Illinois Infantry, Hurlbut's brigade, Corse's division, XV Army Corps.

[3] This ravine is quite a bit larger and deeper than the one utilized by Carlin's division in the battle of March 19. The Confederate position here on March 20 lined the crest of its western slope. Any attacking force would have to negotiate this formidable obstacle before reaching the Confederates, who would be defending the line with a downhill fire.

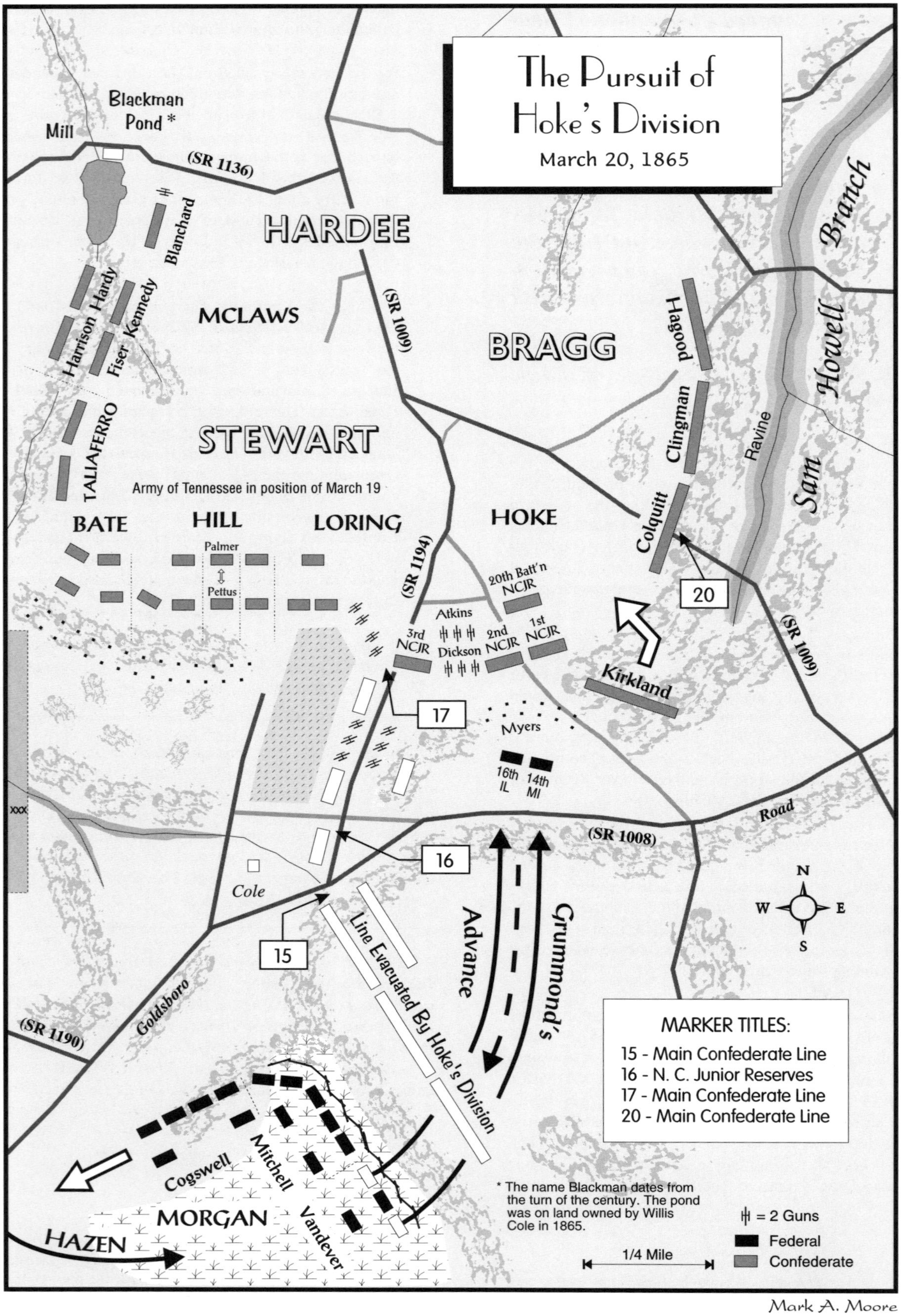
The Pursuit of Hoke's Division
March 20, 1865
Blackman Pond *
Mill
(SR 1136)
Blanchard
HARDEE
Harrison Hardy
Fiser Kennedy
MCLAWS
(SR 1009)
BRAGG
Hagood
Clingman
Ravine
Sam Howell Branch
TALIAFERRO
STEWART
Army of Tennessee in position of March 19
BATE
HILL
LORING
HOKE
Colquitt
Palmer
Pettus
(SR 1194)
20th Batt'n NCJR
Atkins
3rd NCJR
Dickson
2nd NCJR
1st NCJR
20
(SR 1009)
Kirkland
17
Myers
16th IL
14th MI
Road
(SR 1008)
16
Cole
15
Advance
Grummond's
Line Evacuated By Hoke's Division
Goldsboro
(SR 1190)
Cogswell
Mitchell
Vandever
MORGAN
HAZEN
MARKER TITLES:
15 - Main Confederate Line
16 - N. C. Junior Reserves
17 - Main Confederate Line
20 - Main Confederate Line
* The name Blackman dates from the turn of the century. The pond was on land owned by Willis Cole in 1865.
= 2 Guns
Federal
Confederate
1/4 Mile
N
W
E
S

Mark A. Moore

"The men were ordered to lie down behind such obstructions as they could find, and to await the order to fire until the advance came very near to them. When the enemy got within, say 100 yards....the men immediately raised upon their knees and fired a volley full in front of the advancing foe. Their ranks were mowed down like wheat before the scythe....[T]he whole front was covered with the dead and dying, and showed the effect of troops obeying the commands of their officers, to shoot low and wait until the enemy was near upon them."

— **George M. Rose**, Adjutant, 66th North Carolina, Kirkland's Brigade

♦ With the westward advance of the Federal Right Wing threatening the rear of General Bragg's position {15}, Johnston ordered Hoke's Division to swing back north of the Goldsboro Road. This new line would present a direct front to General Howard's column as it arrived from the direction of Cox's Bridge. The North Carolina Junior Reserves {16} pulled back parallel with the Goldsboro Road, their right resting near its position of the previous day {17}. The rest of Hoke's men formed to the left of the Juniors, with the line curving around sharply to the north. Hoke's new front was a strong defensive position, conforming to the western edge of a deep wooded ravine {20}. The Confederates began clearing their immediate front of small trees and underbrush to improve their fields of fire.

♦ As Hoke withdrew, the Army of Tennessee kept its old position of March 19, with Taliaferro's Division on the right. McLaws' Division moved into line on the right of Taliaferro, as General Stewart's troops continued the work of improving their breastworks.[1] General William B. Hazen's exhausted Federal division, having come to Slocum's support during the night, arrived on the battlefield at 6:30 a.m.

♦ South of the Goldsboro Road, Morgan's Federal division remained in line opposite Hoke's original position. Lieutenant Colonel George W. Grummond, commanding the aggressive 14th Michigan (Vandever's brigade), heard *"heavy chopping"* noises emanating from the direction of the enemy, and realized the Confederates were strengthening their works. Around 9:00 a.m. Grummond sent four companies out as skirmishers to annoy their progress. Captain J. Walter Myers advanced the skirmish line, whose fire sent the Rebels scurrying for cover.

♦ Gradually, return fire from Hoke's men began to diminish, and Myers became aware that the Confederates were withdrawing to their right from the main line. Grummond saw this as an opportunity to take the enemy's breastworks, and

informed General Vandever of the situation. Grummond was then ordered to lead the 16th Illinois and 14th Michigan on a charge against the Confederate position. This attack reached the line in time to capture a party of stragglers from Hoke's Division as it pulled out to the north.

♦ With Myers' skirmishers in the lead, the 16th and 14th pushed ahead in pursuit of Hoke's Division, for it looked as though the enemy was in full retreat. The small band of Federals swept across the Goldsboro Road, but promptly fell under a severe fire from Hoke's new position. From a point near Cole's house, Maj. Gen. D. H. Hill heard the *"loud cheers"* of the attackers and crossed over to Hoke's line. Taking matters into his own hands, Hill ordered Dickson's six-gun battery to open on the approaching Union regiments.[2] North of Grummond's right flank, Kirkland's Brigade deployed to cover Hoke's retreat before withdrawing to a gap left for it in the main line. The Federals surged ahead. Although Myers reported that his troops reached the enemy works, the two Federal regiments were forced to withdraw under heavy fire. They fell back across the Goldsboro Road and took position in Hoke's abandoned earthworks. Around 1:00 p.m., as the Federal Right Wing moved up from the east, Hazen's skirmishers began pushing beyond Morgan's right flank.

♦ **NOTE:** For action involving the Federal Right Wing concurrent with Hoke's change of front, see the previous section on Catterson's brigade, pp. 48-49.

"[W]e were met by a withering fire of musketry and....canister from [six] guns, which the enemy had in position on our left flank....[T]he men were completely exhausted by marching at double-quick so long [and] our line was confused, broken, and disorganized....[T]he left of my regiment was within thirty yards of the rebel breast-work, from which we were receiving a most destructive fire....upon our left flank, while another line was pouring it into us directly in front. At this time all of the Fourteenth Michigan on my right had fallen back, [and] I deemed it the wisest course to withdraw the regiment from such a position as speedily as possible." — **Capt. Herman Lund**, commanding the 16th Illinois, Vandever's brigade

---

"[T]here was a line of works across the field, and the [3-inch] rifles were placed in the centre of the field, while the Napoleons were on the left...[T]he portion of our line that was down in the woods on our left, in front of & perpendicular to us, fell back and took position [in] prolongation of our line. The enemy charged before the line was well established and they came so rapidly that the men of Kirkland's Brig[ade] were pressed pretty hard. [W]e opened six pieces on [their] flank, and as the shell[s] commenced bursting amongst them they gave way, and in a few minutes retired entirely."[3] — **Lt. Halcott P. Jones**, Dickson's Battery, (Company E) 13th Battalion North Carolina Light Artillery

---

[1] This was a formidable line of works, however undermanned it may have been. Today the Army of Tennessee line is visible and virtually intact, complete with what appear to be small traverses extending to the north from the main line. This area is not accessible to the general public.

[2] In this instance Hill was issuing orders to troops he did not command, and seems to have provided some much-needed authority on that part of the line.

[3] Interestingly, Lieutenant Jones makes no mention of the Federals reaching his position. Captain Myers reported that *"many of my skirmishers leaped over their defenses, seizing the battery horses and demanding the surrender of the battery."*

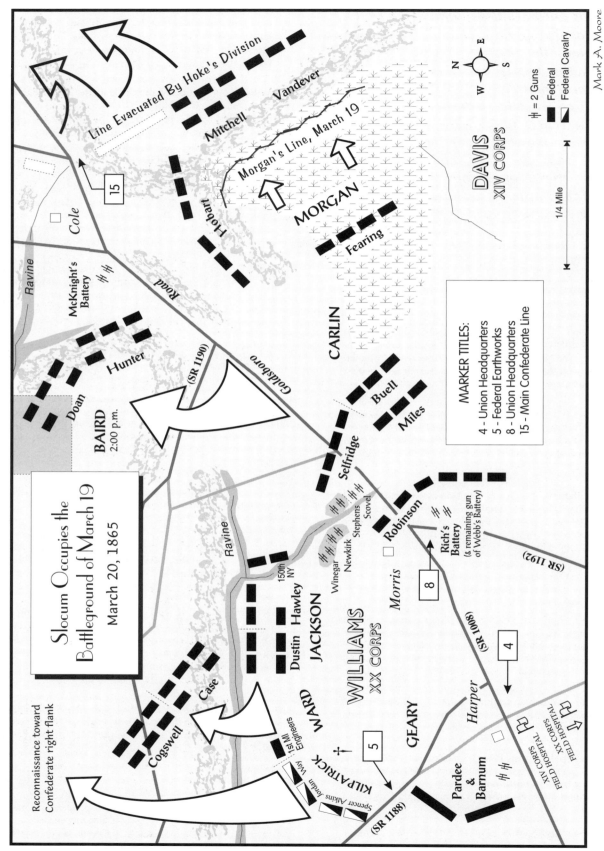

Mark A. Moore

Slocum Occupies the
Battleground of March 19
March 20, 1865

Reconnaissance toward
Confederate right flank

MARKER TITLES:
4 - Union Headquarters
5 - Federal Earthworks
8 - Union Headquarters
15 - Main Confederate Line

= 2 Guns

Federal
Federal Cavalry

N
W E
S

1/4 Mile

Line Evacuated By Hoke's Division

Vandever

Mitchell

Morgan's Line, March 19

Hobart

MORGAN

Cole

Ravine

McKnight's
Battery

Fearing

Road

(SR 1190)

Goldsboro

Hunter

Doan

BAIRD
2:00 p.m.

CARLIN

DAVIS
XIV CORPS

Buell

Miles

Selfridge

Robinson

Winegar Newkirk Stephens Scovel

150th
NY

Dustin Hawley

JACKSON

WILLIAMS
XX CORPS

Morris

Rich's Battery
(& remaining gun
of Webb's Battery)

(SR 1192)

8

Ravine

WARD

Case

Cogswell

1st MI Engineers

Spencer Atkins Jordan Way

KILPATRICK

(SR 1188)

5

GEARY

Harper

(SR 1008)

4

Pardee
&
Barnum

XIV CORPS
FIELD HOSPITAL

XX CORPS
FIELD HOSPITAL

"To-day finds us in a strong position, which the 'Rebs' will not attempt to force. Johnston hoped to catch us, yesterday, and give us 'fits,' but we have repulsed him with a severe loss....To-night the detachments that have been guarding the trains of the 14th and 20th [Corps] have been moved up to our line. We expect some more fun soon."

— **Cpl. Andrew J. Boies**, 33rd Massachusetts, Cogswell's brigade

♦ On March 20, Gen. H. W. Slocum's front saw little fighting but quite a bit of maneuvering. At this point the Left Wing troops fully expected a renewed and fierce confrontation with the enemy. Consequently, they spent the night of March 19 and all day on the 20th strengthening their positions and reconnoitering the battlefield, the details of which are outlined below:

♦ As the March 19 battle drew to a close, the 46th Pennsylvania[1] finally joined Selfridge's brigade. Around 7:00 p.m. Selfridge moved up and relieved Robinson on the front line. He began strengthening the works begun by Robinson's men, who fell back to Selfridge's old position.

♦ Late on March 19 General Sherman had ordered the divisions guarding the Left Wing trains to move up to the support of Slocum at the front. General John W. Geary's XX Corps division arrived at the John Harper farm at 4:30 a.m. on the 20th, along with Capt. Thomas Sloan's Pennsylvania battery. Geary held a reserve position for the remainder of the battle. General William B. Hazen's XV Corps division, having been sent from the Right Wing column by Sherman, arrived at Harper's about 6:30 a.m. and later passed around the right flank of Morgan's division. Hazen would form the link between General Slocum's position and the approaching Federal Right Wing.

♦ When Robert F. Hoke's Confederate Division pulled out of its main line of the previous day {15}, Morgan's division moved up and occupied the abandoned enemy works. Fearing's brigade returned to its original position of March 19, while Carlin's division crossed over to the right of the Goldsboro Road. Cogswell's XX Corps brigade was relieved by Hobart's brigade, and filed around to the left of the army to rejoin Ward's division.

♦ General Absalom Baird's XIV Corps division arrived at 8:00 a.m., and took position behind Carlin's men. At 2:00 p.m. Baird advanced over the battleground of the previous day, and stopped at the unfinished breastworks on the Cole farm begun by Robinson's brigade. Skirmishers were sent forward in reconnaissance of the Confederate position,[2] and Captain Joseph McKnight's 5th Wisconsin Battery unlimbered on the

[1] The 46th Pennsylvania had been detailed to "*hold the Smithfield road*" on March 19, and reached the brigade around 5:00 p.m.
[2] The Confederate line north of the ravine at Cole's farm does not appear on the map. See previous map, p. 50.

ground held previously by Scovel's and Webb's gunners. McKnight fired only 20 rounds during the afternoon, and Baird's troops soon withdrew to their original position behind Carlin. The 150th New York came up on Hawley's line and relieved the 82nd Illinois, which returned to Robinson's brigade. The 82nd had remained separated from the main body of Robinson's troops during the battle of March 19.

♦ The extreme Federal left {5} had not been engaged during the recent battle. Case's and Cogswell's brigades took up advanced positions and sent skirmishers out to explore the Confederate right flank. Likewise, elements of General Kilpatrick's cavalry joined in the reconnaissance. Kilpatrick is shown here in compact form to the left of Ward's division {†}. His troopers were probably spread out a short distance further to the west.

♦ The headquarters sites of Gens. H. W. Slocum {8} and Alpheus S. Williams {4} were established on March 19.

"[O]n the morning of the 20th the enemy had disappeared, leaving their pickets to fall into our hands and their dead unburied. Several [of our men] went out in front and brought in a number of wounded Rebels. One Rebel who was severely wounded would not accept of help. He said he would die rather than accept of a favor from a Yank, and he was as good as his word for he did not accept of even a drink of water, and died in the afternoon....Under one tree lay in death's cold embrace some eight or ten dead Rebels, and all along the road for some distance the Rebels lay dead in twos and threes....The number of the Rebel wounded must have been much larger than the Union, for [our] artillery did terrible execution." — **Sgt. Henry C. Morhous**, 123rd New York, Selfridge's brigade

"The battle yesterday was a terrible one, raging with terrific force all along the lines. The enemy charged our line 7 times in vain to get through and cause a panic in our [wagon] train. Our artillery did good service. When shot and shell failed they took musket balls and made dreadful havoc. The fight was renewed again today [but] the boom of our guns keeps the rebs at proper distance. The loss of the enemy is very great and ours is large but we do not yet know how great, for the rebs hold part of the ground that we occupied. True Barlow, and I were the only ones of our squad who were with us last night....Stragglers keep coming in. Capt. [Silas A.] Yerkes takes command of our Reg. in stead [sic] of Major Eaton who was killed yesterday." — **Pvt. John W. Daniels**, 13th Michigan, Buell's brigade. (Diary entry, March 20, 1865)

"The brunt of this battle was on the Army of Tennessee, and the more praise should be accorded them for their quick recuperation from the disaster at Nashville [Tennessee, December 15-16, 1864]....March 20th Gen. Loring [commanding Stewart's Corps] goes to the rear from sickness, and [General] Walthall succeeds to command. Enemy seem remarkably quiet in our front, but demonstrating heavily on Gen. Bragg, evidently trying to find a weak point. One division of Hardee's [McLaws'] sent to support the left. Skirmishers on our side have advanced to still find a [Federal] force confronting us." — **Maj. Bromfield L. Ridley**, aide to Lt. Gen. A. P. Stewart, commanding the Army of Tennessee

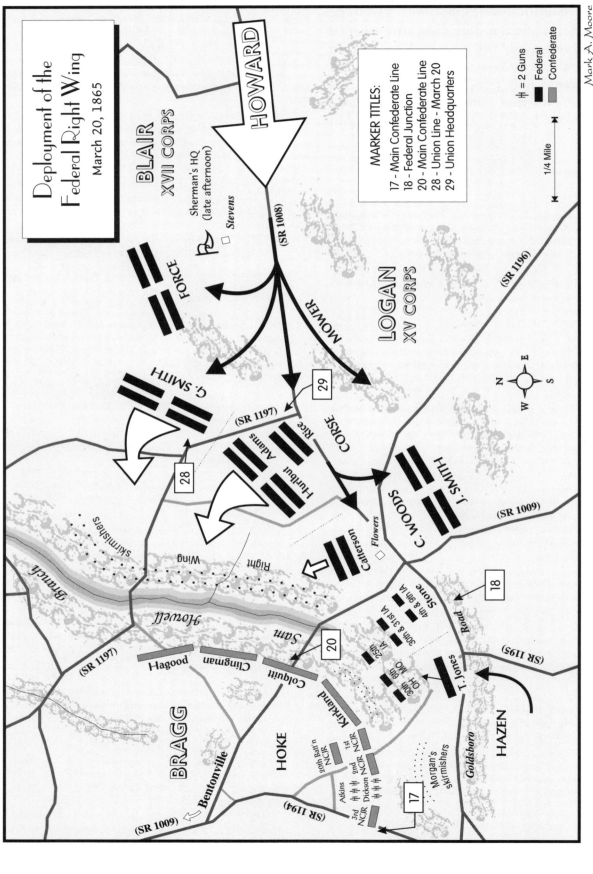

Deployment of the
Federal Right Wing
March 20, 1865

MARKER TITLES:
17 - Main Confederate Line
18 - Federal Junction
20 - Main Confederate Line
28 - Union Line - March 20
29 - Union Headquarters

Ⲏ = 2 Guns
⬛ Federal
▪ Confederate

1/4 Mile

Mark A. Moore

BLAIR
XVII CORPS

HOWARD

Sherman's HQ
(late afternoon)
□ Stevens

(SR 1008)

FORCE

LOGAN
XV CORPS

MOWER

(SR 1196)

G. SMITH

29

(SR 1197)

Rice

CORSE

Hurlbut
Adams

28

N
E
W
S

C. WOODS
J. SMITH

(SR 1009)

Skirmishers

Catterson
□ Flowers

18

Branch

Wing

Right

Stone

4th & 9th IA

Howell

Sam

20

30th & 31st IA

25th IA

(SR 1195)

(SR 1197)

Hagood

Clingman

Colquitt

30th OH

9th MO

T. Jones
Road

HAZEN

Goldsboro

BRAGG

HOKE

Kirkland

Bentonville

20th Batt'n
NCJR

1st
NCJR

2nd NCJR

Atkins

Dickson NCJR

(SR 1194)

3rd
NCJR

17

Morgan's
skirmishers

(SR 1009)

"On the morning of the 20th [our] attack was not renewed. We held our ground, however, in hope that [Sherman's] greatly superior numbers might encourage him to attack, and to cover the removal of our wounded."

— **General Joseph E. Johnston**, commanding Confederate forces at Bentonville

♦ Early in the afternoon two regiments of Maj. Gen. William B. Hazen's division moved out beyond Morgan's XIV Corps line.[1] The 6th Missouri and 30th Ohio of Col. Theodore Jones' brigade advanced in search of the left flank of General Howard's wing, which was beginning to arrive in force on the battlefield. Marching down the Goldsboro Road, Col. George A. Stone's brigade (Woods' division) turned to the north and took up position between Jones and Catterson's brigade. In doing so the 25th Iowa joined Hazen's advance regiments in a charge, forcing back a heavy line of Confederate skirmishers on the right of Hoke's refused position {17}. The main brigade lines followed close behind, and began to dig in above the road. Morgan's skirmishers (from the 10th Michigan) were fanned out to the left of Jones' brigade. By nightfall they would form a tenuous link with the Federal Right Wing {18}.

♦ The remaining divisions of the XV Corps filed down the Goldsboro Road and joined the Federal battle line: General John M. Corse's division formed on the right of Woods, while Gen. John E. Smith's division came up in reserve behind the main line. By mid-afternoon the lead elements of Maj. Gen. Frank P. Blair's XVII Corps arrived on the battlefield, with Gen. Giles Smith's division falling in on the right of Corse {28} and Gen. Manning F. Force's division forming in reserve. Major General Joseph A. Mower's division had arrived first, initially taking position south of the Goldsboro Road with orders to feel for the lines of Slocum's XIV Corps. Mower's skirmishers made contact with the 10th Michigan (Morgan), but when Hazen's advance regiments returned to the main line, Mower pulled out and joined the XVII Corps north of the road.

♦ As Howard's Right Wing deployed for battle, heavy lines of skirmishers were sent out to develop the position of the enemy. They found the Confederates *"admirably posted"* on the far slope of the Sam Howell Branch {20}, and sharp skirmishing prevailed along the lines.

♦ During the day Joe Johnston began the tedious process of evacuating the Confederate wounded, a difficult operation made worse by logistical problems. John T. Darby, medical director for the Army of Tennessee, sent the walking wounded off toward Smithfield. His concern, however, was transportation for the more seriously injured. Darby was anxious for information from Gen. A. P. Stewart regarding time allowed for the evacuation, complaining that *"unless all the wagons are placed at my disposal the wounded cannot be*

removed to-day." At some point on the 20th Johnston's adjutant, Col. Archer Anderson, sent a directive to Braxton Bragg: *"There is great complaint of the treatment the wounded receive in the rear. General Johnston desires you would send a medical officer of experience in the field to Smithfield, to take charge of the whole matter."* This officer was to communicate immediately by telegraph with an engineer in charge of Confederate railroads in Raleigh, *"calling for trains to carry off the wounded as fast as possible."* Perhaps unsure of his future military situation, Johnston insisted that *"any hospital arrangements at Smithfield and the depot should be of a temporary character."*

♦ Johnston sent nearly identical messages to Gen. Robert E. Lee in Virginia and Gen. Pierre G. T. Beauregard at Raleigh, North Carolina: *"I concentrated our troops here yesterday morning and attacked the enemy about 3:00 p.m.; routed him, capturing three guns....Our troops behaved handsomely. This morning enemy was intrenched. We have now the whole [Federal] army in our front....There has, so far, been only skirmishing to-day."* Lee, no doubt hoping for the best from Johnston's front, replied: *"I can but express my hearty congratulations at your victory of the 19th. It was skillfully planned and boldly executed. The gratification it will give to the country will be equaled by the gratification which will be felt for yourself and the brave army that achieved it."* One week later Johnston would again wire Lee in Virginia, this time giving a more complete account of the battle, and lamenting that *"my brief account [of March 20] may have given you an exaggerated idea of our success."*

♦ That afternoon General Sherman established his headquarters at the Stevens house, some distance behind the main Federal battle line {29}. To the east Gen. John Schofield's command drew nearer to Goldsboro and Gen. Alfred Terry's command advanced toward Cox's Bridge. These troops would be available, if needed, to support Sherman's army at Bentonville.[2]

"Another beautiful morn[ing] and warm day....Yesterday's fight [between Johnston and Slocum] was severe—much loss—a draw game....At noon (out 10 miles) we struck the Rebs['] flank near where they fought yesterday—The army rapidly formed in line of battle & threw up breastworks in several lines—Little artillery but rapid skirmish fighting all day—Hence all excitement and no rest—I was so tired I lay on [the] ground & slept several naps—All last night I lay out too cold to sleep (without overcoat & blankets[,] the waggons [sic] not having come up)—& too tired to stand up—Thus has passed this day but we little know what is to happen tonight or what the fate of tomorrow." — **E. P. Burton**, surgeon in the 7th Illinois, Hurlbut's brigade (Diary entry of March 20)

---

[1] Morgan's men had by this time advanced to the line of breastworks abandoned by Hoke's Division earlier in the day. See previous section on the Federal Left Wing, pp. 52-53.

[2] While forced to confront Johnston's army at Bentonville, Sherman's anticipated concentration with Schofield and Terry at Goldsboro remained foremost in the general's mind. He informed General Terry early on March 20: *"By to-night I will know whether Joe Johnston intends to fight me in force, when I will communicate further. Until you know the result, you and General Schofield should work up to my support south of the Neuse [River]."* That afternoon Sherman told Schofield: *"You can march into Goldsborough without opposition....I have ordered [Terry] to Cox's Bridge till the present action [at Bentonville] is over....After occupying Goldsborough, if you hear nothing to the contrary, join a part of your forces with General Terry's and come to me wherever I may be."*

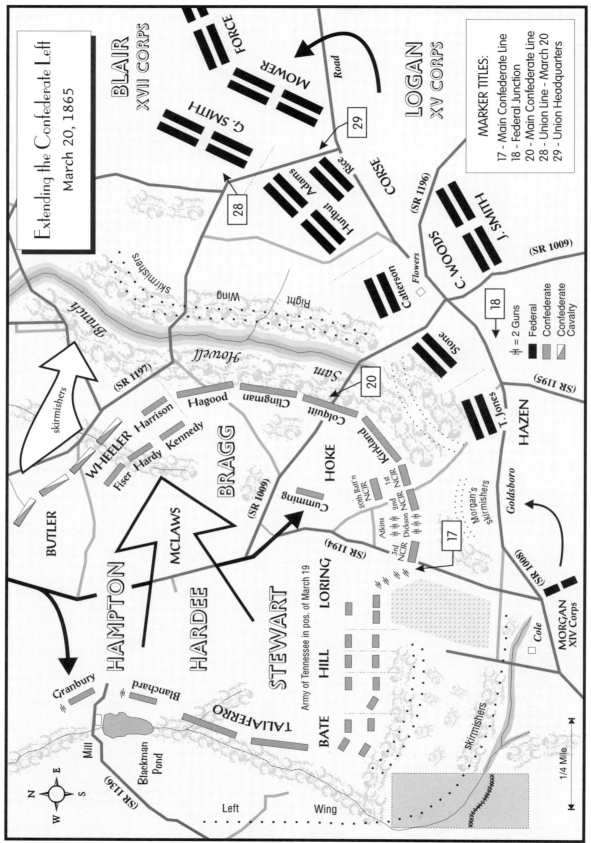

Extending the Confederate Left
March 20, 1865

Mark A. Moore

MARKER TITLES:
17 - Main Confederate Line
18 - Federal Junction
20 - Main Confederate Line
28 - Union Line - March 20
29 - Union Headquarters

⊞ = 2 Guns

Federal
Confederate
Confederate Cavalry

"During the formation of the [XVII Corps] line, as well as in the evening and late into the night, the musketry fire on the skirmish line was vigorously kept up, intermingled with heavy cannonading....which often reminded us of the old times before Atlanta."

— **Brig. Gen. William W. Belknap**, commanding Third Brigade, Fourth Division, XVII Corps

◆ As Sherman's Right Wing arrived in force on the battlefield, forming a junction with General Slocum's XIV Corps {18}, Johnston was compelled to add more weight to the left of his line. Accordingly, Gen. Lafayette McLaws' Division was pulled from its position on the Confederate right and sent to the left of Hoke's Division {17-20}. Lieutenant General Wade Hampton's cavalry further prolonged the line to the north, and skirmishers were sent forward to confront those of the enemy across the Sam Howell Branch. When McLaws withdrew from the right, Gen. William B. Taliaferro's command stretched out to the north to cover the vacated space. McLaws left one brigade (Blanchard's)[1] and a section of artillery in position east of the mill pond on Taliaferro's right.

◆ During the morning General Johnston received some welcome reinforcements. Granbury's and Cumming's brigades had traveled by rail from Raleigh to Smithfield, and thence on foot to Bentonville.[2] Cumming's Brigade, commanded by Col. Robert J. Henderson, was in position behind Hoke's Division by 1:30 p.m., while Granbury's Brigade formed in reserve a little further to the north. These were brigades in name only, numbering altogether about 500 men. Their scant addition counted little against the powerful masses of the enemy. At 2:30 p.m. Johnston's adjutant, Col. Archer Anderson, appealed to General Beauregard's headquarters: *"Send all troops of Army of Tennessee this way as soon as they arrive, not to march, however, after night."*[3]

◆ Sherman's headquarters {29} were established some distance behind Frank Blair's XVII Corps line {28}. That night, as the skirmish fire rolled along the opposing lines, Sherman sent a note to the Federal Left Wing headquarters of Gen. H. W. Slocum: *"We struck the enemy on his left rear about noon and have pressed him pretty hard, and have dislodged him from all his barricades except the line constructed as against you....for our men find parapets from the [Goldsboro] road well down to Mill Creek. Johnston hoped to overcome your wing before I could come to your relief. Having failed in that, I cannot see why he remains....I would rather avoid a general battle.... [but] in case of being forced to fight the enemy here we must*

send our [wagon] trains to Kinston for supplies....Make no orders as yet, till to-morrow reveals the purpose of our enemy."

◆ At midnight, from his headquarters on the Morris farm, Slocum replied to Sherman: *"I can, at any time, move this wing to the Goldsborough road without a fight....The enemy has a good road leading from his position to Smithfield, with intrenchments covering it*[4]*....Johnston was too slow; he allowed me to discover his strength before he made any strong efforts, and then found my men behind a very strong line of works. I have an excellent line, and the men were very industrious yesterday afternoon and last night."*[5]

"Heavy fighting continues on our left. All day we take the [Goldsboro] road....and camp early at Mills Creek [sic]. We move in onto the line and the 17th Corps becomes engaged with the enemy who seems concentrating at this point for a decisive battle....The 20th is sent out on a scout to the right [toward Bentonville]. Many women and children are seen wandering about having been driven from their homes by the flying bullets." — **Allen Morgan Geer**, 20th Illinois mounted provost guard, 3rd Division (Force's), XVII Corps (Diary entry of March 20)

"As soon as the train stopped [at Smithfield] we could hear the boom! boom! of cannon away off to the right down in the swampy, turpentine lagoon country about old Bentonville. We knew that Johnston and Sherman were at it again. The sound was familiar. We arrived on the battlefield [and] passed near where Gen. Johnston was standing, and the boys cheered him lustily—the first thing of the kind we had witnessed since the beginning of the campaign in Tennessee under Gen. [John Bell] Hood. The main battle....had been fought the day before our arrival, and Johnston had set [Slocum] back on his haunches....Under almost any other commander but Gen. Joseph E. Johnston, the Confederates at Bentonville, N. C., would have become demoralized at once....His lines were in the shape of a horse shoe [sic], with two ugly, muddy, deep creeks in his rear.[6] *Sherman kept pressing our line all round on the outside.* — **Lt. R. M. Collins**, 15th Texas, Granbury's Brigade.[7]

---

[1] Brigadier General Albert G. Blanchard commanded a brigade of South Carolina reserves, composed of young boys and old men. McLaws seems to have made an effort to keep these troops away from any confrontation with the enemy, and doesn't mention them at all in his writings on the action of March 19.

[2] These brigades were deployed independent of their normal commands: Cumming belonged to Carter L. Stevenson's Division, and Granbury to Cleburne's Division, Army of Tennessee.

[3] The concentration of Confederate forces at Bentonville was a partial one, and troops of the Army of Tennessee were still trickling in from the west.

[4] This was Johnston's *only* avenue of retreat, and thus of vital importance to the Confederate army. Inaccurate maps of North Carolina were a source of confusion for both armies, and initially Sherman was unaware of this road's existence. Similarly, when O. O. Howard received early reports on March 19 that Slocum's command was driving a band of Confederate cavalry eastward, he thought Johnston's force might retreat via Cox's Bridge on the Goldsboro Road.

[5] This statement by Slocum is of interest. The only portion of the XX Corps line with *"a very strong line of works"* was that which formed behind the ravine on the Morris farm. This line was not engaged. The Confederate attacks at this place were directed only at Robinson's brigade and the XX Corps artillery, and Robinson lay behind incomplete rail works at best. The artillery had more to do with Slocum's successful defense of the Morris farm than any Federal breastworks. Likewise, Cogswell's brigade lay down in the wooded swamps below the Goldsboro Road while battling with Loring's and Kennedy's commands. See map titled *Bate's Attack at Morris' Farm*, p. 42.

[6] Mill Creek and Hannah's Creek. See map titled *Howard Turns West Toward Bentonville*, p. 46.

[7] Lieutenant Collins' story checks out well enough with the facts, but his treatment of dates and names is atrocious.

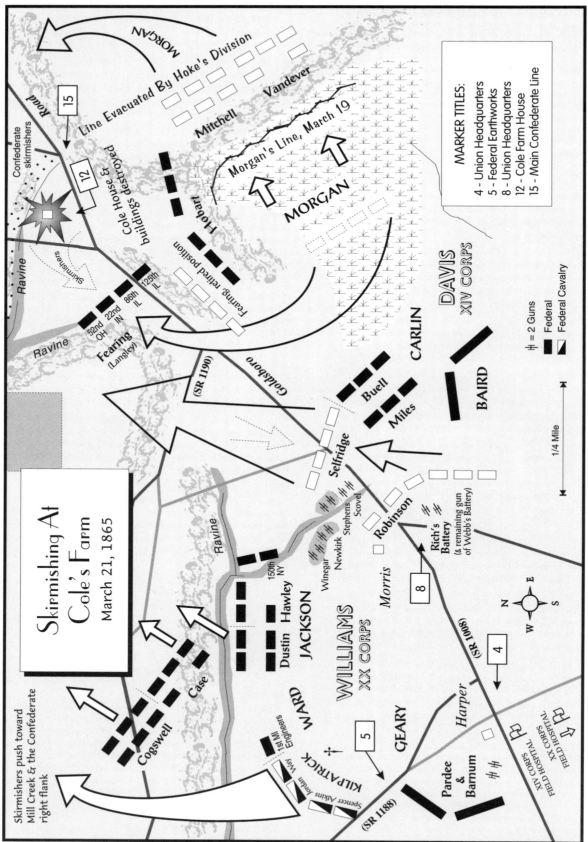

Skirmishing At
Cole's Farm
March 21, 1865

MARKER TITLES:

4 - Union Headquarters
5 - Federal Earthworks
8 - Union Headquarters
12 - Cole Farm House
15 - Main Confederate Line

Mark A. Moore

"[I]n our front [the enemy] were little affected by [the arrival of the Federal Right Wing], keeping up a bold front, using their artillery savagely. A large house [Cole's], situated half way between the picket lines, was secured by a few of our boys, who, from the second story windows annoyed the rebels by shooting down in their works, killing many artillery horses. This, it seems, they could not bear, so they advanced a line of battle, driving in our skirmishers, and burnt the house."

— **Capt. W. C. Robinson**, 34th Illinois, Mitchell's brigade, witness to the skirmishing at Cole's Farm

♦ During the day on March 21, the Federal Left Wing troops again pressed forward to develop the position and purpose of the Confederates. General Alpheus Williams' XX Corps line {5} and Kilpatrick's cavalry[1] {†} sent skirmishers out to reconnoiter the right flank of the enemy, whose entrenchments were wrongly assumed to extend as far north as Mill Creek. In truth, the Confederate line extended roughly half that far, prompting Gen. William Bate to report that the *"enemy can come in there with impunity."*

♦ General James D. Morgan, from a position in Robert F. Hoke's abandoned earthworks {15}, swung his command around to the north and formed a new line parallel to the Goldsboro Road. The XIV Corps line, however, still did not make a solid connection with the Federal Right Wing to the east.

♦ During the night of March 20, Col. James W. Langley (commanding Fearing's brigade) sent two regiments out to Robinson's old works of March 19. These trenches had been recently vacated by the troops of Gen. Absalom Baird. Langley's remaining two regiments followed on the morning of the 21st, and skirmishers were advanced out into the fields of Cole's farm. Many of these took aim at the enemy from the protective cover of the Cole house {12} and surrounding buildings. Though Robinson and Selfridge had earlier been sent to support the line, they were as quickly withdrawn. Langley's position now attracted the attention of XIV Corps commander Jefferson C. Davis, who warned that the brigade was *"entirely exposed to the attack of the enemy at any time they may choose to make it."* Mindful that Carlin's division had been similarly exposed in the battle of March 19, Davis ordered the command to fall back south of the Goldsboro Road. Before long a heavy force of skirmishers from the Army of Tennessee advanced, forcing their Federal counterparts to withdraw. The Confederates then set fire to the Cole house and buildings, burning them to the ground.

♦ The headquarters sites of Generals H. W. Slocum {8} and Alpheus Williams {4} were established on March 19.

♦ William T. Sherman was impatient for Johnston to pull up stakes and retreat to Smithfield. He complained to Gen. John Schofield, whose command was approaching Goldsboro: *"I thought Johnston, having failed, as he attempted to crush one of my wings, finding he had not succeeded but that I was present with my whole force, would withdraw, but he has not, and I must fight him here."* Accordingly, Slocum and Howard were ordered to send wagons to Kinston for supplies. Slocum also detached his pontoon train to the area of Cox's Bridge[2] so that Alfred H. Terry's command, advancing from the direction of Wilmington, would have a means of crossing the Neuse River.

♦ Sherman also made plans to withdraw the Left Wing from the battlefield. With Kilpatrick's skirmishers acting as a screen, Slocum was to put the XX Corps on the road to Goldsboro on March 22. Staying behind to cover the withdrawal, the XIV Corps would follow on March 23. Sherman was anxious to get to Goldsboro and unite his forces with those of Generals Schofield and Terry, and thus found Johnston's delay in leaving the battlefield a source of great irritation.

"[O]n March 21st....We had heavy firing again all along the line. I was selected as corps officer of the day and refer to....Major-General D. H. Hill's report. He said: 'There was a great deal of heavy firing on our left line [Hoke, McLaws, and Hampton], but no attack upon my command this day. My skirmish line, under Major [L. P.] Thomas, as corps officer of the day, was advanced that afternoon in connection with the skirmish line of Generals Walthall and Bate, and with small loss drove the Yankee's from their position about Cole's house. All the buildings were burned to prevent their further use by the Yankee sharp-shooters,' and thus we were bringing matters to the close." — **Maj. Lovick P. Thomas**, commanding the 42nd Georgia, Stovall's Brigade, Army of Tennessee

---

"We remain [south of the Goldsboro Road on March 20] until dark then move out on the front line....My men buried 26 dead rebels in our front. I was out showing the men where and how to bury them, found a dead boy laying close by a dead officer, supposed it was his father. We could only dig the depth of a spade and the water would fill up the ditch. We laid them side by side and covered them the best we could. I found many wounded and one man, a Virginian, Capt. John Hall made him some coffee and dressed his wound. I had my men carry back to the ambulances 15 wounded rebels and we allowed the enemy to carry back all their wounded during the night and what they left on the field was so badly wounded they could not move them....Tuesday morning [March 21] cloudy and warm. I advanced [Company I] within one hundred yards of the rebel skirmishers....shortly after the enemy's artillery opened up on us....driving our men back to our main line....It rained in torrents, the enemy shelling us doing no damage." — **Lt. Col. Allen L. Fahnestock**, commanding the 86th Illinois, Fearing's brigade (Diary entries of March 20-21)

---

[1] Kilpatrick's brigades are shown here in compact form to the left of Ward's XX Corps division. They were probably spread out further to the west.

[2] Cox's Bridge had been burned by Col. John N. Whitford's Brigade on March 20, in an effort to keep the Federals south of the Neuse River.

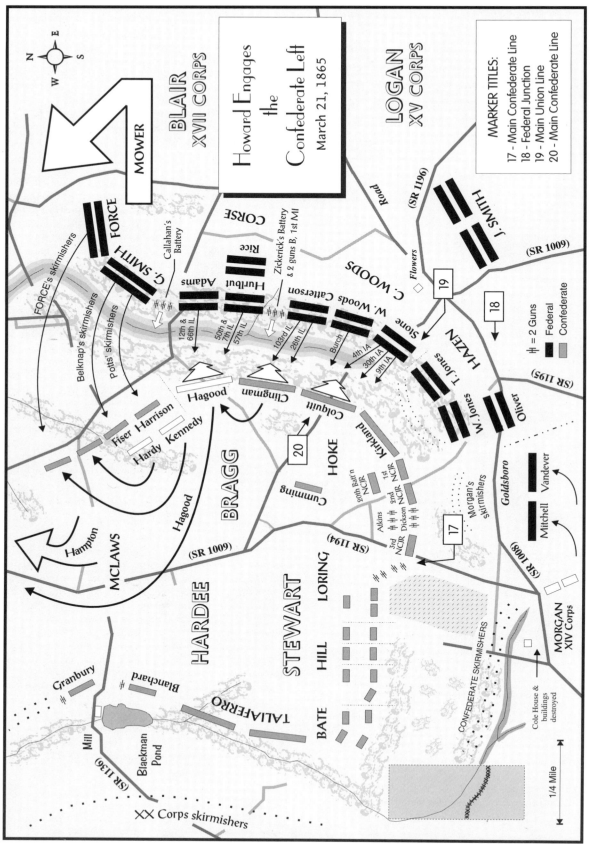

Mark A. Moore

Howard Engages
the
Confederate Left
March 21, 1865

BLAIR
XVII CORPS

MOWER

LOGAN
XV CORPS

MARKER TITLES:
17 - Main Confederate Line
18 - Federal Junction
19 - Main Union Line
20 - Main Confederate Line

⫲ = 2 Guns   Federal Confederate

FORCE

G. SMITH

Callahan's Battery

CORSE

Rice

Zickerick's Battery
& 2 guns B, 1st MI

Adams

Hurlbut

FORCE's skirmishers

Belknap's skirmishers

Potts' skirmishers

12th & 66th IL

50th & 7th IL

57th IL

103rd IL

26th IL

Burch

W. Woods Catterson

Stone

C. WOODS

J. SMITH

(SR 1196)

(SR 1009)

Flowers

19

18

(SR 1195)

4th IA
30th IA
9th IA

T. Jones

HAZEN

W. Jones

Oliver

Hagood

Clingman

Colquitt

Fiser Harrison

Hardy Kennedy

Hagood

Hampton

MCLAWS

BRAGG

20

HOKE

Cumming

Kirkland

20th Batt'n NCJR

1st NCJR

2nd NCJR Dickson

Atkins

3rd NCJR

Morgan's skirmishers

Goldsboro Vandever

Mitchell

17

(SR 1008)

MORGAN
XIV Corps

HARDEE

STEWART

LORING

HILL

BATE

(SR 1194)

Cole House & buildings destroyed

CONFEDERATE SKIRMISHERS

Granbury

Blanchard

TALIAFERRO

Mill

Blackman Pond

(SR 1136)

XX Corps skirmishers

1/4 Mile

"As the boys mounted our works and advanced, a private in Company C lagged behind his comrades and finally got behind a tree and stayed. Col. Wayne ordered the 1st sergeant of his company to shoot [the private], but he begged the colonel to excuse him. Col. Wayne ordered the sergeant to hand him his rifle [and] Col. Wayne placed the gun to his shoulder and called to the fellow behind the tree to advance, which he did in double-quick time. He knew it was death in the rear and he might stand some showing on the front."

— **Sgt. William H. Andrews**, 1st Georgia Regulars, Fiser's Brigade

♦ At 2:00 a.m. on March 21 Gen. Evander Law (commanding Butler's division of cavalry) sent a note to the headquarters of Lt. Gen. Wade Hampton: *"My scouts have just returned from the right of the enemy's lines. They report no retrograde movement of the enemy; on the contrary, the indications are that he will fight to-day."* Sherman's army stood united in Johnston's front, with Federal skirmishers pressing forward in close reconnaissance of the thin Confederate line. With both flanks refused sharply to the north, Johnston clung to his tenuous position guarding Mill Creek Bridge and the road to Smithfield. Around 7:20 a.m. he informed Gen. Robert E. Lee in Virginia: *"We are remaining here to cover the removal of our wounded to the railroad at Smithfield. The enemy's intrenched position and greatly superior number....make further offensive impracticable."* Outnumbered and no longer holding the advantage of surprise, Johnston could only hope that his own entrenched army would repulse any Federal attempt of a general assault.

♦ Oliver O. Howard's Right Wing skirmishers pushed forward at first light, developing the enemy line crowning the slope west of the Sam Howell Branch. The Hoke-McLaws defensive position was a strong one. Arrayed near the base of the ravine was a series of rifle pits, followed by a line of abatis[1] further up the ridge near the main Confederate line {17-20}. At 10:00 a.m. Howard's two corps advanced to the eastern edge of the ravine {19}, in close support of the Federal skirmishers. The brigades of William Woods, John Oliver and Wells Jones now joined the main battle line from positions in the rear. But the gap between Sherman's Right and Left Wings remained: the left of Hazen's division was several hundred yards in advance of Vandever's XIV Corps brigade. Rather than connect the lines at a sharp angle, Hazen placed Oliver's brigade in reserve to watch the interval {18}. Several batteries were advanced with the Federal line, and soon added their fire to that of the skirmishers. Around noon a heavy rain set in that would last the entire day.

♦ Sherman reported that on this day *"my orders were to avoid a general battle, till we could be sure of Goldsboro', and of opening up a new base of supply."* By 1:30 p.m., however, news had come back that Gen. Joseph Mower's division had driven around the Confederate left, threatening the bridge across Mill Creek—the only avenue of escape for Johnston's army. Accordingly, General Howard issued orders for the Right Wing to engage the Confederates in support of Mower's breakthrough. Severe skirmishing erupted along the Sam Howell Branch, with each side alternately trading possession of the Confederate rifle pits in the ravine. The advance of Frank Blair's XVII Corps skirmishers required McLaws to shift his line to the left to meet them. Wade Hampton's cavalry was stretched out to the north of McLaws, holding a key position between Mower's attacking division and Mill Creek Bridge. As the afternoon wore on, Hagood's Brigade was called away to help shore up the defense of the bridge, and Hoke's Division stretched itself even thinner to cover the resulting gap in the line. These movements well illustrate just how dangerous a position Johnston occupied.

♦ At 3:00 p.m. an agitated Sherman sent instructions to cavalry commander Judson Kilpatrick, who held the extreme left of the Union army: *"I think General Mower has got around the flank toward Mill Creek, threatening the enemy's line of retreat. Look out, and in case of a general battle hold your cavalry massed and dash at infantry toward the Mill Creek bridge on the road from Bentonville to Smithfield."*

"Although raining, a fire was burning the pine leaves between the lines, and near my station it burned over the bodies of several dead....Confederates, which in the fog made a terrible stench....[The 100th Indiana] was relieved at daylight. The 103rd Illinois was thrown forward as skirmishers and drove the enemy from a strong line of rifle pits, covering the ground occupied by their medical corps as a field hospital the day before, where was strewn around their amputating tables....many legs and arms which had been amputated, and a large number of bodies of men who had died of wounds while waiting attention." — **Capt. Eli J. Sherlock**, 100th Indiana, Catterson's brigade

---

"Late in the day the enemy made a spirited attack upon us....giving us a rattling fire from their sharpshooters. [My skirmishers] were fighting with a glee and abandon I never saw equaled. I am sorry to say that several of these young men, who had left their homes so far behind, were killed and many wounded....The sun of the Confederacy, notwithstanding the hopes of our Generals, the determination of the troops, and the prayers of the [Southern] people, was fast sinking in the west. The glorious rising on the plains of Manassas had gone down among the pine barriers of North Carolina. The last stroke had been given, and destiny seemed to be against us....The tattered battle flags waved as triumphantly over the heads of the shattered ranks of the battle-scared [sic] veterans here in the pine barriers as it ever did on the banks of the Rapidan [in Virginia]."[2] — **Capt. D. Augustus Dickert**, 3rd South Carolina, Kennedy's (Conner's) Brigade

---

[1] Defensive obstacles consisting of felled trees with sharpened branches, designed to impede the progress of an enemy assault.

[2] Lieutenant John P. Fort, of the 1st Georgia Regulars (Fiser), offers a more pragmatic view of Bentonville: *"It was a bloody, indecisive battle, and ought never to have been fought. We were confronted by a force over four times our superior in number and ten times in equipment. No valor or strategy could overcome such immense odds."*

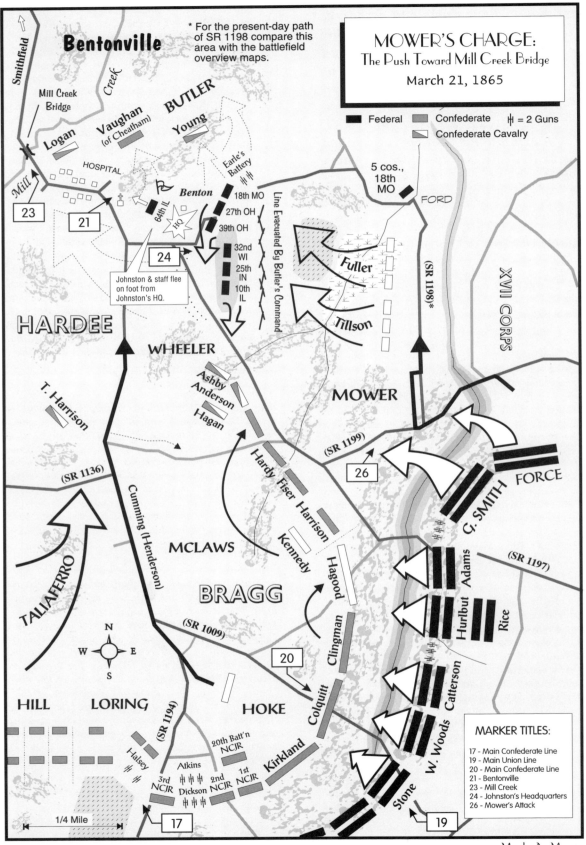

Bentonville

Mill Creek
Bridge

Creek

BUTLER

Vaughan
(of Cheatham)

Young

Logan

* For the present-day path
of SR 1198 compare this
area with the battlefield
overview maps.

MOWER'S CHARGE:
The Push Toward Mill Creek Bridge
March 21, 1865

■ Federal   ▬ Confederate   ⊢⊢ = 2 Guns
◳ Confederate Cavalry

HOSPITAL

Mill

23

21

Benton

64th IL

HQ

24

Johnston & staff flee
on foot from
Johnston's HQ.

Earle's
Battery

18th MO

27th OH

39th OH

32nd
WI

25th
IN

10th
IL

5 cos.,
18th
MO

FORD

Fuller

Tillson

(SR 1198)*

XVII
CORPS

HARDEE

WHEELER

Ashby
Anderson

Hagan

T. Harrison

MOWER

(SR 1199)

26

G. SMITH FORCE

Hardy
Fiser
Harrison

Kennedy

MCLAWS

BRAGG

(SR 1136)

Cumming (Henderson)

(SR 1009)

20

Hagood

Clingman

Colquitt

(SR 1197)

Adams

Hurlbut

Rice

Catterson

W. Woods

TALIAFERRO

N
W   E
S

HILL   **LORING**   **HOKE**

(SR 1194)

Halsey

Atkins

3rd
NCJR   Dickson

20th Batt'n
NCJR

2nd
NCJR   1st
NCJR

Kirkland

Stone

17

19

1/4 Mile

MARKER TITLES:

17 - Main Confederate Line
19 - Main Union Line
20 - Main Confederate Line
21 - Bentonville
23 - Mill Creek
24 - Johnston's Headquarters
26 - Mower's Attack

Line Evacuated By Butler's Command

Smithfield

Mark A. Moore

"On the morning of the 21st of March....learning that a road leading from the right of the line crossed Mill Creek at a ford,[1] I pushed my command down that road for the purpose of closing in on the enemy's flank."

— **Maj. Gen. Joseph A. Mower**, commanding the 1st Division, XVII Corps

♦ When Gen. Joseph A. Mower received instructions for deployment on the Federal right, he secured permission from XVII Corps commander Frank Blair to undertake *"a little reconnaissance."* By 11:00 a.m. Mower's division was on the move, swinging around the extreme right flank of the army. It soon found a road leading northward which crossed a ford over a tributary of Mill Creek. Mower placed five companies of the 18th Missouri just north of this ford, to guard his right flank against any Confederate advance from that direction. The rest of the command deployed parallel to the road and prepared for a westward advance. Colonel John Tillson's brigade held the left while Gen. John W. Fuller's brigade held the right of Mower's line. By noon the command was pushing ahead in reconnaissance of the Confederate left flank.

♦ Opposite Mower's command was the lightly entrenched line of Butler's dismounted cavalry division, commanded by Gen. Evander M. Law. These troopers made no connection with Joseph Wheeler's command on their right—which Wheeler felt was stretched thin enough. Soon Law's videttes reported the enemy advancing in considerable force across the swamp in their front. General Wade Hampton hastened to inform Joe Johnston of the situation, reminding him that there was not sufficient force on the left to withstand an enemy assault.

♦ Painfully cognizant of the importance of safeguarding Mill Creek Bridge[2], Johnston began planning for an all-out defense of his line of retreat {23}. As the Federal Left Wing (Slocum) was showing no signs of a general advance in Stewart's front, Johnston called for several commands on the right of the army to be moved over to the left. The weakened Army of Tennessee line was forced to spread out to cover the vacated spaces, but Johnston's gambling instincts would pay dividends before the day was through.

♦ The Confederates received the last of their infantry reinforcements from Smithfield when Gen. Frank Cheatham arrived at Bentonville with Brown's Division, plus Lowrey's Brigade of Cleburne's Division[3]. It was a timely arrival, providing an additional 1,000 men to help defend Mill Creek Bridge.

♦ On the Federal right, Mower's troops advanced with great difficulty, negotiating a dense swamp before breaking into open ground to the west. Emerging from the swamp his skirmishers immediately received artillery fire from Earle's Battery,[4] one gun of which held an advanced position on Butler's skirmish line. Mower, who had kept up with the advance, promptly ordered his men to charge. The troops rushed forward with a shout {26}. Butler's thin line of dismounted cavalry broke for the rear as the Federals surged westward. Earle's Battery limbered up and hastily retreated, but a reserve caisson fell into the hands of Fuller's brigade.

♦ Butler's Brigade (Gen. Thomas Logan) stampeded all the way back through Bentonville {21}, while Young's Brigade, commanded by Col. Gilbert Wright, swung back parallel to Mill Creek. Vaughan's Brigade, having recently arrived with Brown's Division, was forced back through the fields of the Benton farm. The 64th Illinois, equipped with Henry rifles, pushed rapidly toward Bentonville and overran Johnston's headquarters {24}. The general and his entourage were forced to head for the rear on foot.

♦ Mower's main line halted at the crest of a ridge east of Bentonville. While in this position he was informed that the left of his command did not connect with the skirmishers of Gen. Manning Force's division. Having come within a few hundred yards of the bridge over Mill Creek, Mower began to backpedal, ordering his brigades to shift to the left toward the main Federal line. The division was well in advance of the nearest supporting troops.

♦ Around 2:00 p.m. Col. Robert J. Henderson (commanding Cumming's Brigade) received word that he was now subject to the orders of Gen. William J. Hardee, whom Johnston had charged with collecting reserves to defend Mill Creek Bridge. From his position behind Hoke's Division, Henderson filed onto the road and hurried northward toward Bentonville.

♦ **NOTE:** For concurrent action between the Federal Right Wing {19} and the Hoke-McLaws line {17-20}, see the previous section titled *Howard Engages the Confederate Left*, pp. 60-61.

"[We] form line of battle in a heavily wooded country and move forward....Nothing joins our extreme left—skirmishers engaged—as we advance rebel batteries shell us—we push forward rapidly—[striking a] line of rebels behind log breastworks; [We were] onto them so quick we captured half of them....[O]ur skirmishers got into Joe Johnston's headquarters tents." — **Lt. Matthew H. Jamison**, 10th Illinois, Tillson's brigade (Diary entry)

"[O]ne gun of Earle's Battery, placed upon the skirmish line in a commanding position by order of Gen. Law, and commanded by Capt. [William] Earle in person, opened, and Gen. Law rode direct to it at a gallop, and seeing the moving line of [Y]ankee infantry, said: 'Capt. Earle, get your gun out of here.' This was done, but the reserve caisson, in turning, got a tree between the wheel and the limber chest....The enemy in line of battle—how many lines deep I could not see—swept our line back until it reached our field hospital on the side of the road leading to the bridge, and in sight of it." — **James G. Holmes**, staff of Gen. Evander Law

---

[1] Mower mistakenly refers to this swampy tributary as Mill Creek. The branch actually fed into Mill Creek some distance north of the ford.

[2] Frequent rains during the campaign had rendered Mill Creek impassable in the vicinity of the battlefield. The lone bridge at Bentonville was the only way out for Johnston's wagons and artillery.

[3] Cheatham arrived by rail at Smithfield late in the afternoon of March 20. The command marched for Bentonville on the morning of the 21st.

[4] Earle's Battery had rejoined Butler's Division on March 20.

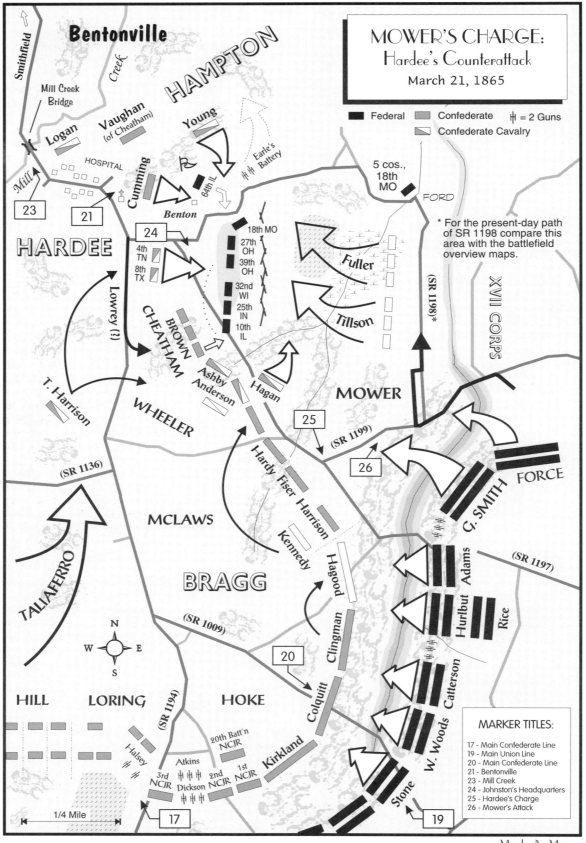

Bentonville

HAMPTON

Smithfield

Mill Creek Bridge

Creek

MOWER'S CHARGE:
Hardee's Counterattack
March 21, 1865

■ = Federal ▨ = Confederate ╫ = 2 Guns
▧ = Confederate Cavalry

Vaughan (of Cheatham)

Young

Earle's Battery

Mill

HOSPITAL

Cumming

Benton

64th IL

5 cos., 18th MO

FORD

(SR 1198)*

XVII CORPS

23

21

24

* For the present-day path of SR 1198 compare this area with the battlefield overview maps.

HARDEE

4th TN

8th TX

18th MO
27th OH
39th OH
32nd WI
25th IN
10th IL

Fuller

Tillson

Lowrey (?)

BROWN
CHEATHAM

Ashby
Anderson

Hagan

MOWER

T. Harrison

WHEELER

25

(SR 1199)

26

(SR 1136)

Hardy
Fiser
Harrison

G. SMITH
FORCE

(SR 1197)

MCLAWS

Kennedy

Adams

Rice

BRAGG

Hagood

Hurlbut

TALIAFERRO

Clingman

W. Woods
Catterson

(SR 1009)

20

Colquitt

N
W E
S

HILL

LORING

HOKE

(SR 1194)

20th Batt'n NCJR

Kirkland

Halsey

Atkins

3rd NCJR Dickson 2nd NCJR 1st NCJR

Stone

MARKER TITLES:
17 - Main Confederate Line
19 - Main Union Line
20 - Main Confederate Line
21 - Bentonville
23 - Mill Creek
24 - Johnston's Headquarters
25 - Hardee's Charge
26 - Mower's Attack

1/4 Mile

17

19

Mark A. Moore

"With a charge rarely equaled and never surpassed in impetuosity and daring, the Texans under Doc. Mathews' [sic] leadership threw themselves upon [Mower's] infantry with a recklessness that indicated do or die on their part. The enemy were greatly confused and wavered for a moment and then began to give back. The Texans still pressing....drove the enemy clear off the field and the [Mill Creek] bridge was saved to us for our use."

— **J. K. P. Blackburn**, 8th Texas Cavalry, Thomas Harrison's Brigade, Army of Tennessee

♦ With Cumming's Brigade advancing northward in line of battle, the 64th Illinois (Fuller) began to fall back from the village of Bentonville {21}. As the 64th pulled out, Col. Robert J. Henderson turned Cumming's Brigade to the right, in pursuit of the retreating Federals.

♦ Harrison's cavalry brigade, commanded by Col. Baxter Smith, was lying in reserve about a half-mile below Bentonville when Mower's division attacked {26}. A member of General Hardee's staff rode up with orders calling for Smith's command to help defend the bridge over Mill Creek {23}, and the 8th Texas and 4th Tennessee Cavalry regiments sped off toward the firing around Bentonville.[1]

♦ When Colonel Smith's regiments arrived at the scene of action, Hardee ordered them to attack the advancing enemy. In a pelting rain Hardee himself led the charge of the 8th Texas and 4th Tennessee, crashing through Tillson's skirmishers and bearing down on the gap between Mower's two brigades {25}.

♦ Joining Hardee's counterattack to the right of the 8th Texas was Brown's Division, of Cheatham's Corps.[2] The division went into line with the three brigades of Strahl, Gist, and Maney. Frank Cheatham advanced his command in two lines of battle against the left flank and front of Tillson's brigade. The fourth brigade of Brown's Division (Vaughan's) had earlier been driven from the vicinity of Johnston's headquarters {24}, but soon joined in the Confederate advance.

♦ Young's Brigade, having regrouped after falling back before Mower's attack, swept down on the right flank of the 64th

Illinois. The 64th fell back under fire toward Mower's position to the south. On Cheatham's right, Joseph Wheeler called Hagan's Alabama brigade up from its reserve position behind Anderson's Brigade, and ordered it to advance upon the left and rear of the attacking enemy.

♦ Mower's two brigades were now virtually surrounded by the surging Confederates, with no immediate support available. Clinging to its position on the ridge east of Bentonville, Mower's line began to break.

♦ **NOTE:** For concurrent action between the Federal Right Wing {19} and the Hoke-McLaws line {17-20}, see the section titled *Howard Engages the Confederate Left*, pp. 60-61)

"After a somewhat lengthy delay, during which we were subjected to a steady shelling from the enemy in front....the command moved on through an exceedingly miry and tangled swamp, almost impassable for horsemen....The main line, on emerging from the swamp, came up with the advance, which had been held at bay by a thick and well-filled line of rifle-pits, and carried the pits at once, though stubbornly held....On closing with [Fuller's] Brigade (about 150 yards forward of the rifle-pits) I was directed to move by the left flank, thus obliquing slightly to the rear for nearly the length of my brigade. The line was then halted and brought to a front. Hardly was this done when the skirmishers on the left were driven in, and being urged forward again, fell back, reporting heavy odds before them. Just at this time also both the commanders of the two right skirmishing companies came in reporting their lines broken by a cavalry charge and an advance of infantry on both flanks." — **Col. John Tillson**, commanding the 3rd Brigade, 1st Division, XVII Corps

"[W]e heard the boom of artillery directly in our rear. Every man pricked up his ears, for we knew that it meant something serious....In less time than it takes to tell it, we were mounted and racing to the rear. Within about half a mile of the bridge we passed a small brigade of infantry [Cumming's] 'double quicking' in the same direction. We saluted each other with a cheer as we passed, for all felt that it was a critical time in the battle. As we came upon some rising ground we had a good view of the enemy across an open field about 500 yards distant....It looked like the old regiment was this time surely going to its grave. Everything was so plain and clear you could see the [Federals] handling their guns and hear their shouts of command. Without a moment's hesitation Captain [Doc] Matthews gave the order....and with that wonderful yell we charged across the 500 yards of open field upon and among the mass of Yankees. We rode them down and emptied our pistols at close range." — **Lieutenant Briscoe**, 8th Texas Cavalry, Thomas Harrison's Brigade, Army of Tennessee

"I was just a common private soldier who never missed a roll call or detail, nor a service in which my company was in, and received an honorable discharge on the last day, without a cent and thirteen hundred miles from home....The saddest incident of my army life, is that of Dave Ross, a member of my company [D], who had served with zeal and honor throughout the war and was killed at Bentonville, in the very last engagement. Such a useless sacrifice to the demon of war, and so near his return to his family and home." — **R. C. Johnson**, 51st Alabama Cavalry, Hagan's Brigade, Army of Tennessee

---

[1] Smith's remaining two regiments, the 3rd Arkansas and 11th Texas Cavalry, had earlier been sent out toward Wheeler's skirmish line.

[2] Cheatham's command arrived after a harried journey to the battlefield. While waiting to board a train at Salisbury, North Carolina, for the ride to Smithfield, Frank Cheatham became impatient. *"[E]verything seemed to be delayed,"* recounted a member of the 19th Tennessee, *"officers as well as men [were] anxious to be away, [and] none more so than Gen. Cheatham, who began to get into a great bluster."* The men were exhausted by the time they reached Bentonville, and many collapsed and went to sleep amid the sounds of battle. The remainder of Cheatham's Corps was in line with the Army of Tennessee, having fought at Bentonville under the command of Gen. William B. Bate.

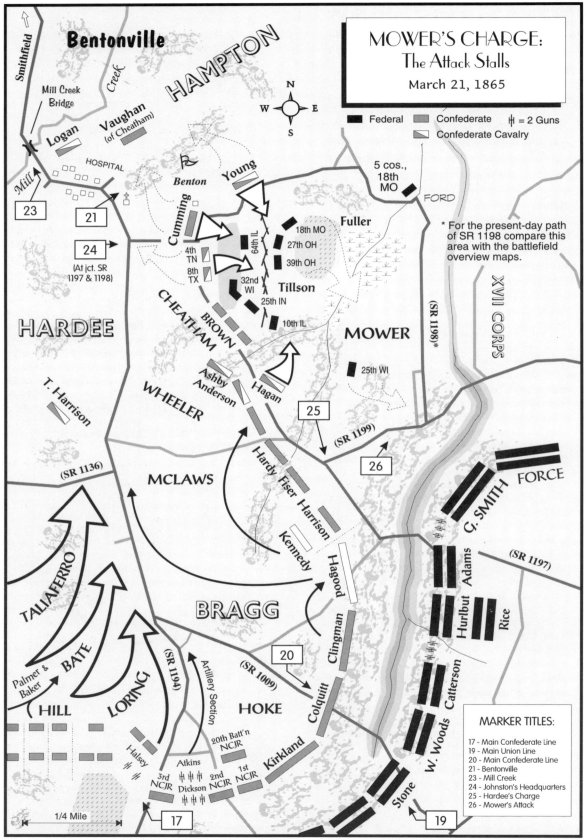

MOWER'S CHARGE:
The Attack Stalls
March 21, 1865

■ Federal   ▬ Confederate   ⊞ = 2 Guns
▨ Confederate Cavalry

* For the present-day path of SR 1198 compare this area with the battlefield overview maps.

MARKER TITLES:

17 - Main Confederate Line
19 - Main Union Line
20 - Main Confederate Line
21 - Bentonville
23 - Mill Creek
24 - Johnston's Headquarters
25 - Hardee's Charge
26 - Mower's Attack

Mark A. Moore

"As we marched past Gen. Johnston's headquarters, a joyous yell was heard along the whole line. The firing is hot in front. The enemy....forced our line in the form of a horse shoe [sic], leaving only the open end of the shoe unguarded....Hardee, in person, at the head of a Texas brigade of Cavalry[1], charged the line of [Mower's] infantry and drove them back, when the Nineteenth with others, doubled quicked to prevent a reoccupation. The retreat of the foe was so precipitate that they left all of their picks and shovels, of which we took possession, and at once threw up earth works [sic]."

— **Col. C. W. Heiskell**, commanding the 19th Tennessee, Strahl's Brigade

♦ As Young's Brigade bore down on the right flank of Mower's line, Gen. John W. Fuller ordered his right to swing backward and confront the advancing enemy head on. While this change of front was in progress, however, Cumming's Brigade struck the left of Fuller's command and drove the Federals from the crest of the ridge. Fuller withdrew to the line of Confederate rifle pits earlier abandoned by Butler's cavalry. Young's Brigade attacked this new position, but was easily repulsed by a volley from Fuller's main line.

♦ On Cumming's right the 8th Texas and 4th Tennessee Cavalry broke through Col. John Tillson's skirmish line. Many of the troopers passed through the gap between Mower's brigades before quickly withdrawing toward their own lines. With the cavalry falling back on both his flanks, Col. Robert J. Henderson ordered Cumming's Brigade to pull out as well. As the Confederates fell back in front of Mower's right, the 64th Illinois followed up and reoccupied the crest of the ridge east of Bentonville.

♦ On Mower's left, Tillson's brigade was struggling to hold its ground. As Cheatham's command advanced upon Tillson's left, it was joined on the right by Hagan's Alabama brigade and a few troopers from Ashby's command. With the 25th Indiana wavering in the center, the 10th Illinois broke for the rear. The 10th halted at the abandoned line of Confederate works at the base of the ridge, and the 25th Indiana fell back to join on its right. While steadily firing upon this refused line, the Confederates made no further attempt to drive Tillson from his position.

♦ As the firing slackened Joe Mower ordered Fuller's brigade to pass around to the rear and left of Tillson's brigade. As Fuller fell back the 25th Wisconsin, having earlier advanced in tentative support of Mower's breakthrough, withdrew from the field and returned to the XVII Corps trains in the rear.[2] Having thus shifted closer to the main Federal line, Mower was eager to launch a second assault on the Confederate left. General Sherman, however, had received word of the attack and was just as eager for Mower to withdraw altogether. *"I ordered him back to connect with his own corps,"* Sherman wrote of Mower, *"and, lest the enemy should concentrate on him, ordered the whole rebel line to be engaged with a strong skirmish-fire."* To the bitter disappointment of Mower and Right Wing commander Oliver O. Howard, the promise of crushing the Confederate army at Bentonville slipped away. *"[A]t the moment,"* continued Sherman, *"I preferred to make junction with Generals Terry and Schofield [at Goldsboro], before engaging Johnston's army, the strength of which was utterly unknown."*[3]

♦ As the fight with Mower drew to a close, the reinforcements called for by Joe Johnston earlier in the afternoon began arriving in the vicinity of Bentonville. Having stripped his right flank, Johnston meant to assure the safety of his line of retreat {23} by shoring up the Confederate left.

♦ In the affair known as Mower's Charge {26} the advance of the 64th Illinois through Johnston's headquarters {24} and into Bentonville {21} marked the zenith of the attack. As it turned out, Hardee's counterattack {25} guaranteed that Johnston's army would live to fight another day (if necessary). *"I think I made a mistake there,"* Sherman later wrote of Johnston's escape, *"and should rapidly have followed Mower's lead with the whole of the right wing, which would have brought on a general battle, and it could not have resulted otherwise than successfully to us, by reason of our vastly superior numbers."*[4]

♦ **NOTE:** For concurrent action between the Federal Right Wing {19} and the Hoke-McLaws line {17-20}, see the section titled *Howard Engages the Confederate Left*, pp. 60-61).

"I directed the right of the line to swing back....As this movement was taking place the enemy attacked. A portion of the line was thrown into confusion, as the regiments which were swinging could not be immediately halted....In spite of the temporary confusion our right oblique fire was so sharp as to halt the enemy's line and cause him to retire." — **Brig. Gen. John W. Fuller**, commanding the 1st Brigade, 1st Division, XVII Corps

---

"With a wild shout we rushed through the woods....The whole [of Mower's] line partook of the confusion and panic, and were driven back hastily....[W]e rode in among them, using our 'navies,' [and] scattered them and forced them back to their main line....There can be no doubt but that this charge saved our little army from destruction at Bentonville." — **Capt. George B. Guild**, 4th Tennessee Cavalry, Thomas Harrison's Brigade, Army of Tennessee

---

[1] Thomas Harrison's Brigade, commanded by Col. Baxter Smith, was often referred to as the Texas Brigade.
[2] The 25th Wisconsin belonged to Mower's 2nd Brigade (Montgomery's), which was on train guard duty.

[3] During the battle the Federal high command received exaggerated reports of Confederate strength; some estimates ran as high as 40,000 men present with Johnston.
[4] Sherman met with U. S. Grant and President Abraham Lincoln on March 27-28, 1865, aboard the steamer *River Queen* at City Point, Virginia. He later remembered: *"Both General Grant and myself supposed that one or the other of us would have to fight one more bloody battle, and that it would be the last. Mr. Lincoln exclaimed, more than once, that there had been blood enough shed, and asked us if another battle could not be avoided. I remember well to have said that we could not control that event....and I inferred that [the enemy] would be forced to fight one more desperate and bloody battle. I rather supposed it would fall on me, somewhere near Raleigh."*

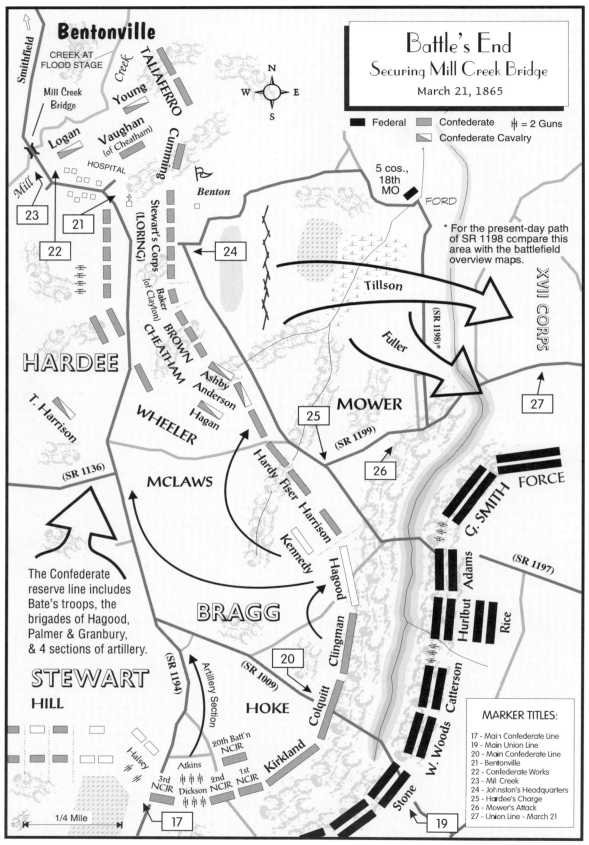

Bentonville

Smithfield

CREEK AT
FLOOD STAGE

Creek

TALIAFERRO

Young

Mill Creek
Bridge

Vaughan
(of Cheatham)

Logan

HOSPITAL

Cumming

Mill

23

21

22

Stewart's Corps

(LORING)

24

Benton

Battle's End
Securing Mill Creek Bridge
March 21, 1865

■ Federal   ■ Confederate   ⫪ = 2 Guns
▨ Confederate Cavalry

5 cos.,
18th
MO

FORD

* For the present-day path
of SR 1198 compare this
area with the battlefield
overview maps.

Tillson

(SR 1198)*

XVII CORPS

Baker
(of Clayton)

BROWN
CHEATHAM

HARDEE

Ashby
Anderson

Hagan

T. Harrison

WHEELER

(SR 1136)

MCLAWS

Fuller

MOWER

25

27

(SR 1199)

26

Hardy Fiser Harrison

G. SMITH   FORCE

Kennedy

Hagood

(SR 1197)

Hurlbut   Adams

Rice

The Confederate
reserve line includes
Bate's troops, the
brigades of Hagood,
Palmer & Granbury,
& 4 sections of artillery.

STEWART

HILL

(SR 1194)

Artillery Section

BRAGG

(SR 1009)

20

Clingman

HOKE

Colquitt

Catterson

W. Woods

1/4 Mile

Halsey

3rd
NCJR

Atkins

Dickson

20th Batt'n
NCJR

2nd
NCJR

1st
NCJR

Kirkland

Stone

17

19

MARKER TITLES:

17 - Main Confederate Line
19 - Main Union Line
20 - Main Confederate Line
21 - Bentonville
22 - Confederate Works
23 - Mill Creek
24 - Johnston's Headquarters
25 - Hardee's Charge
26 - Mower's Attack
27 - Union Line - March 21

Mark A. Moore

"At nightfall all the wounded that could bear transportation had been removed; so that we had no object for remaining in a position made very hazardous by the stream behind us [Mill Creek], rendered unfordable by recent rain."

— **Gen. Joseph E. Johnston**, commanding Confederate forces at Bentonville

♦ With the engagement ended, Gen. Joseph Mower's command withdrew to a position north of Force's XVII Corps division, and just east of the Sam Howell Branch {27}.

♦ Joe Johnston went about massing his reserves on the Confederate left, and the troops began to dig in {22}.[1] As Gens. William J. Hardee and Wade Hampton conferred over the success of the recent counterattack on Mower's division, Hardee learned that his only son, Willie Hardee, had been mortally wounded in the charge of the 8th Texas Cavalry.

♦ On the Confederate right, Gen. William B. Bate worried over the thin condition of his lines. Roughly half of the Army of Tennessee had been shifted to the left near Bentonville. At 5:00 p.m. Bate penned a dispatch to the headquarters of Gen. A. P. Stewart, commanding the Army of Tennessee: *"I have just been making disposition of what force I have left. I am from three to five feet apart in single rank."*[2] Bate had retained Taliaferro's skirmishers when that command departed for the Confederate left. These skirmishers, with Stewart's, were deployed to watch for signs of movement from the Federal Left Wing, commanded by Gen. Henry W. Slocum. Having gambled by stripping his right flank to protect his left, Johnston was pleased to learn that Slocum's wing was *"drawn back and formed obliquely to the general line; the left retired, and intrenched."* Slocum had no intention of assaulting the Confederate right. In fact, he worried over a renewed Confederate attack on his own lines. Perhaps because of the incident on March 19, when Confederate prisoners accurately informed him of Johnston's presence and intentions[3], Slocum was still placing great stock in the warnings of Confederate POWs. Echoing his earlier missives, he wrote General Sherman that afternoon: *"A deserter from Cheatham's command has just come into our lines....He says two divisions from [Robert E.] Lee's army have just arrived. Came last evening and this morning....He is intelligent and I am disposed to believe him."* (See pp. 60-61 for Stewart's position, and pp. 58-59 for Slocum's).

♦ During the afternoon Gen. John Schofield, commanding the XXIII Corps, occupied Goldsboro with minimal resistance from a small force of Confederate cavalry.[4] Twelve miles west of Goldsboro, Gen. Alfred H. Terry's Provisional Corps arrived at the crossroads below Cox's Bridge. At 6:00 p.m. Sherman communicated with Terry: *"It is manifest that we are not to be favored with weather. After raining for six weeks it has apparently set in for another six weeks."* Mower's Charge notwithstanding, Sherman continued: *"We have had some pretty sharp skirmishing all round the line, but nothing material either way. If I could get the railroad [repaired] to Goldsborough I would be better off than Johnston, as he has the same weather and, I think, a worse road to his base at Smithfield—both distances twenty miles. I am very anxious to hear of General Schofield at Goldsborough, and especially that the railroad is done to that point."*[5]

♦ Sherman's caution had thus far spared Johnston's army from destruction, and soon the Confederate commander would oblige Sherman and slip away during the night. During the afternoon Johnston learned that communication by telegraph with Goldsboro had abruptly ceased, indicating the Federal occupation of that town. The Confederates spent the remainder of the day and evening evacuating those of their wounded who could bear transportation to Smithfield. (The remainder would be left in and around the village of Bentonville). Johnston's only option was to retreat. At 10:00 p.m. the Confederates began pulling out toward Smithfield, finally making use of the little bridge for which so much effort had been expended.

"As we returned to our lines, which we did in a leisurely way and with little or no order, notwithstanding the enemy's shells were singing a dirge in the treetops overhead, I rode through [a swamp] with two men of my regiment. In going through my horse shied, and, looking around, I saw a Federal lieutenant of infantry leaning against a tree, badly wounded, with bloody water all around. I checked my horse, returned to him, and offered to place him on my horse and carry him to our division hospital, where he would be immediately cared for. His answer was: 'You go to h[ell], you d[amned] Rebel. I had rather die and go to h[ell] than have your polluted hands touch me.' [H]e grew worse and worse and cursed the South and all Confederate soldiers. So we left him to his fate. He was about twenty-two years of age, well dressed and very handsome." — **J. A. Jones**, 51st Alabama Cavalry, Hagan's Brigade, Army of Tennessee

---

"It is now raining and night has let her curtains fall. We are ordered to dig rifle-pits and remain on the line all night. It is a dark night, a cold March rain is falling upon the tired soldiers. The chilling winds make mournful music through the branches of the tall pines. The rebels are entrenched close to our lines and until three o'clock in the morning there is a continual firing. The Seventh pumped the death dealing elements from their sixteen-shooters with such a vim that it made the enemy think that the whole army was on the line of battle. Three o'clock in the morning the firing ceased, and at the first gray dawn of morning light the enemy is discovered to be gone and on the retreat. Thus ends our battle near Bentonville, North Carolina, which proves to be our last encounter with the rebel army in the war for the Union." — **D. Leib Ambrose**, 7th Illinois, Hurlbut's brigade

---

[1] The map interprets the Confederate left as arrayed from left to right. The exact positions of the individual units are unknown.

[2] A portion of Bate's command was sent to the Confederate left as a reserve.

[3] Maj. William G. Tracy, of Slocum's staff, had recognized one of these "galvanized Yankees" as a former acquaintance. Thus Slocum was inclined to take the man at his word.

[4] Under command of Col. Thomas J. Lipscomb, of the 2nd South Carolina Cavalry, Department of North Carolina.

[5] Schofield's forces were repairing the Atlantic & North Carolina Railroad for Federal use between New Bern, Kinston and Goldsboro.

Aftermath

As the Confederate army began its retreat toward Smithfield the artillery left first, followed by the masses of infantry. General Joseph Wheeler's cavalry remained in its entrenchments, with orders to "gradually fall back, checking the enemy should he follow us," reported Wheeler. While the Army of Tennessee filed across the bridge at Mill Creek, skirmishing between the Hoke-McLaws line and Sherman's Right Wing continued into the small hours of March 22. A cold rain was falling, but the woods around Bentonville were swept with fire ignited by exploding artillery rounds. "The night was a wild one," recalled Col. William P. Bishop, commanding Vaughan's Brigade. "The pine-forest had taken fire, and at frequent intervals the crash of burning, falling trees mingled with the roar of musketry and the occasional boom of cannon. Slowly the defeated army filed along the road lighted by tens of thousands of blazing torches."

At 5:30 a.m. Gen. Wade Hampton informed Wheeler that the Confederate infantry had completed its crossing, and gave orders to destroy the bridge and post videttes along Mill Creek. Having been slowly pressed back by Federal skirmishers, Wheeler's command tore the flooring from the bridge and set it on fire before retreating.

For Sherman's Right Wing skirmishers, the first light of morning brought evidence of the Confederate evacuation. "They left during the night," remembered Sgt. Alexander G. Downing of the 11th Iowa. "The fire [in the pine woods] compelled them to fall back, and they left their dead and wounded on the battlefield, to the mercy of the flames; the clothing was entirely burned off some of the bodies."

Over on the XV Corps front Col. Robert F. Catterson's brigade pushed beyond the empty works of the enemy, sending the 26th Illinois rapidly up the road toward Bentonville. They reached the bridge over Mill Creek only "a very few moments after the enemy's rear guard had crossed," reported Catterson. The bridge was on fire, and the 26th rushed to extinguish the flames before it was consumed. The men pushed the burning barrels of rosin set by Wheeler's command over the side and into the creek. Wheeler had not had enough time to wreck the bridge, and a short while later Hampton reported to Joseph E. Johnston that "I suppose infantry can cross." As the Confederate cavalry fell back toward Smithfield, Catterson's brigade followed in close pursuit.

One mile to the north the men of Granbury's Texas Brigade were encamped near the bridge over Hannah's Creek. The Texans, numbering only about 160 men, were among the first to pull out from Bentonville during the night of March 21. They bivouacked on the north side of the creek and dug rifle pits in the sandy soil. Before dawn the weather began to break: "The clouds rolled by, the big moon came out, and the drops of rain yet on the deep foliage around looked like millions of diamonds," wrote Lt. R. M. Collins of the 15th Texas. "We slept quite soundly that night." In the Texans' camp, the bright morning of March 22 was disrupted by the sound of gunfire, and soon a squad of Confederate cavalry came thundering up from the south toward the bridge at Hannah's Creek. It was Wheeler. Lt. Collins noted that "the bridge had been covered about two feet deep with pine tops and sand, and that lots of people and things had crossed it the night before, and sure enough the whole of Johnston's army had crossed it that night, passing within 200 yards of us, and we knew nothing about it."

Wheeler's men swiftly crossed over and set fire to the bridge, with Lt. Col. Ira J. Bloomfield's 26th Illinois following close behind. A severe skirmish erupted as the Illinoisans stormed the bridge and began dousing the flames. Granbury's men fled into a swamp to the north. The affair at the bridge was over quickly, but

not before the colors of the 26th Illinois lay floating in the waters of Hannah's Creek, and Col. Bloomfield's horse had been shot from beneath him. Several members of Company E managed to recover the flag of the 26th before the Confederates could get to it. Catterson's men were soon called back to Mill Creek, and Joe Johnston's rear guard continued to Smithfield unmolested.

Back at Bentonville the Federals found the village and vicinity teeming with the dead and wounded of both sides. "[I saw] a dead Rebel and one of our men with his foot cut half off, one of his toes cut off, several more cuts on his body, and a bullet hole in his temple," remembered Maj. Charles Wills of the 103rd Illinois. "Some of the boys saw one of our men with [a] leg cut off in five places. Some surgeon had probably been practicing on the last two men."[1] That night the 100th Indiana would build "fires on the battlefield along our picket line," according to Capt. Eli Sherlock, "so that we could move about without stumbling over graves or dead bodies."

During the day William T. Sherman finally got his army moving again. Though the rain had ceased, Lt. Matthew Jamison of the 10th Illinois found it a "miserable day," with the "wind blowing a hurricane [and] sand flying in clouds." While the Right Wing held its ground, the Left Wing took up the march for Goldsboro, where the army would get the rest and refitting it so badly needed. Oliver O. Howard's Right Wing would follow on March 23. For all his later attempts to downplay the threat to his army at Bentonville, Sherman officially congratulated his men for defeating the concentrated forces of the enemy upon their own chosen ground. Anxious for provisions at Goldsboro, Sherman was irritated to learn that the railroad running inland from Morehead City and New Bern was still not fully operational. "At all events," he informed Gen. U. S. Grant on March 23, "we have now made a junction of all the armies, and if we can maintain them will in a short time be in position to march against Raleigh, or Gaston, or Weldon, or even Richmond, as you may determine."

Frederick E. Pimper of the 39th Ohio was glad to see the ordeal ended: "[T]he day of jubilee is coming and I hope that it aint very far off," he would write from Goldsboro. "[E]verybody here is in the best of spirits and the wildest rumors are going around among the boys daily....Mr. Johnston has pulled up stakes in our front and left his fortified position, as he didn't think it very safe to remain and get perhaps between 2 of our armies [sic]."[2]

Pimper's "day of jubilee" was little more than a month away. On April 26, 1865, Joseph E. Johnston would lay down Confederate arms on Sherman's terms, in the largest troop surrender of the Civil War. But for now, "Old Joe" looked to Gen. Robert E. Lee in Virginia for his next course of action. From Smithfield, where his battered army recuperated and reorganized, Johnston wired Lee on March 23: "Troops of Tennessee army have fully disproved slanders that have been published against them [but] Sherman's course cannot be hindered by the small force I have. I can do no more than annoy him. I respectfully suggest that it is no longer a question whether you leave present position [at Petersburg, Virginia]; you have only to decide where to meet Sherman. I will be near him."

Lee's own Army of Northern Virginia was on its last legs, and his response must not have been very encouraging to Johnston: "I am delighted at conduct of Tennessee army. I hope you will be able often to repeat your blow and finally shiver enemy. Still we must meet the question. Where, in your opinion, can we best meet Sherman?"

---

[1] For a more ominous explanation see Mark Bradley's passage on atrocities at Bentonville, beginning on page 402 of *Last Stand in the Carolinas*.
[2] The forces of Sherman and Gen. John Schofield.

Appendix A — Contemporary Views and Drawings of the Battlefield

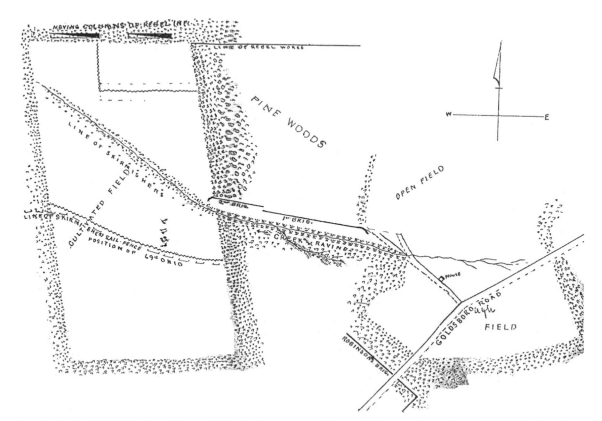

In his report on the battle, Bvt. Brig. Gen. George P. Buell twice refers to an attached "diagram." Though a footnote in the published version explains that the diagram was to *"appear in the Atlas,"* Buell's map, shown above, was never included in the *Atlas to Accompany the Official Records of the Union and Confederate Armies*. Pictured are the positions of Buell's (2nd) brigade and Briant's wing of Hobart's (1st) brigade, the Cole House, position of the 69th Ohio, Capt. George M. Rowe's skirmish line, Robinson's brigade (which did *not* extend below the Goldsboro Road), and the Confederate Army of Tennessee line to the north. The caption at the top left of the drawing reads "moving columns of rebel inf."—that is, Taliaferro's Division. Note that on the Goldsboro Road someone inserted the letters "ugh" to complete the archaic spelling of the town. The sketch was unearthed by Mark Bradley at the National Archives, along with Buell's manuscript report. (Compare with maps titled *Carlin's Probing Attack,* p. 24, and *Robinson's Advance,* p. 26). —Record Group 94, Vol. 47, Box 109, Report Number 617, Office of the Adjutant General, Union Battle Reports. National Archives, Washington, D.C.

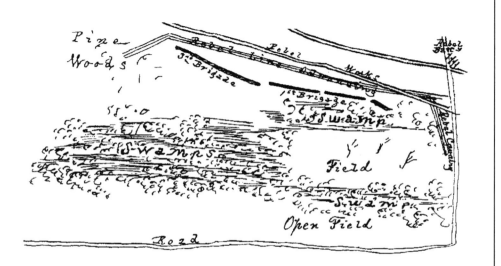

The sketch at left was drawn by Pvt. William David Evans of the 27th Ohio, Fuller's brigade, Mower's division. The scene illustrates Fuller's (1st) and Tillson's (3rd) brigades during Mower's Charge. They are advancing from east to west. Also pictured are the line of rail works originally occupied by Butler's Confederate cavalry, and the Confederate lines during Hardee's counterattack (labeled "Rebel Line Advancing" and "Rebel Cavalry"). The position labeled "Rebel Batty" at the top right denotes William Earle's South Carolina Battery. (Compare with the maps on Mower's Charge, pp. 62-67). —William David Evans Papers, The Western Reserve Historical Society, Cleveland, Ohio.

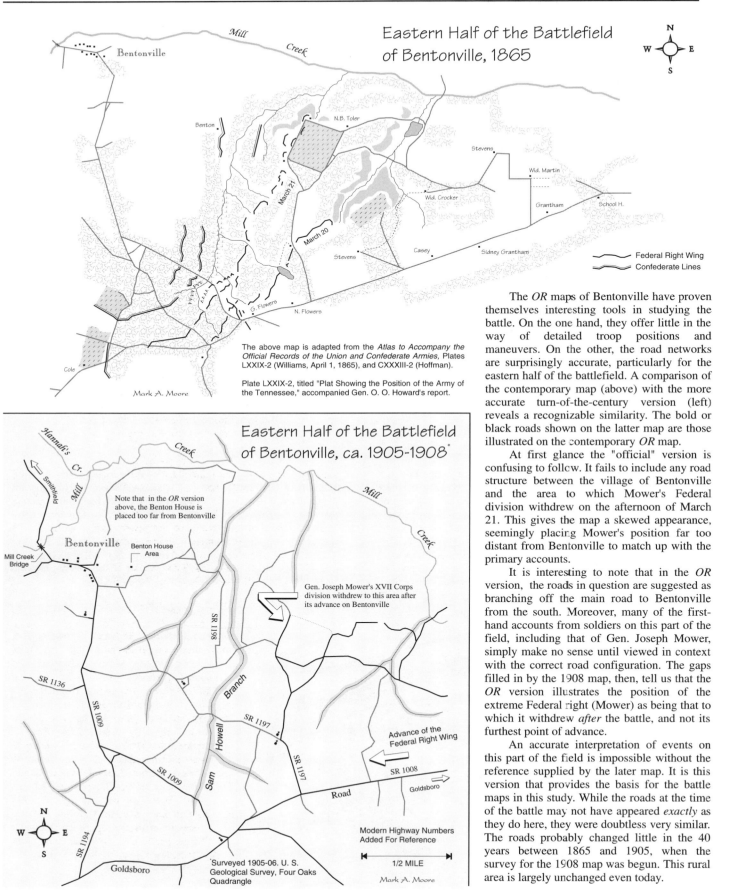

Eastern Half of the Battlefield of Bentonville, 1865

Federal Right Wing
Confederate Lines

The above map is adapted from the *Atlas to Accompany the Official Records of the Union and Confederate Armies*, Plates LXXIX-2 (Williams, April 1, 1865), and CXXXIII-2 (Hoffman).

Plate LXXIX-2, titled "Plat Showing the Position of the Army of the Tennessee," accompanied Gen. O. O. Howard's report.

Mark A. Moore

Eastern Half of the Battlefield of Bentonville, ca. 1905-1908

Note that in the *OR* version above, the Benton House is placed too far from Bentonville

Gen. Joseph Mower's XVII Corps division withdrew to this area after its advance on Bentonville

Advance of the Federal Right Wing

Modern Highway Numbers Added For Reference

Surveyed 1905-06. U. S. Geological Survey, Four Oaks Quadrangle

1/2 MILE

Mark A. Moore

The *OR* maps of Bentonville have proven themselves interesting tools in studying the battle. On the one hand, they offer little in the way of detailed troop positions and maneuvers. On the other, the road networks are surprisingly accurate, particularly for the eastern half of the battlefield. A comparison of the contemporary map (above) with the more accurate turn-of-the-century version (left) reveals a recognizable similarity. The bold or black roads shown on the latter map are those illustrated on the contemporary *OR* map.

At first glance the "official" version is confusing to follow. It fails to include any road structure between the village of Bentonville and the area to which Mower's Federal division withdrew on the afternoon of March 21. This gives the map a skewed appearance, seemingly placing Mower's position far too distant from Bentonville to match up with the primary accounts.

It is interesting to note that in the *OR* version, the roads in question are suggested as branching off the main road to Bentonville from the south. Moreover, many of the first-hand accounts from soldiers on this part of the field, including that of Gen. Joseph Mower, simply make no sense until viewed in context with the correct road configuration. The gaps filled in by the 1908 map, then, tell us that the *OR* version illustrates the position of the extreme Federal right (Mower) as being that to which it withdrew *after* the battle, and not its furthest point of advance.

An accurate interpretation of events on this part of the field is impossible without the reference supplied by the later map. It is this version that provides the basis for the battle maps in this study. While the roads at the time of the battle may not have appeared *exactly* as they do here, they were doubtless very similar. The roads probably changed little in the 40 years between 1865 and 1905, when the survey for the 1908 map was begun. This rural area is largely unchanged even today.

Appendix B

The Opposing Forces in the Battle of Bentonville

ORGANIZATION OF UNION FORCES[1]
Maj. Gen. William T. Sherman, Commanding

Headquarters Guard
7th Company, Ohio Sharpshooters

Engineers and Mechanics
1st Michigan
1st Missouri (five companies)

RIGHT WING
Army of the Tennessee
Maj. Gen. Oliver O. Howard
(Total Casualties: 383)

Escort
15th Illinois Cavalry
4th Company Ohio Cavalry

Pontoon Train Guard
14th Wisconsin (Company E)

FIFTEENTH ARMY CORPS
Maj. Gen. John A. Logan
(Casualties: 190)

First Division (119)
Bvt. Maj. Gen. Charles R. Woods

First Brigade (23)
Bvt. Brig. Gen. William B. Woods
12th Indiana	26th Iowa
27th Missouri	76th Ohio
31st/32nd Missouri (six companies)	

Second Brigade (33)
Col. Robert F. Catterson
26th Illinois	40th Illinois
103rd Illinois	97th Indiana
100th Indiana	6th Iowa
46th Ohio	

Third Brigade (63)
Col. George A. Stone
4th Iowa	9th Iowa
25th Iowa	30th Iowa
31st Iowa	

Second Division (34)

Maj. Gen. William B. Hazen

First Brigade (22)
Col. Theodore Jones
55th Illinois	116th Illinois
127th Illinois	30th Ohio
57th Ohio	
6th Missouri (Cos. A and B, 8th Missouri attached)	

Second Brigade (11)
Col. Wells S. Jones
111th Illinois	83rd Indiana
37th Ohio	47th Ohio
53rd Ohio	54th Ohio

Third Brigade (1)
Brig. Gen. John M. Oliver
48th Illinois	90th Illinois
99th Indiana	15th Michigan
70th Ohio	

Third Division (In Reserve)
Bvt. Maj. Gen. John E. Smith

First Brigade (0)
Brig. Gen. William T. Clark
63rd Illinois	48th Indiana
59th Indiana	4th Minnesota
93rd Illinois (with detachment nonveterans of 18th Wisconsin)	

Second Brigade (0)
Col. Clark R. Wever
56th Illinois	10th Iowa
80th Ohio	
17th Iowa (one company)	
26th Missouri (two companies, and detachment 10th Missouri)	

Fourth Division (32)
Bvt. Maj. Gen. John M. Corse

First Brigade (1)
Brig. Gen. Elliott W. Rice
52nd Illinois	66th Indiana
2nd Iowa	7th Iowa

Second Brigade (9)
Col. Robert N. Adams
12th Illinois	66th Illinois
81st Ohio	

Third Brigade (22)
Col. Frederick J. Hurlbut
7th Illinois	50th Illinois
57th Illinois	39th Iowa

Unassigned (Not Engaged)
110th United States Colored Troops

ARTILLERY (5)

---

[1] This order of battle is based on *OR* 47, pt. 1, pp. 46-55, with corrections based on additional sources. Casualty figures appear as "officially" reported, and are thus subject to minor inaccuracies. They reflect the categories of killed, wounded, and "captured or missing." *OR* 47, pt 1, pp. 67-76.

Lt. Col. William H. Ross

1st Michigan Light, Battery B (Wright's)
1st Illinois Light, Battery H (De Gress')
1st Missouri Light, Battery H (Callahan's)
12th Wisconsin Battery (Zickerick's)

Unassigned (0)
29th Missouri (Mounted)

SEVENTEENTH ARMY CORPS
Maj. Gen. Frank P. Blair, Jr.
(Casualties: 193)

Escort
11th Illinois Cavalry (Company G)

First Division (150)
Maj. Gen. Joseph A. Mower

First Brigade (54)
Brig. Gen. John W. Fuller
| 64th Illinois | 18th Missouri |
| 27th Ohio | 39th Ohio |

Second Brigade[2] (1)
Col. Milton Montgomery
| 35th New Jersey | 43rd Ohio |
| 63rd Ohio | 25th Wisconsin |

Third Brigade (95)
Col. John Tillson
| 10th Illinois | 25th Indiana |
| 32nd Wisconsin | |

Third Division (13)[3]
Brig. Gen. Manning F. Force

Provost Guard
20th Illinois

First Brigade
Col. Cassius Fairchild
30th Illinois	31st Illinois
45th Illinois	12th Wisconsin
16th Wisconsin	

Second Brigade
Col. Greenberry F. Wiles
| 20th Ohio | 68th Ohio |
| 78th Ohio | 17th Wisconsin |

Fourth Division (30)
Bvt. Maj. Gen. Giles A. Smith

First Brigade (4)
Brig. Gen. Benjamin F. Potts
| 53rd Illinois | 23rd Indiana |
| 53rd Indiana | 32nd Ohio |

14th/15th Illinois (battalion)

Third Brigade (26)
Brig. Gen. William W. Belknap
11th Iowa	13th Iowa
15th Iowa	16th Iowa
32nd Illinois	

ARTILLERY (0)
Maj. Allen C. Waterhouse

1st Michigan Light, Battery C (Hyser's)
1st Minnesota Battery (Clayton's)
15th Ohio Battery (Burdick's)

Unassigned (0)
9th Illinois (mounted)

LEFT WING
Army of Georgia
(Late Army of the Cumberland)
Maj. Gen. Henry W. Slocum
(Total Casualties: 1,144)

Pontoniers
58th Indiana

FOURTEENTH ARMY CORPS
Bvt. Maj. Gen. Jefferson C. Davis
(Casualties: 886)

First Division (453)
Brig. Gen. William P. Carlin

First Brigade (159)
Bvt. Brig. Gen. Harrison C. Hobart
104th Illinois	88th Indiana
33rd Ohio	94th Ohio
21st Wisconsin	42nd Indiana

Second Brigade (205)
Bvt. Brig. Gen. George P. Buell
| 13th Michigan[4] | 21st Michigan |
| 69th Ohio | |

Third Brigade (89)
Lt. Col. David Miles (W)
Lt. Col. Arnold McMahan
| 38th Indiana[5] | 21st Ohio |
| 79th Pennsylvania | 74th Ohio[6] |

Second Division (410)[7]
Brig. Gen. James D. Morgan

---

[2] The 25th Wisconsin was the only regiment of Montgomery's brigade to reach the battlefield. The remaining regiments served as train guard.
[3] Losses in Force's division not reported in detail.

---

[4] Commander Maj. Willard G. Eaton killed.
[5] Commander Capt. James H. Low killed.
[6] The 74th Ohio remained in the rear as train guard. Owens, Ira S. *Green County Soldiers*. Dayton: Christian Publishing House, 1884, p. 102.
[7] Number of wounded includes two of Morgan's staff.

Provost Guard
110th Illinois (Company B; Company A, 24th Illinois attached)

First Brigade (149)
Brig. Gen. William Vandever

16th Illinois	60th Illinois
10th Michigan	14th Michigan
17th New York	

Second Brigade (160)
Brig. Gen. John G. Mitchell

34th Illinois	78th Illinois
98th Ohio	108th Ohio
113th Ohio	121st Ohio

Third Brigade (99)
Bvt. Brig. Gen. Benjamin D. Fearing (W)
Lt. Col. James W. Langley

86th Illinois	125th Illinois
22nd Indiana	52nd Ohio
85th Illinois[8]	
37th Indiana (one company)	

Third Division[9] (9)
Bvt. Maj. Gen. Absalom Baird

First Brigade (7)
Col. Morton C. Hunter

82nd Indiana	17th Ohio
31st Ohio	89th Ohio
23rd Missouri (four companies)	
92nd Ohio (11th Ohio attached)	

Second Brigade (2)
Lt. Col. Thomas Doan

75th Indiana	87th Indiana
101st Indiana	2nd Minnesota
105th Ohio	

Third Brigade (Not Engaged)
Col. George P. Este

74th Indiana	18th Kentucky
14th Ohio	38th Ohio

ARTILLERY (14)
Maj. Charles Houghtaling

1st Illinois Light, Battery C (Scovel's)
2nd Illinois Light, Battery I (Rich's)
19th Indiana Battery (Webb's)[10]
5th Wisconsin Battery (McKnight's)

TWENTIETH CORPS
Bvt. Maj. Gen. Alpheus S. Williams
(Casualties: 258)

First Division (117)
Brig. Gen. Nathaniel J. Jackson

First Brigade (3)
Col. James L. Selfridge

5th Connecticut	123rd New York
141st New York	46th Pennsylvania

Second Brigade (7)
Col. William Hawley

2nd Massachusetts	13th New Jersey
107th New York	150th New York
3rd Wisconsin	

Third Brigade (107)
Brig. Gen. James S. Robinson

82nd Illinois	143rd New York
61st Ohio	82nd Ohio
31st Wisconsin	101st Illinois

Second Division[11] (Not Engaged)
Bvt. Maj. Gen. John W. Geary

First Brigade
Bvt. Brig. Gen. Ario Pardee, Jr.

5th Ohio	29th Ohio
66th Ohio	28th Pennsylvania
147th Pennsylvania	

Second Brigade
Col. George W. Mindil

33rd New Jersey	119th New York
134th New York	154th New York
73rd Pennsylvania	
109th Pennsylvania	

Third Brigade
Bvt. Brig. Gen. Henry A. Barnum

60th New York	102nd New York
137th New York	149th New York
29th Pennsylvania	
111th Pennsylvania	

Third Division (139)
Bvt. Maj. Gen. William T. Ward

First Brigade (2)
Col. Henry Case

70th Indiana	79th Ohio
102nd Illinois	105th Illinois
129th Illinois	

Second Brigade (0)
Col. Daniel Dustin

33rd Indiana	85th Indiana
19th Michigan	22nd Wisconsin

Third Brigade (137)

---

[8] The 85th Illinois remained in the rear as train guard. *OR* 47, pt. 1, p. 534.
[9] The Third Division remained with the trains on March 19, and arrived at the battlefield on March 20. The Third Brigade remained in the rear on train guard duty.
[10] Commander Lt. Samuel D. Webb killed.

[11] The Second Division remained in the rear as train guard. The First and Third Brigades reached the battlefield on March 20.

Bvt. Brig. Gen. William Cogswell
20th Connecticut   55th Ohio
73rd Ohio   136th New York
26th Wisconsin
33rd Massachusetts

ARTILLERY (2)
Maj. John A. Reynolds

1st New York Light, Battery I (Winegar's)
1st New York Light, Battery M (Newkirk's)
1st Ohio Light, Battery C (Stephens')
Pennsylvania Light, Battery E (Sloan's)[12]

CAVALRY

Third Division[13]
Bvt. Maj. Gen. Judson Kilpatrick

First Brigade
Col. Thomas J. Jordan
8th Indiana   2nd Kentucky
3rd Kentucky   9th Pennsylvania
3rd Indiana (battalion)

Second Brigade
Bvt. Brig. Gen. Smith D. Atkins
9th Ohio   10th Ohio
9th Michigan
92nd Illinois (mounted)
McLaughlin's Squadron (Ohio)

Third Brigade
Col. George E. Spencer
1st Alabama   5th Kentucky
5th Ohio

Fourth Brigade (provisional)[14]
Lt. Col. William B. Way
1st Regiment   2nd Regiment
3rd Regiment

ARTILLERY

10th Wisconsin Battery (Beebe's)

Bentonville's Medal of Honor Winners

Pvt. Peter T. Anderson: 31st Wisconsin, Robinson's brigade, for single-handedly saving one gun and team of the 19th Indiana Battery during the rout of Carlin's division. Received personal thanks of Sherman. Commissioned captain. (Issued June 16, 1865).

Cpl. George W. Clute: 14th Michigan, Vandever's brigade, for capturing the regimental flag of the 40th North Carolina from a lieutenant who carried and defended it. (Applied for through Congress and issued August 26, 1898).

Lt. Allan H. Dougall: Adjutant, 88th Indiana, Hobart's brigade, for voluntarily returning to the fallen color bearer to save the regimental flag from capture. (Applied for through Congress and issued February 16, 1897).

Pvt. Henry E. Plant: 14th Michigan, Vandever's brigade, for rescuing the regimental colors when the bearer, Sgt. Ezra Davis, was mortally wounded. (Applied for through Congress and issued April 27, 1896).

---

[12] Not engaged. The battery arrived with Geary on March 20.
[13] Not actively engaged.
[14] Composed of dismounted men from the Third Division, with regimental numbers coinciding with the parent brigade numbers.

State Archives of Michigan

Maj. Willard G. Eaton: A native of New York, Willard Gould Eaton (above) was residing in Otsego, Michigan, at the outbreak of the Civil War. When the 13th Michigan Infantry was mustered in at nearby Kalamazoo in 1862, he entered the service as 1st Lieutenant of Company I, leaving behind a wife and two young daughters. He was 40 years old. Like many soldiers of his era, Eaton was a faithful writer of letters. As his regiment passed through the great campaigns and battles of the Western Theater, he diligently recorded scenes of war and camp life for loved ones on the home front. And he yearned for their replies. "I hear from my family often," he wrote in 1862. "They are very anxious for my return and I am sure it will be a pleasure....to once more have the privilege of enjoying home and the society of friends." That summer he confided to his niece, Elizabeth, that "one consideration only keeps me here—my country."

By the summer of 1863, Eaton had risen to the rank of major. After the Battle of Chickamauga, in which the 13th suffered a casualty rate of nearly 50 percent, his attitude toward war changed from fascination to grim pragmatism: "Surely we are not exempt from death anywhere," he explained to his daughter and son-in-law that November, "but while it comes singly in civil life it is sown broadcast here. In civil life a single corpse fills a man's mind with horror, while here he will take shelter from a storm of bullets behind them, wishing there was more, making his bed among them for the night without a thought even that he may be counted amongst them the next hour."

By January 1865, Willard was due to leave the army. "I have not fully decided whether I shall go home on the 17th," he wrote. "My time is out then." His impending discharge notwithstanding, March 19, 1865, found Maj. Eaton in command of the 13th Michigan in North Carolina, and preparing to attack the Confederate Army of Tennessee at Bentonville.

When the 21st Michigan and 69th Ohio were roughly handled that morning by Confederates concealed in the woods to their front, the 13th Michigan charged through the front rank and assaulted the Rebel position. The attack crested in front of Henry Clayton's and Pat Cleburne's divisions, and the 13th's color bearer was severely wounded. Willard Eaton, shot through the brain, fell dead at the head of his regiment. Buell's brigade, to which the 13th Michigan belonged, fell back and was soon driven from the field by the last grand charge of the Army of Tennessee. The 13th suffered 106 casualties, the highest loss of any Federal regiment at Bentonville.

On the morning of March 22, the 13th's Charles F. Bowman was out with a burial party and "found Major Eaton stripped of all but underclothes [and] covered in a hole with 7 others." The late lamented major would not remain long in a Southern grave. His body was retrieved by family members and taken home to Michigan, where he is buried in his home town of Otsego. Prior to Bentonville, Eaton had been promoted to the rank of colonel, but his commission did not arrive until after his death.

ORGANIZATION OF CONFEDERATE FORCES[15]
Gen. Joseph E. Johnston, Commanding

ARMY OF TENNESSEE
Lt. Gen. Alexander P. Stewart
(Total Casualties: 1,227)

LEE'S CORPS (761)
Maj. Gen. D. H. Hill

Stevenson's Division (366)
Maj. Gen. Carter L. Stevenson

Palmer's Brigade
Brig. Gen. Joseph B. Palmer

3rd Tennessee	18th Tennessee
26th Tennessee	32nd Tennessee
45th Tennessee	46th Tennessee[16]
54th Virginia	63rd Virginia

58th North Carolina
60th North Carolina
23rd Tennessee Battalion

Pettus' Brigade
Brig. Gen. Edmund W. Pettus (W)

20th Alabama	23rd Alabama
30th Alabama	31st Alabama

46th Alabama

Cumming's Brigade (Arrived on the battlefield March 20)
Col. Robert J. Henderson

34th Georgia	36th Georgia
39th Georgia	56th Georgia

Clayton's Division (290)
Maj. Gen. Henry D. Clayton

Stovall's Brigade
Col. Henry C. Kellogg

40th Georgia	41st Georgia
42nd Georgia	43rd Georgia

52nd Georgia

Jackson's Brigade
Lt. Col. Osceola Kyle

25th Georgia	29th Georgia
30th Georgia	66th Georgia

1st Confederate
1st Battalion Georgia Sharpshooters

Baker's Brigade

Brig. Gen. Alpheus Baker

37th Alabama	40th Alabama
42nd Alabama	54th Alabama

Hill's Division (105)
Col. John G. Coltart

Deas' Brigade
Col. Harry T. Toulmin

19th Alabama	22nd Alabama
25th Alabama	39th Alabama

50th Alabama

Manigault's Brigade
Lt. Col. John C. Carter

24th Alabama	34th Alabama

10th South Carolina
19th South Carolina

STEWART'S CORPS (223)
Maj. Gen. William W. Loring

Loring's Division (153)
Col. James Jackson

Adams' Brigade
Lt. Col. Robert J. Lawrence

6th Mississippi	14th Mississippi
15th Mississippi[17]	20th Mississippi
23rd Mississippi	43rd Mississippi

Scott's Brigade
Capt. John A. Dixon

27th Alabama	35th Alabama
49th Alabama	55th Alabama
57th Alabama	12th Louisiana

Featherston's Brigade
Maj. Martin A. Oatis

1st Mississippi	3rd Mississippi
22nd Mississippi	33rd Mississippi
31st Mississippi	40th Mississippi

1st Mississippi Battalion

Walthall's Division (70)
Maj. Gen. Edward C. Walthall

Reynolds' Brigade
Brig. Gen. Daniel H. Reynolds (W)
Col. Henry G. Bunn (W)
Lt. Col. Morton G. Galloway

4th Arkansas	9th Arkansas

25th Arkansas
1st Arkansas Mounted Rifles (dismounted)
2nd Arkansas Mounted Rifles (dismounted)

Quarles' Brigade

---

[15] Regiments, battalions and batteries are listed individually to credit all units represented on the field of battle. By March 1865, many of these depleted and campaign-weary entities were consolidated, with some brigades having two or more units combined under a single commander. Thus Bentonville-specific command structures at the regimental level cannot be determined in every case. The army was partly reorganized at the end of March and again, more radically, April 9, 1865. Casualty figures appear as "officially" reported, and are thus subject to minor inaccuracies. They reflect the categories of killed, wounded, and missing. See *OR* 47, pt. 1, pp. 1060-1066, and *OR* 47, pt. 3, pp. 732-736.

[16] The Confederate troop roster for March 31, 1865, lists the 46th Tennessee simultaneously in Palmer's and Quarles' Brigades. *OR* 47, pt. 3, pp. 733, 735.

[17] The Confederate troop roster for March 31, 1865, lists the 15th Mississippi simultaneously in Adams' and Lowrey's Brigades. *OR* 47, pt. 3, pp. 734, 736.

Brig. Gen. George D. Johnston

1st Alabama	17th Alabama
29th Alabama	42nd Tennessee
48th Tennessee	49th Tennessee
53rd Tennessee	55th Tennessee

CHEATHAM'S CORPS (243)
Maj. Gen. William B. Bate

Cleburne's Division (112)[18]
Brig. Gen. James A. Smith

Govan's Brigade
Col. Peter V. Green

1st Arkansas	2nd Arkansas
5th Arkansas	6th Arkansas
7th Arkansas	8th Arkansas
13th Arkansas	15th Arkansas
19th Arkansas	24th Arkansas
3rd Confederate	

Smith's Brigade
Capt. J. R. Bonner

54th Georgia	57th Georgia
63rd Georgia	
1st Georgia (Volunteers)	

Granbury's Brigade
Maj. William A. Ryan

35th Tennessee	6th Texas
7th Texas	10th Texas
15th Texas	17th Texas
18th Texas	24th Texas
25th Texas	5th Confederate

Lowrey's Brigade[19]
(Arrived on the battlefield March 21)
Lt. Col. John F. Smith

3rd Mississippi	8th Mississippi
16th Alabama	32nd Mississippi

Bate's Division (131)[20]
Col. D. L. Kenan (W)

Tyler's Brigade
Maj. W. H. Wilkinson (K)

2nd Tennessee	10th Tennessee
15th Tennessee	20th Tennessee
30th Tennessee	37th Tennessee
37th Georgia	
4th Georgia Battalion Sharpshooters	

Finley's Brigade
Lt. Col. Eli Washburn

1st Florida	3rd Florida
4th Florida	6th Florida
7th Florida	
1st Florida Cavalry (dismounted)	

Brown's Division[21]
Brig. Gen. Roswell S. Ripley

Gist's Brigade
Col. Hume R. Feild

46th Georgia	65th Georgia
16th South Carolina	
24th South Carolina	
3rd Georgia Battalion	
2nd Battalion Georgia Sharpshooters	

Maney's Brigade
Lt. Col. Christopher C. McKinney

1st Tennessee	8th Tennessee
16th Tennessee	27th Tennessee
28th Tennessee	

Strahl's Brigade
Col. James D. Tillman

4th Tennessee	5th Tennessee
19th Tennessee	24th Tennessee
31st Tennessee	33rd Tennessee
38th Tennessee	41st Tennessee

Vaughan's Brigade
Col. William P. Bishop

11th Tennessee	12th Tennessee
13th Tennessee	29th Tennessee
47th Tennessee	51st Tennessee
52nd Tennessee	154th Tennessee

DEPARTMENT OF NORTH CAROLINA
Gen. Braxton Bragg
(Total Casualties: 740)

Hoke's Division[22] (734)
(From the Army of Northern Virginia)
Maj. Gen. Robert F. Hoke

Clingman's Brigade
Col. William S. Devane (W)

8th North Carolina	31st North Carolina
51st North Carolina	61st North Carolina[23]

Kirkland's Brigade

---

[18] Casualty figure for March 19 only (i.e., Smith and Govan).

[19] Lowrey appears as "Lowry" on the Confederate troop roster for March 31, 1865. *OR* 47, pt. 3, p. 736.

[20] Casualty figure for March 19 only.

[21] Frank Cheatham led Brown's Division into the fight. This division was officially reported as "not engaged," and its casualty figures are thus omitted. Though it saw limited action on March 21, the unit did suffer casualties: Col. William P. Bishop, commanding Vaughan's Brigade, reported "half a dozen brave fellows killed, and as many more wounded" in his command alone. *OR* 47, pt. 1, p. 1060; Lindsley, *Military Annals of Tennessee.*

[22] Though Hoke's Division belonged to the Army of Northern Virginia, it was operating at Bentonville with several local detachments. These included three companies of the 13th Battalion North Carolina Light Artillery, three regiments and one battalion of North Carolina Junior Reserves, and two regiments and one battalion from the Cape Fear coastal artillery garrisons (brigaded with Johnson Hagood's South Carolinians). Also attached was the brigade of Col. John N. Whitford, consisting of the 67th and 68th North Carolina Regiments. Whitford's units were formed late in the war from North Carolina local defense troops. They were actively engaged at Cox's Bridge on March 20, 1865.

[23] Commander Lt. Col. Edward G. Mallett killed.

Brig. Gen. William W. Kirkland
17th North Carolina
42nd North Carolina
66th North Carolina

Hagood's Brigade
Brig. Gen. Johnson Hagood

Contingent of Lt. Col. James H. Rion:

11th South Carolina	21st South Carolina
25th South Carolina	27th South Carolina

7th South Carolina Battalion

Contingent of Lt. Col. John D. Taylor (W):
36th North Carolina
1st North Carolina Battalion Heavy
Artillery (9th North Carolina Battalion)
Adams' Battery (Company D, 13th
Battalion North Carolina Light Artillery)

Contingent of Maj. William A. Holland:
40th North Carolina

Colquitt's Brigade
Col. Charles T. Zachry

6th Georgia	19th Georgia
23rd Georgia	27th Georgia
28th Georgia	

North Carolina Junior Reserves Brigade
Col. John H. Nethercutt
70th North Carolina (1st Junior Reserves)
71st North Carolina (2nd Junior Reserves)
72nd North Carolina (3rd Junior Reserves)
20th Battalion North Carolina Junior Reserves

ARTILLERY[24]

13th Battalion NC Light Artillery[25] (6)
Lt. Col. Joseph B. Starr

Atkins' Battery (Company B)
Dickson's Battery (Company E)

---

[24] The following artillery batteries may have been present with Hoke's Division: *3rd NC Battalion* Co. A, Capt. Andrew J. Ellis; Co. B, Capt. William Badham, Jr.; and detachments, Co. C, Lt. Alfred M. Darden. *10th NC (detachment)* Co. I, Capt. Thomas J. Southerland; *Sampson Artillery*, Capt. Abner M. Moseley; and the *Staunton Hill (Virginia) Battery*, Capt. Andrew B. Paris. If these units were present, no accounts have surfaced to state specifically where on the field, or with what brigade, they served. It is also unclear whether they served as infantry or artillery. See *OR* 47, pt. 3, p. 1155.

[25] The six companies of this battalion were widely scattered in March 1865. Company F was attached to James Longstreet's Corps of the Army of Northern Virginia; Company A was operating out of Weldon, North Carolina; and one section of Company C, known as Cumming's Battery, was stationed at Kinston, North Carolina. It may have been this section of Cumming's Battery that, with Col. John Whitford's Brigade, opposed the Federal Right Wing at Cox's Bridge near Goldsboro. Of the three companies present at Bentonville Company D (Adams' Battery) probably fought as infantry with Hagood's Brigade, while Companies B and E (Atkins' and Dickson's Batteries) fought as artillery under the direct command of Colonel Starr. Manarin, *North Carolina Troops.* 1, pp. 551, 558, 568, 576, 585, 594.

DEPARTMENT OF SOUTH CAROLINA, GEORGIA, AND FLORIDA

HARDEE'S CORPS
Lt. Gen. William J. Hardee
(Total Casualties: 526)

Taliaferro's Division (323)
Brig. Gen. William B. Taliaferro

Elliott's Brigade
Brig. Gen. Stephen Elliott, Jr. (W)
22nd Georgia Battalion
28th Georgia Battalion (Bonaud's)
2nd South Carolina Heavy Artillery
Hanleiter's Battalion
Gist Guard Artillery

Rhett's Brigade
Col. William Butler
1st South Carolina Infantry (Regulars)
1st South Carolina Heavy Artillery
Lucas' South Carolina Battalion

McLaws' Division (203)
Maj. Gen. Lafayette McLaws

Conner's Brigade
Brig. Gen. John D. Kennedy

2nd South Carolina	3rd South Carolina
7th South Carolina	8th South Carolina
15th South Carolina	20th South Carolina
3rd South Carolina Battalion	

Fiser's Brigade
Col. John C. Fiser

1st Georgia Regulars	5th Georgia Reserves
6th Georgia Reserves	27th Georgia Battalion
2nd Georgia Battalion Reserves	

Harrison's Brigade
Col. George P. Harrison

5th Georgia	32nd Georgia
47th Georgia	

Hardy's Brigade
Col. Washington Hardy
50th North Carolina
10th North Carolina Battalion
77th North Carolina (7th Senior Reserves)

Blanchard's Brigade (Not Engaged)
Brig. Gen. Albert G. Blanchard
1st Battalion South Carolina Reserves
2nd Battalion South Carolina Reserves
6th Battalion South Carolina Reserves
7th Battalion South Carolina Reserves
Kay's Company, South Carolina Reserves

Battalion Artillery
Maj. A. Burnet Rhett

LeGardeur's Battery
H. M. Stuart's Battery (Beaufort Light Artillery)

CAVALRY COMMAND
Lt. Gen. Wade Hampton
(Total Casualties: 113)

WHEELER'S CORPS (61)
Maj. Gen. Joseph Wheeler
(Army of Tennessee)

Humes' Division
Col. Henry M. Ashby

Thomas Harrison's Brigade
Col. Baxter Smith
3rd Arkansas Cav.   4th Tennessee Cav.
8th Texas Cav.   11th Texas Cav.

Ashby's Brigade
Lt. Col. James H. Lewis
1st Tennessee Cav.   2nd Tennessee Cav.
5th Tennessee Cav.
9th Tennessee Battalion

Allen's Division
Brig. Gen. William W. Allen

Hagan's Brigade
Col. D. G. White
1st Alabama Cav.   3rd Alabama Cav.
9th Alabama Cav.   12th Alabama Cav.
51st Alabama Cav.   53rd Alabama Cav.
24th Alabama Battalion

Anderson's Brigade
Brig. Gen. Robert H. Anderson
3rd Confederate Cav.   8th Confederate Cav.
10th Confederate Cav.
5th Georgia Cav.

Dibrell's Division
Col. George G. Dibrell

Dibrell's Brigade
Col. William S. McLemore
4th Tennessee (McLemore's) Cav.
13th Tennessee Cav.
Shaw's Tennessee Battalion

Breckinridge's Brigade (formerly Lewis')
Col. W. C. P. Breckinridge
1st Kentucky Cav.   2nd Kentucky Cav.
9th Kentucky Cav.
2nd Kentucky Mounted Infantry
4th Kentucky Mounted Infantry
5th Kentucky Mounted Infantry
6th Kentucky Mounted Infantry
9th Kentucky Mounted Infantry

Butler's Division (45)

Maj. Gen. M. C. Butler
Brig. Gen. Evander M. Law
(From the Army of Northern Virginia)

Young's Brigade
Col. Gilbert J. Wright
10th Georgia Cav.   Jeff Davis Legion
Cobb's Georgia Legion
Phillips' Georgia Legion

Butler's Brigade
Brig. Gen. Evander M. Law
Brig. Gen. Thomas M. Logan
4th South Carolina Cav.
5th South Carolina Cav.
6th South Carolina Cav.

HORSE ARTILLERY

Earle's South Carolina Battery
Hart's (Halsey's) South Carolina Battery (7)

Brig. Gen. Daniel H. Reynolds: Reynolds' Brigade joined the Army of Tennessee's line north of the Cole farm on March 19, 1865, amid incoming rounds from Lt. Palmer Scovel's Federal battery: "Here old Bob, General Reynolds' horse, that he had ridden since the spring of 1862....was killed," remembered Robert Dacus of the 1st Arkansas Mounted Rifles, "and General Reynolds lost one of his legs at the same time." "[The shell] entered my horse's breast," wrote Reynolds (above), "& came out....tearing off a great part of the calf of [my] leg & then killed a horse standing next to mine....I threw myself out of the saddle, falling on the dead horse, the blood from my Horse's side spurting over me....the noble animal still standing tho' a stream of blood larger than my arm was gushing from his breast."—Robert H. Dacus. *Reminiscences of Company "H," First Arkansas Mounted Rifles.* Dardanelle, Ark.: Post-Dispatch Print, 1897. / D. H. Reynolds Diary, March 19, 1865, D. H. Reynolds Papers, University of Arkansas, Fayetteville, Arkansas.

Appendix C — Historical Marker Reference Guide

The table below lists the battlefield markers with reference to where each can be found on a map.

Battle of Bentonville

Highway Historical Markers	Map Titles/Page Numbers
Bentonville (21)	Mower's Charge: The Push Toward Mill Creek Bridge / 62 Mower's Charge: Hardee's Counterattack / 64 Mower's Charge: The Attack Stalls / 66 Battle's End: Securing Mill Creek Bridge / 68
Cole Farmhouse (12)	Carlin Deploys to Clear the Road / 22 Carlin's Probing Attack / 24 Robinson's Advance / 26 Last Grand Charge of the Army of Tennessee / 28 Skirmishing at Cole's Farm / 58
Confederate Attacks (10)	Taliaferro Moves on the XX Corps at Morris' Farm / 40 Bate's Attack at Morris' Farm / 42 Hardy & Harrison Advance at Nightfall / 44
Confederate Cemetery (7)	Battlefield of Bentonville (only) / 18
Confederate Hospital (3)	Battlefield of Bentonville (only) / 18
Confederate Main Charge (11)	Last Grand Charge of the Army of Tennessee / 28 Fearing's Counterattack / 30 Morgan's Stand: Hoke's Frontal Assault / 32 Morgan's Stand: Hill's Advance from the Rear / 34 Morgan's Stand: Cogswell's Advance & Vandever's Counterattack / 36 McLaws' Advance / 38 Taliaferro Moves on the XX Corps at Morris' Farm / 40 Bate's Attack at Morris' Farm / 42 Hardy & Harrison Advance at Nightfall / 44
Confederate Works (22)	Battle's End: Securing Mill Creek Bridge / 68
Federal Artillery (9)	Morgan's Stand: Hill's Advance from the Rear / 34 Morgan's Stand: Cogswell's Advance & Vandever's Counterattack / 36 McLaws' Advance / 38 Taliaferro Moves on the XX Corps at Morris' Farm / 40 Bate's Attack at Morris' Farm / 42 Hardy & Harrison Advance at Nightfall / 44
Federal Earthworks (5)	Taliaferro Moves on the XX Corps at Morris' Farm / 40 Bate's Attack at Morris' Farm / 42 Hardy & Harrison Advance at Nightfall / 44 Slocum Occupies the Battleground of March 19 / 52 Skirmishing at Cole's Farm / 58
Federal Junction (18)	Deployment of the Federal Right Wing / 54 Extending the Confederate Left / 56 Howard Engages the Confederate Left / 60
Fighting Below the Road (13)	Morgan's Stand: Hoke's Frontal Assault / 32 Morgan's Stand: Hill's Advance from the Rear / 34 Morgan's Stand: Cogswell's Advance & Vandever's Counterattack / 36

Mower's Attack (26)	Mower's Charge: The Push Toward Mill Creek Bridge / 62
	Mower's Charge: Hardee's Counterattack / 64
	Mower's Charge: The Attack Stalls / 66
	Battle's End: Securing Mill Creek Bridge / 68
N. C. Junior Reserves (16)	Carlin Deploys to Clear the Road / 22
	Carlin's Probing Attack / 24
	Robinson's Advance / 26
	Last Grand Charge of the Army of Tennessee / 28
	Fearing's Counterattack / 30
	Morgan's Stand: Hoke's Frontal Assault / 32
	Morgan's Stand: Hill's Advance from the Rear / 34
	Morgan's Stand: Cogswell's Advance & Vandever's Counterattack / 36
	The Pursuit of Hoke's Division / 50
Sherman (1)	Howard Turns West Toward Bentonville / 46
Union Headquarters (29)	Deployment of the Federal Right Wing / 54
	Extending the Confederate Left / 56
Union Headquarters (4)	Morgan's Stand: Hill's Advance from the Rear / 34
	Morgan's Stand: Cogswell's Advance & Vandever's Counterattack / 36
	McLaws' Advance / 38
	Taliaferro Moves on the XX Corps at Morris' Farm / 40
	Bate's Attack at Morris' Farm / 42
	Hardy & Harrison Advance at Nightfall / 44
	Slocum Occupies the Battleground of March 19 / 52
	Skirmishing at Cole's Farm / 58
Union Headquarters (8)	Morgan's Stand: Hoke's Frontal Assault / 32
	Morgan's Stand: Hill's Advance from the Rear / 34
	Morgan's Stand: Cogswell's Advance & Vandever's Counterattack / 36
	McLaws' Advance / 38
	Taliaferro Moves on the XX Corps at Morris' Farm / 40
	Bate's Attack at Morris' Farm / 42
	Hardy & Harrison Advance at Nightfall / 44
	Slocum Occupies the Battleground of March 19 / 52
	Skirmishing at Cole's Farm / 58
Union Hospital (2)	Battlefield of Bentonville (only) / 18
Union Hospital (6)	Battlefield of Bentonville (only) / 18
Union Line — March 20 (28)	Deployment of the Federal Right Wing / 54
	Extending the Confederate Left / 56
Union Line — March 21 (27)	Battle's End: Securing Mill Creek Bridge / 68

Battle of Averasboro

Highway Historical Markers	**Map Titles/Page Numbers**
Battle of Averasboro — **Phase One** (2)	Battlefield of Averasboro (only) / 8
Battle of Averasboro — **Phase Two** (8)	Battle of Averasboro: Case's Attack / 12
	Battle of Averasboro: Arrival of the XIV Corps / 14

Confederate First Line (3)	Battle of Averasboro: Case's Attack / 12
	Battle of Averasboro: Arrival of the XIV Corps / 14
Confederate Second Line (7)	Battle of Averasboro: Case's Attack / 12
	Battle of Averasboro: Arrival of the XIV Corps / 14
Federal Artillery (6)	Battle of Averasboro: Case's Attack / 12
	Battle of Averasboro: Arrival of the XIV Corps / 14
Federal Hospital (11)	Battlefield of Averasboro (only) / 8
Lebanon (10)	Battlefield of Averasboro (only) / 8
Oak Grove (5)	Battle of Averasboro: Case's Attack / 12
	Battle of Averasboro: Arrival of the XIV Corps / 14
Prelude to Averasboro (1)	Battlefield of Averasboro (only) / 8
Rhett's Brigade (4)	Battle of Averasboro: Case's Attack / 12
	Battle of Averasboro: Arrival of the XIV Corps / 14
Union Headquarters (9)	Battle of Averasboro: Arrival of the XIV Corps / 14

Harper's Weekly

Village of Bentonville

The above sketch was made just after the battle by Theo Davis, a civilian artist employed by *Harper's Weekly,* who was traveling with Sherman's headquarters staff. The view faces west, with mounted soldiers standing in the road. Just beyond the background, the road curved to the north before crossing the "rude bridge of logs" over Mill Creek. Today the road is SR 1009 (the Devil's Racetrack).

"Bentonville is a wretched village of five or six mud hovels, in Johnston County, North Carolina. It is five miles south of the Neuse River, and twenty miles west of Goldsboro. Mill Creek is a small, shallow, stream of water, hardly reaching the dignity of a creek.[1] It is skirted generally by lowlands and considerable swamps."—**Capt. George W. Pepper**, war correspondent traveling with the Federal Right Wing. *Personal Recollections of Sherman's Campaigns in Georgia and the Carolinas.* Zanesville, Ohio: Hugh Dunne, 1866.

E. D. Westfall, a *New York Herald* correspondent accompanying the Federal Left Wing, referred to this tiny hamlet as "the spot on the map known as Bentonsville [sic]."[2] "[John A.] Logan's [XV] corps went into Bentonsville," he wrote, "and brought off a large number of our wounded left by the enemy in his hasty flight. Many of their wounded were found and paroled, and everywhere along the line of their retreat dead rebels were found....[N]o point could be selected in that pine woods where rebel dead were not in view." —*New York Herald*, March 30, 1865.

Passing through several weeks later, one of A. H. Terry's soldiers noted that Bentonville consisted of "scarcely a dozen small unpainted weather-beaten dwellings. Two or three of these primitive tenements were still occupied by several severely wounded rebel soldiers. They were destitute of hospital conveniences." —Mowris, J. A. *History of the One Hundred and Seventeenth New York Volunteers.* Hartford: Case, Lockwood & Company, 1866.

---

[1] Captain Pepper seems to describe either the Sam Howell Branch or Mill Creek at its normal level—a condition he did not witness. Mill Creek was at flood stage during the battle, making the safety of Mill Creek Bridge Joseph E. Johnston's highest priority on March 21, 1865.

[2] "Bentonsville" was a commonly used early spelling. This was how William T. Sherman and many other participants referred to the battle.

Appendix D

Casualties and Other Numbers

At the beginning of March 1865, the effective strength of Sherman's "army group" was reported as follows:[1]

RIGHT WING (Army of the Tennessee)

Corps	Infantry	Cavalry	Artillery	Total
XV Corps (Logan)	14,809	14	362	15,185
XVII Corps (Blair)	11,116	46	271	11,433
	25,925	60	633	**26,618**

LEFT WING (Army of Georgia)

Corps	Infantry	Artillery	Total
XIV Corps (Slocum)	12,763	445	13,208
XX Corps (Williams)	12,910	504	13,414
	25,673	949	**26,622**

	Cavalry	Artillery	Total
Kilpatrick *(Third Division)*	4,341	95	4,436
		Aggregate =	**57,676**

Johnston's approximate effective force at Bentonville:[2]

Command	Strength
Army of Tennessee	4,500
Hoke's Division	5,557
Hardee's Corps	5,955
Hampton's Cavalry	4,000
Aggregate =	**20,012**

On March 19 Johnston carried about 16,000 infantry into the fight, and by late afternoon Slocum's Federal Left Wing had about 20,000 men on the field. Johnston received some 1,500 additional reserve troops during March 20-21, a portion of which saw limited action. (See Appendix B: *The Opposing Forces in the Battle of Bentonville.* For a discussion of Monroe's Crossroads, see p. 5.)

CASUALTIES[3]

AVERASBORO:

Command	Loss	Engaged
Official Union loss	682[4]	12,000 (principal)[5]
Confederate loss	500 (approx.)	6,455 (plus Wheeler)
Aggregate =	**1,182** (approx.)	

---

[1] See *OR* 47, pt. 1, p. 43.

[2] Bradley, *Last Stand,* p. 138. *OR* 47, pt. 2, p. 1424. By March 15, 1865, Hardee's Corps had dwindled to approximately 6,455 effectives. The figure 5,955 listed above is less Hardee's approximate loss of 500 at Averasboro, March 16. *OR* 47, pt. 2, pp. 1386, 1397. *OR* 47, pt. 3, p. 707.

[3] As officially reported: *OR* 47, pt. 1, pp. 63-76, 1060.

[4] 95 killed, 533 wounded, and 54 captured or missing. *OR* 47, pt. 1, p. 66.

[5] Two XX Corps divisions and Kilpatrick's cavalry. Bradley, *Last Stand,* p. 123. Specific losses reported: XX Corps = 485; XIV Corps = 116; Kilpatrick = 81. *OR* 47, pt. 1, p. 66. By day's end the Federals fielded some 20,000 men.

BENTONVILLE:

FEDERAL:

Type	Number
Killed	194
Wounded	1,112
Captured or Missing	221
Aggregate =	**1,527**

CONFEDERATE:

Type	Number
Killed	239[6]
Wounded	1,694
Missing	673
Aggregate =	**2,606**
Grand Total =	**4,133**

The exact number of casualties on both sides at Bentonville will never be known. Records are sketchy at best, and there are many conflicting reports. In their post-war memoirs both Sherman and Johnston published figures that differ from those in the *Official Records.* Sherman put the Federal loss at 1,604, while Johnston stated a Confederate loss of 2,343. Johnston further claimed a total of 903 Union prisoners, while Sherman claimed only 296 missing. These figures for captured and missing do not match the official numbers. Sherman's estimate of Confederate prisoners is far too high, as he mistakenly uses Oliver O. Howard's figure for the entire campaign (1,287). Slocum reported capturing 338 prisoners at Bentonville.[7]

The official tallies are probably low. Even if they were increased an additional ten percent, the numbers pale when compared to those of larger battles fought earlier in the war. Such comparisons have given rise to a sort of "Gettysburg mentality" among enthusiasts of the conflict, whereby a battle's importance and interest-holding qualities are based largely upon its casualty returns. Bentonville occurred in the twilight of the rebellion, by which time ideals, attitudes and methods of combat had undergone drastic changes. Battles fought in 1865 were different from those of 1862.

As always, terrain played a significant role. The dense pine woods and thickets around Bentonville helped absorb projectiles that might have done more damage to troops fighting on open ground. This was especially true south of the Goldsboro Road—in the engagement between Hoke and Morgan, as well as that between Cogswell and the Confederate commands of Loring, Walthall and Kennedy. An exception to this was the fight at Morris' Farm. Here the inexperienced Confederate garrison troops of Taliaferro's Division, together with Bate's veterans, attacked a portion of the Federal XX Corps. These assaults met with disaster in a large open field, where Robinson's brigade and the massed artillery of the XX Corps held commanding positions.

While figures for all three engagements remain inexact, the combined losses for Monroe's Crossroads, Averasboro and Bentonville equal close to 6,000 men.

---

[6] The battlefield monument erected by the Goldsboro Rifles in 1893 claims to mark a mass grave containing 360 Confederates who died at Bentonville.

[7] Johnston, *Narrative,* p. 393; Sherman, *Memoirs,* 2, p. 305. The author's own casualty study (some 1,600 names to date) reveals minor inconsistencies among recorded small unit losses.

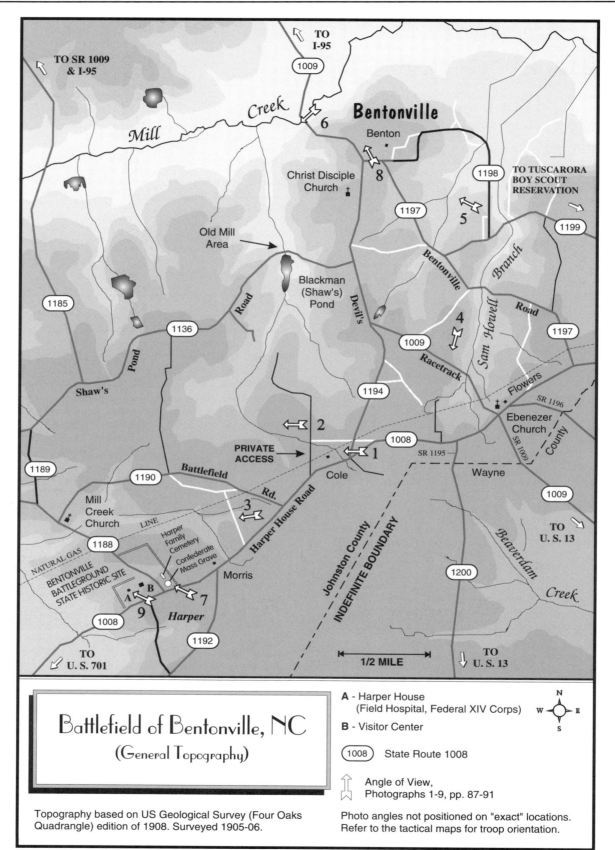

TO I-95

1009

TO SR 1009 & I-95

Mill Creek

6

Bentonville

Benton

8

Christ Disciple Church

1198

TO TUSCARORA BOY SCOUT RESERVATION

1197

5

1199

Old Mill Area

Blackman (Shaw's) Pond

Devil's

Road

Bentonville

Branch

Sam Horvell

Road

1185

1136

1009

4

1197

Shaw's

Pond

Racetrack

Flowers

SR 1196

1194

Ebenezer Church

SR 1009

PRIVATE ACCESS

2

1008

SR 1195

1189

Battlefield

1

Cole

Wayne

1190

Rd.

Harper House Road

Johnston County

1009

Mill Creek Church

3

TO U.S. 13

LINE

1188

Harper Family Cemetery

Confederate Mass Grave

Morris

INDEFINITE BOUNDARY

1200

Beaverdam

Creek

NATURAL GAS

BENTONVILLE BATTLEGROUND STATE HISTORIC SITE

A B

7

9

Harper

1008

1192

TO U.S. 701

1/2 MILE

TO U.S. 13

Battlefield of Bentonville, NC
(General Topography)

A - Harper House
(Field Hospital, Federal XIV Corps)

B - Visitor Center

N W E S

1008   State Route 1008

Angle of View,
Photographs 1-9, pp. 87-91

Topography based on US Geological Survey (Four Oaks Quadrangle) edition of 1908. Surveyed 1905-06.

Photo angles not positioned on "exact" locations. Refer to the tactical maps for troop orientation.

Mark A. Moore

Appendix E — Views of the Battlefield

1. View from the position of the 1st N.C. Junior Reserves: As Briant's wing of Hobart's brigade advanced toward the Cole House on March 19, 1865, it fell under fire from Atkins' Battery and the N.C. Junior Reserves. The house stood across a ravine, beyond the modern copse of trees on the left of the photograph. The Juniors were criticized by D. H. Hill when a portion of the command broke under fire at Wyse Fork, March 8-10, but they performed well in limited action at Bentonville: "Their conduct in camp, on the march and on the battlefield, was everything that could be expected of them, and....was equal to that of the old soldiers who had passed through four years of war."— Gen. Robert F. Hoke. Clark, *Histories.* (See map on page 22)

2. Army of Tennessee: A portion of the Army of Tennessee advanced from right to left across this view on March 19: "The charge was made with great spirit and dash," wrote Maj. George W. F. Harper, commanding the 58th North Carolina, "and the enemy entrenched and with a high fence built in their front, gave way before inflicting great loss on their assailants. In the pursuit which followed, two pieces of artillery, limbering with all haste to the rear, were captured and driven back into our lines with their teams complete. In running down and taking the guns some of the artillerymen were shot while on the chests, and the old pine field was strewn with blankets, provisions and plunder of all sorts thrown away by the flying foe."— Clark, *Histories.* (See map on page 28)

Brig. Gen. William P. Carlin: The last grand charge of the Army of Tennessee sent Carlin's division reeling backward to the Morris farm, one mile to the west. As it turned out, Carlin's command absorbed the shock of the Confederate onslaught, while Morgan's XIV Corps division and Jackson's of the XX Corps squelched the Confederate advance late on March 19. The perceived disgrace inherent in being driven from the field had a profound effect on Carlin. In the 1880s he published several accounts of the battle in which he sought to shift the blame for the rout to others, especially Gen. George P. Buell, one of his brigade commanders.

Carlin (left) was with Buell's brigade when the attack came, and later claimed that Buell retreated without orders. "I turned to my right and saw the rebel flag flying at the breastworks that had been thrown up by Robinson's brigade," wrote Carlin. "The enemy had the breastworks on the right and left of my position, and were not thirty steps from me....One thinks very rapidly while facing great danger, and I decided to make the attempt to rejoin my command [which was stampeding to the rear]....I was not molested till I had passed about one hundred yards from the rebel lines....It was then that a regular fusilade [sic] from at least a hundred guns was opened on me, cutting the twigs and bushes all around me, and throwing up black dirt around my feet."— William P. Carlin. "The Battle of Bentonville," *Sketches of War History, 1861-1865.*

3. Morris' Farm: A portion of Taliaferro's Division attacked from right to left across this view on the afternoon of March 19, 1865. Elliott's Brigade had the advance: "The men started at the double-quick, steadily, and in good order from the woods into the field," recalled Cpl. A. P. Ford of Elliott's Brigade, "when they were met with rapid volleys of grape and canister shot, besides a heavy rifle-fire. The men held on well until within about fifty yards of the Federal line, when they suddenly wavered, halted, and then retired with the utmost precipitation. A panic had seized this brigade, incomprehensible as it was inexcusable. But it was simply the fact."—"The Last Battles of Hardee's Corps," *The Southern Bivouac*, 1 (New Series: June 1885-May 1886) pp. 140-143.

Elliott and Rhett attacked Robinson's position and the massed Federal artillery, passing at right angles to the 13th New Jersey and 82nd Illinois regiments: "[T]he enemy appeared in front of the 13th [New Jersey]," wrote Thomas R. Devor, "moving forward at a double-quick, being unconscious of the presence of the regiment, and thinking themselves on the left of the line....Waiting until they approached within easy range, the 13th opened on them, instantly throwing them into disorder [and] causing the enemy to seek shelter in the woods, and finally to disappear from our front. A battery on our right did splendid service on this occasion." A ditch and thin line of trees (above), indistinguishable from the heavier woods in the background, mark the path of an old wagon road which cut through the Morris farm. Beyond the ditch, the positions of the 13th and 82nd face the viewer from the distant tree line.—"The Twentieth Corps at Bentonville," *National Tribune*, June 3, 1897. (See map on page 40)

4. Hoke-McLaws Line, March 20-21, 1865: This long and formidable line of breastworks still dominates the crest of a large wooded ravine, at the bottom of which flows the Sam Howell Branch. The view faces southwest and shows a portion of the line occupied by Hoke's Division. From this line, faced toward the left of the photograph, Confederate troops sparred with the aggressive skirmishers of the Federal Right Wing. Near the base of the ravine were arrayed a series of rifle pits, which the Federals had to capture in order to ascend the slope toward the main Confederate line: "[T]he rebel skirmish pits were so near their main works that nothing could be done without much loss of life," reported Lt. Col. Henry Van Sellar, commanding the 12th Illinois, Adams' brigade—*Official Records*, Vol. 47, pt. 1. (No public access)

General Johnson Hagood, commanding a brigade in Hoke's Division, remembered that this new line was "scarcely taken when the enemy on the right attacked partially but heavily....On the left he deployed heavy skirmish lines....[T]he respective skirmishers were engaged all day and night [March 20] along the whole line."—Hagood, *Memoirs*.

Many of the rifle pits changed hands several times as the battle raged along the ravine, but Federal skirmishers did not stand long in front of the Confederate line. A soldier in the 50th Illinois, Hurlbut's brigade, recalled that "the main works of the enemy were too near, not over seventy-five yards distant, and heavily manned."—Charles F. Hubert. *History of the Fiftieth Regiment Illinois Volunteer Infantry in the War for the Union.* Kansas City, Mo.: Western Veteran Publishing Company, 1894.

"We took their skirmish pits along the whole front of our division [Woods']," wrote Maj. Charles Wills of the 103rd Illinois, "but they were very close to their main line and we did have a very interesting time holding them, I assure you."—Wills, *Army Life.* (See map on page 60)

5. Mower's Attack: A portion of Mower's Federal division advanced toward the background of this view while attacking Johnston's left on March 21, 1865. Beyond the distant tree line lies a swampy tributary of Mill Creek: "In our front the marsh was so deep and such a tangle of vines," noted Col. Charles Sheldon of the 18th Missouri, "that all the mounted officers were speedily on foot, and the intrenching tools thrown away." Earle's Confederate Battery was "all the time shelling from the high ground on the opposite side of the swamp," remembered the 18th's Elias Perry. As Mower emerged onto dry ground, Johnston was preparing for an all-out defense of his left flank.—Leslie Anders. *The Eighteenth Missouri.* Indianapolis: The Bobbs-Merrill Co., 1968. (See map on page 62)

Maj. Gen. Joseph A. Mower: Although Mower (right) undertook his "little reconnaissance" on the afternoon of March 21, 1865, the last thing William T. Sherman wanted was a general engagement with Johnston's Confederates. "General Mower, ever rash, broke through the rebel line on [its] extreme left flank," wrote Sherman, "and was pushing straight for Bentonsville [sic] and the bridge across Mill Creek." Fearing Confederate retaliation, Sherman called Mower off, but the Federal advance had posed a grave threat to Johnston's sole line of retreat. "Old Joe" was allowed to escape on the night of March 21 and, barring the hindsight later afforded by Five Forks and Appomattox, Sherman missed an opportunity to end the war in his theater of operations.—Sherman, *Memoirs*.

Opposing Mower's Federal advance was Lt. Gen. **William J. Hardee** (above), whom Johnston had entrusted with collecting reserves to defend Mill Creek Bridge on March 21. Hardee led the attack at the head of the 8th Texas and 4th Tennessee Cavalry. General **Wade Hampton** (right), who had conceived the plan for Johnston's attack on March 19, led the attack of Young's cavalry brigade. This counterstroke succeeded in stalling Mower's two brigades before Sherman called a halt to the operation. / Like Mower, Right Wing commander **Oliver O. Howard** (far right) was bitterly disappointed that Sherman chose to let Johnston escape at Bentonville. Years later Howard became reconciled to Sherman's decision, but he also confessed that "None of [Sherman's] reasons [for allowing Johnston's army to escape] satisfied me at the time."—*Autobiography of Oliver Otis Howard, Major General United States Army, 1862-1865*. Vol. 2, New York: Baker and Taylor, 1907.

Wade Hampton remembered that "General Hardee, who assumed command when he reached the field, led this charge [against Mower] with his usual conspicuous gallantry; and as he returned from it successful, his face bright with the light of battle, he turned to me and exclaimed: 'That was Nip and Tuck, and for a time I thought Tuck had it.' A sad incident marred his triumph, for his only son, a gallant boy of sixteen, who had joined the 8th Texas Cavalry two hours before, fell in the charge led by his father."—Wade Hampton, "The Battle of Bentonville," in R. U. Johnson and C. C. Buel, eds., *Battles and Leaders of the Civil War*, 4, pp. 700-705. 4 vols. New York: The Century Company, 1884-1889. Willie Hardee died in Hillsborough, North Carolina—probably at the Kirkland family home of Ayr Mount—on March 24, 1865. He is buried in the cemetery of St. Matthews Episcopal Church in Hillsborough.

6. Mill Creek: A bridge across this creek (left), which was at flood stage in March 1865, was the Confederate army's only means of egress from the battlefield of Bentonville. This view faces westward from the modern bridge. "The enemy's line of retreat toward Smithfield is open," noted the Federal Right Wing's chief of artillery on March 21, "and General Sherman thinks it so covered by Mill Creek that he cannot cut it. The position is so covered with earth works [sic] that we must lose too many men to care to break it, and we have no fears of Johnston making another attack on us."—Maj. Thomas Osborn. Richard Harwell, and Philip N. Racine, eds. *The Fiery Trail, A Union Officer's Account of Sherman's Last Campaigns.* Knoxville: The University of Tennessee Press, 1986. (See maps pp. 62-68)

7. Confederate Mass Grave: The monument above, erected by the Goldsboro Rifles and dedicated on March 20, 1895, marks the common grave of some 360 Confederates who fell in the Battle of Bentonville. General Wade Hampton was present for the dedication. The Reverend John J. Harper, "son of the venerable couple at Bentonville," whose own home in that village had been destroyed during the battle, offered a prayer for the occasion: "O merciful Father, grant the strength of Thy guiding hand to this great nation....Preserve us from complications and internal strife and from war. Give to the American Republic peace and prosperity and a greater purity."—*Confederate Veteran*, 3, no. 8 (August 1895), p. 231.

8. Original Building: It is believed that the small structure shown at right, minus the tin awning, was standing at the time of the battle. It sits behind the present-day community building in Bentonville. Today the village survives in name only.

An 1860s marketplace for naval stores, Bentonville was also the home and place of business of carriage maker John C. Hood. In 1927 Hood's daughter, then in her seventies, recalled the chaotic scenes she witnessed in the village as an impressionable ten-year-old: "The battle raged. Homes and out houses of all kinds were filled with the wounded, dead and dying....It seems I can almost hear the groans of the wounded, even yet, it was stamped on my mind so forcibly as they were brought to my father's wash shelter....Many houses were being burned and people lived continually in the fear of seeing their homes go up in flames....My father's shops and storehouses were burned. Our home and a few more were the only ones left standing." The Hood family and several neighbors took shelter under their house. This reminiscence is also surprisingly accurate regarding the alleged atrocities inflicted upon several Union prisoners during the battle.—Dora Hood Kirkman, *Smithfield Herald*, September 13, 1927.

9. Harper House: Built in the late 1850s, this farm house was the home of John and Amy Harper. When the Federal XIV Corps field hospital at Morris' farm was evacuated on March 19, it was relocated to this house. More than 500 Union casualties were treated here March 19-21, 1865. Jeff Davis' XIV Corps medical staff employed the four downstairs rooms as operating and recovery areas, using the interior doors of the house as operating tables. The surrounding grounds and outbuildings were also utilized. Six of the nine Harper children were at home during the battle, and were kept upstairs while their parents did all they could to help the wounded. **LOWER LEFT**: ca. 1890s view showing John and Amy on the front porch. **LOWER RIGHT**: ca. 1950s view showing twentieth-century addition to west side and altered facade. **LEFT**: modern view showing the house restored to its original appearance.

North Carolina Division of Archives and History

North Carolina Division of Archives and History

When the Federal army advanced to Goldsboro following the battle, the Harper House became a recovery ward for a few wounded Confederates, some of whom lingered in convalescence for weeks: "My scout sent....to the battle-field near Bentonville has returned," reported Lt. Col. J. W. Griffith, 1st Kentucky Cavalry, on March 27. "There are forty-five of the wounded of our army at the house of Mr. Harper (exclusive of those left at Bentonville). They are in a suffering condition for the want of proper supplies, and there is no surgeon to attend them. Mr. Harper and family are doing all their limited means will allow for the sufferers. Their wounds have been dressed and six or eight amputations performed skillfully by the surgeons of the enemy. There were no supplies left either with the wounded or in the country....Citizens report that [the Federals] employed all their ambulances and 200 wagons constantly and actively, from Sunday afternoon until Thursday night, removing their dead and wounded." Several of the soldiers buried in the Confederate mass grave died here of wounds received at Bentonville.—*Official Records,* Vol. 47, pt. 3.

The Harper House is the most prominent feature of Bentonville Battleground State Historic Site. The downstairs rooms are furnished to interpret a functioning Civil War field hospital, while the upstairs rooms have period domestic furnishings. The site hosts yearly special events, which in the past have included excellent interpretive programs on Civil War medicine. Tours of the house by site staff are conducted daily for the public. Admission is free. HOURS: Tuesday-Saturday, 9:00 a.m.-5:00 p.m.; Sunday, 1:00 p.m.-5:00 p.m. (Winter Hours, November 1-March 31: Tuesday-Saturday, 10:00 a.m.-4:00 p.m.; Sunday, 1:00 p.m.-4:00 p.m.) Closed Monday. For information contact: Bentonville Battleground, 5466 Harper House Road, Four Oaks, North Carolina, 27524. Telephone: (910) 594-0789.

Selected Bibliography—This list does not include every source consulted in making the battle maps. Full citations on the photograph captions are sources that do not appear on this list. Abbreviated citations are from sources listed here.

Ambrose, Daniel Leib. *History of the Seventh Regiment Illinois Volunteer Infantry.* Springfield, Ill.: Illinois Journal Company, 1868.

Andersen, Mary Ann, ed. *The Civil War Diary of Allen Morgan Geer, Twentieth Regiment, Illinois Volunteers.* Denver: Robert C. Appleman, 1977.

Andrews, William H. *Footprints of a Regiment: A Recollection of the First Georgia Regulars 1861-1865.* Edited by Richard M. McMurray. Marietta, Ga.: Longstreet Press, 1992.

Arbuckle, John C. *Civil War Experiences of a Foot-Soldier Who Marched with Sherman.* Columbus, Ohio: n.p., 1930.

Belknap, William W., and Tyler, Loren S., eds. *History of the Fifteenth Regiment, Iowa Veteran Volunteer Infantry.* Keokuk, Iowa: R. B. Ogden and Son, 1887.

Beyer, W. F., and Keydel, O. F., eds. *Deeds of Valor from Records in the Archives of the United States Government.* The Perrien-Keydel Company, 1907.

Blackburn, J. K. P. "Reminiscences of the Terry Rangers," *The Southwestern Historical Quarterly*, 22 (July and October 1918), pp. 38-77, 143-79.

Boies, Andrew J. *Record of the Thirty-Third Massachusetts Volunteer Infantry, From Aug. 1862 to Aug. 1865.* Fitchburg: n.p., Printed by the Sentinel Printing Company, 1880.

Bowman Family Papers. Charles F. Bowman Diary, March 22, 1865. United States Army Military History Institute, Carlisle Barracks, Pennsylvania.

Bradley, Mark L. *Last Stand in the Carolinas, The Battle of Bentonville.* Campbell, Cal.: Savas Woodbury Publishers, 1996.

Philo B. Buckingham Papers. P. B. Buckingham to My Dear Wife, March 26, 1865. American Antiquarian Society, Worcester, Massachusetts.

Burton, E. P. *Diary of E. P. Burton.* Des Moines: The Historical Records Survey, 1939.

Carlin, William P. "The Battle of Bentonville," *Sketches of War History, 1861-1865. Papers Prepared for the Ohio Commandery of the Loyal Legion of the United States*, 3, pp. 231-251. 6 vols. Cincinnati: Robert Clark and Company, 1888-1908.

Civil War Collection. Diary of William T. Clark, Book 6, February 12, 1865-May 1, 1865. Lancaster County Historical Society, Lancaster, Pennsylvania.

Clark, Olynthus B., ed. *Downing's Civil War Diary.* Des Moines: The Historical Department of Iowa, 1916.

Clark, Walter A. *Under the Stars and Bars, or Memories of Four Years' Service with the Oglethorpes of Augusta, Georgia.* Augusta: Chronicle Printing Company, 1900.

Clark, Walter, ed. *Histories of the Several Regiments and Battalions from North Carolina in the Great War 1861-'65.* Written by Members of the Respective Commands. 5 vols. Goldsboro, N.C.: Nash Brothers, 1901.

Collins, R. M. *Chapters from the Unwritten History of the War Between the States.* St. Louis: Nixon-Jones Printing Company, 1893.

Committee of the Regiment. *A Condensed History of the 143rd Regiment New York Volunteer Infantry.* n.p.: Newburgh Journal Printing House and Book Bindery, 1909.

Corn, Thomas Jefferson. "In Enemy's Lines With Prisoners," *Confederate Veteran*, 11, no. 11 (November 1903), pp. 506-507.

"R. S. Cowles," in Colleen Morse Elliott and Louise Armstrong Moxley, eds. *The Tennessee Civil War Veterans Questionnaires*, 2, pp. 574-578. 5 vols. Easley, S.C.: Southern Historical Press, 1985.

John W. Daniels Diary. March 19, 20, 1865, Bentley Historical Library, University of Michigan, Ann Arbor, Michigan.

Dickert, D. Augustus. *History of Kershaw's Brigade, with Complete Roll of Companies, Biographical Sketches, Incidents, Anecdotes, Etc.* Newberry, S.C.: Elbert H. Aull Company, 1899.

Dougall, Allan H. "Bentonville," *War Papers Read Before the Indiana Commandery, Military Order of the Loyal Legion of the United States*, pp. 212-219. Indianapolis: Published by the Commandery, 1898.

Diary of Allen L. Fahnestock, March 20, 21, 1865. (Transcription on microfilm). North Carolina Division of Archives and History, Raleigh, North Carolina.

Fitch, Michael H. *Echoes of the Civil War as I Hear Them.* New York: R. F. Fenno and Company, 1905.

Ford, Arthur P. and Ford, Marion J. *Life in the Confederate Army.* New York: Neale Publishing Company, 1905.

Fort, John Porter. *A Memorial and Personal Reminiscences.* New York: The Knickerbocker Press, 1918.

Giles, L. B. *Terry's Texas Rangers*, n.p., 1911.

Guild, George B. "Battle of Bentonville: Charge of the Fourth Tennessee and Eighth Texas Cavalry," *The Annals of the Army of Tennessee and Early Western History*, 1, No. 2, (May 1878), pp. 62-64.

—. *A Brief Narrative of the Fourth Tennessee Cavalry Regiment.* Nashville: n.p., 1913.

Hagood, Johnson. *Memoirs of the War of Secession, from the Original Manuscripts of Johnson Hagood.* Columbia, S.C.: The State Company, 1910.

Halsey, Ashley, ed. *A Yankee Private's Civil War by Robert Hale Strong.* Chicago: Henry Regnery Company, 1961.

Hinson, J. "Bentonville. The Commander of the 33rd Ohio Gives a Graphic Account of the Battle," *National Tribune*, July 8, 1886.

Holmes, James G. "The Artillery at Bentonville," *Confederate Veteran*, 3, no. 4 (April 1895), p. 103.

Jamison, Matthew H. *Recollections of Pioneer and Army Life.* Kansas City, Mo.: Hudson Press, 1911.

Johnson, W. A. "Closing Days With Johnston," *National Tribune*, May 22, 29, June 5, 1902.

Johnston, Joseph E. *Narrative of Military Operations During the Civil War.* New York: Da Capo Press, 1990 (Reprint of original 1874 edition).

Jones, J. A. "An Incident of Bentonville," *Confederate Veteran*, 21, (1913), p. 125.

Halcott P. Jones Journal. March 20, 1865, North Carolina Division of Archives and History, Raleigh, North Carolina.

Lambert, R. A. "In the Battle of Bentonville," *Confederate Veteran*, 37, no. 6, (June 1929), pp. 221-223.

Lane, Mills, ed. *"Dear Mother: Don't grieve about me. If I get killed, I'll only be dead." Letters from Georgia Soldiers in the Civil War.* Savannah: The Beehive Press, 1977. (Original Gardner letter located at the Georgia Department of Archives and History).

Lindsley, John Berrien, ed. *The Military Annals of Tennessee. Confederate. First Series. Embracing a View of Military Operations, with Regimental Histories and Memorial Roles, Compiled from Original and Official Sources.* Nashville: J. M. Lindsley and Company, 1886.

McClurg, Alexander. "The Last Chance of the Confederacy," *The Atlantic Monthly*, 50 (September 1882), pp. 389-400.

McLaws, Lafayette. *Order Book*, March 19, 1865, McLaws Papers, Southern Historical Collection, University of North Carolina, Chapel Hill.

Monnet, Howard Norman, ed. "'The Awfulest Time I Ever Seen': A Letter from Sherman's Army," *Civil War History*, 8, no. 3, (September 1962), pp. 283-289.

Morhous, Henry C. *Reminiscences of the 123rd Regiment, N. Y. S. V., Giving a Complete History of Its Three Years Service in the War.* Greenwich, N.Y.: People's Book and Job Office, 1879.

New York Herald (March 30, 1865). E. D. Westfall Correspondence.

Oates, Warren C. *The War Between the Union and the Confederacy.* New York and Washington: The Neale Publishing Company, 1905.

Osborn, Hartwell, and Others. *Trials and Triumphs. The Record of the Fifty-Fifth Ohio Volunteer Infantry.* Chicago: A. C. McClurg and Company, 1904.

Payne, Edwin W. *History of the Thirty-Fourth Regiment of Illinois Volunteer Infantry.* Clinton, Iowa: Allen Printing Company, 1903.

Pimper Manuscripts. Frederick to My Dear Friend, April 8, 1865. Lilly Library, Indiana University, Bloomington, Indiana.

Quaife, Milo M., ed. *From the Cannon's Mouth: The Civil War Letters of General Alpheus S. Williams.* Detroit: Wayne State University Press and the Detroit Historical Society, 1959.

Report of the Adjutant General of the State of Illinois Containing Reports for the Years 1861-1866. Revised by Brigadier General J. W. Vance, Adjutant General. 2, Springfield, Ill.: H. W. Rokker, State Printer and Binder, 1886.

Ridley, Bromfield. *Battles and Sketches of the Army of Tennessee.* Mexico, Mo.: Missouri Printing and Publishing Company, 1906.

Robertson, John H., ed. *Michigan in the War.* Lansing: W. S. George and Company, 1882.

Roster of the Survivors of the 86th Illinois Infantry, With the Post Office Addresses as Far as Known, Together With the Proceedings of the Reunion Held at Peoria, ILL., August 27, 1887. Peoria: J. W. Franks & Sons, n.d.

Sanders, Robert W. "The Battle of Bentonville," *Confederate Veteran*, 34, no. 8 (August 1926), pp. 299-300.

—. "More About the Battle of Bentonville," *Confederate Veteran*, 37, no. 12 (December 1929), pp. 460-461.

Ursula Scott Collection. William Kemp to Mother and Sister, March 27, 1865. Western Historical Manuscript Collection, University of Missouri-Columbia, Columbia, Missouri.

Sherlock, Eli J. *Memorabilia of the Marches and Battles in Which the One Hundredth Regiment of Indiana Infantry Volunteers Took an Active Part.* Kansas City, Mo.: Gerard-Woody Printing Company, 1896.

Sherman, William T. *Memoirs.* 2 vols. New York: Da Capo Press, 1984 (Reprint of original 1875 edition).

Shingleton, Royce, ed. "'With Loyalty and Honor as a Patriot': Recollections of a Confederate Soldier," *Alabama Historical Quarterly*, 33, nos. 3-4 (Fall-Winter 1971), pp. 240-263.

Slocum, Henry W. "Sherman's March from Savannah to Bentonville," in Robert U. Johnson and Clarence C. Buel, eds., *Battles and Leaders of the Civil War*, 4, pp. 681-695. 4 vols. New York: The Century Publishing Company, 1884-1889.

A Study in Valor: Michigan Medal of Honor Winners in the Civil War, n.p., Michigan Civil War Centennial Observance Commission, 1966.

Thomas, L. P. "Their Last Battle," *Southern Historical Society Papers*, 29, (1901), pp. 215-222.

—. Scrapbooks, 2, p. 148, L. P. Thomas Papers, Atlanta Historical Society, Library and Archives Room, Atlanta, Georgia.

United States War Department. *The War of the Rebellion: A Compilation of the Official Records of the Union and Confederate Armies*, 128 vols., Washington, D. C.: Government Printing Office, 1880-1901.

—. *Atlas to Accompany the Official Records of the Union and Confederate Armies.* Washington, D.C.: Government Printing Office, 1891-1895.

Lola J. Warrick Collection. Willard G. Eaton Letters, *Sargent County Teller*, Milnor, N.D., January 12, 19, 1928. W. G. Eaton to Brother Rico [?], May 25, 1862; to Brother Rice and Elizabeth, July 15, 1862; to William and Vesta, November 1, 1863; to Brother Rice, January 6, 1865. Regional History Collections, Western Michigan University, Kalamazoo, Michigan.

Westervelt, William B. *Lights and Shadows of Army Life, as Seen by a Private Soldier.* Marlboro, N.Y.: C. H. Cochrane, 1886.

Wills, Charles W. *Army Life of an Illinois Soldier.* Washington, D. C.: Globe Printing Company, 1906.

Winkler, William K., ed. *Letters of Frederick C. Winkler, 1862-1865.* n.p., 1963.

Winther, Oscar Osburn, ed. *With Sherman to the Sea. The Civil War Letters, Diaries, and Reminiscences of Theodore F. Upson.* Baton Rouge: Louisiana State University Press, 1943.

Worsham, W. J. *The Old Nineteenth Tennessee Regiment, C. S. A.* Knoxville, Tenn.: Press of Paragon Printing Company, 1902.

Wright, Henry H. *A History of the Sixth Iowa Infantry.* Iowa City: State Historical Society of Iowa, 1923.

Wynne, Lewis N. and Taylor, Robert A. *This War So Horrible: The Civil War Diary of Hiram Smith Williams.* Tuscaloosa, Ala.: The University of Alabama Press, 1993.

Yeary, Mamie, ed. *Reminiscences of the Boys in Gray.* Dallas, Tex.: Smith & Lamar, 1912.

Index

Orders of Battle unit / commander entries not included.